Joyce/Shakespeare

Irish Studies

James MacKillop, *Series Editor*

Joyce /Shakespeare

EDITED BY

L A U R A   P E L A S C H I A R

Syracuse University Press

∞ The paper used in this publication meets the minimum requirements
of the American National Standard for Information Sciences—Permanence
of Paper for Printed Library Materials, ANSI Z39.48-1992.

For a listing of books published and distributed by Syracuse University Press,
visit www.SyracuseUniversityPress.syr.edu.

ISBN: 978-0-8156-3389-1 (paperback)   978-0-8156-5312-7 (e-book)

Library of Congress Cataloging-in-Publication Data

Joyce/Shakespeare / edited by Laura Pelaschiar. — First edition.
pages cm. — (Irish studies)
Includes bibliographical references and index.
ISBN 978-0-8156-3389-1 (pbk. : alk. paper) — ISBN 978-0-8156-5312-7 (e-book)
1. Joyce, James, 1882–1941—Criticism and interpretation.   2. Shakespeare, William,
1564–1616—Influence.   I. Pelaschiar, Laura, editor.
PR6019.O9Z66956 2015
823'.912—dc23   2015008853

Manufactured in the United States of America

Contents

Introduction

LAURA PELASCHIAR

Shakespeare's presence in Joyce is such an overwhelming affair that introducing a collection of essays which courageously attempt to focus on this nexus is indeed a hard task.

A vindication of the title could perhaps be a good starting point. Joyce/ Shakespeare: how should one translate the connection that the silent slash is meant to represent? To which preposition or conjunction does the symbol give voice? Shakespeare in Joyce? Shakespeare through Joyce? Joyce through Shakespeare? Joyce versus Shakespeare? Joyce after Shakespeare? Joyce and Shakespeare? Joyce beside Shakespeare? Joyce despite Shakespeare? Joyce's Shakespeare? The impression is that any of them, and others as well, would validly direct the critic or reader to equally plausible and fertile perspectives.

Shakespeare's existence in Joyce is tentacular and functions on many different levels: cultural, structural, political, thematic, contrapuntal, imitational, quotational/misquotational, stylistic, lexical, psychological, or psycholiterary. The J/S nexus is a fascinating and inexhaustible literary workground *also* because of the tricky nature of the relationship that Joyce formed with the Bard. In comparison to any other literary bond, Homer included, the Shakespearean one is for Joyce much more complex, extends more widely, and "feels" less "controllable." The inkling is that Shakespeare represented a sort of psychoartistic inevitability, a "something" Joyce did not *want* to love so much and yet that he could only love so much despite himself. In order to roughly symbolize this dynamic, a pseudo-Freudian *Verneinung* of "I love thee (not)" might be adopted: on the one hand, Joyce voiced objections to Shakespeare's art throughout his life; on the other hand, in his own texts the love he felt for the English writer emerges clearly as artistic creation. It is also important to observe and keep in mind that while his art was becoming more sophisticated, complex, and demanding, and he was metamorphosing from being the writer of *Dubliners* to that of *Portrait of the Artist as a Young Man* and later of *Ulysses* and *Finnegans Wake*, Joyce needed Shakespeare more and more for and within his creative process. This is why *Ulysses* and *Finnegans Wake* are more Shakespearean than his earlier texts.

Yet Joyce's skepticism of Shakespeare remained a constant element and manifested itself very early on, in his 1899 University College Dublin paper on the dramatic inadequacies of *Macbeth* (Ellmann 1982, 58) and his contextual anti-Stratfordian positions (59). This early anti-Bardism should not be simply dismissed as juvenile competitive literary opining because Joyce continued to find imperfections, failures, and implausibilities in Shakespeare's works, objecting in particular to flaws in *Hamlet* (Stanislaus's Trieste Diary [Joyce 1908]) and *Othello* (Budgen 1972, 179) and asserting Ibsen's superiority as a playwright with unabashed confidence throughout his life. His admiration for the Norwegian giant is certainly sincere and profound, but it is impossible not to notice how instrumental it also was in enabling Joyce to articulate a contextual critique of Shakespeare's dramatic art.

Harold Bloom calls *Ulysses* and *Finnegans Wake* "Shakespeare-soaked epics" (Bloom 1994, 506). Bloom is the critic who, more than any other, reads the Joyce/Shakespeare nexus in psycholiterary terms. Of course he is motivated by his own agenda and by his idea of literature, which is agonistic and competitive rather than contaminative. No surprise, then, that chapter 18 of his *Western Canon*, "Joyce's Agon with Shakespeare," rests on the contention that "James Joyce, who rarely lacked audacity, conceived of Shakespeare as Virgil to himself as Dante" (413). Yet Bloom's vision is too limited. In his view, Joyce's struggle with Shakespeare happens mainly at a linguistic level: in the *Wake* Joyce finally manages to give full form to his envy by breaking away from "the English of Shakespeare," and his desire "to play at replacing English with the dialect of the *Wake*, the language of the outlaw" becomes detectable (428).

Shakespeare's presence in Joyce amounts to so much more than a competition for the possession/dominance/invention of an "English" artistic language. Of course Joyce's attitude toward Shakespeare cannot but be complicated by the colonial history of Ireland, and his Shakespeare-skepticism must *also* be comprehended within a postcolonial framework of reference. Yet the impression is that his antagonism transcends postcolonial boundaries, and if there is any parallel—rather than competition—concerning their national significance as writers, it is related to the fact that the forging of the uncreated conscience of his race which Joyce's alter ego, Stephen, identifies as his spiritual, cultural, and artistic mission at the end of *Portrait* turned out also to have been Shakespeare's own achievement or accomplishment for England, even if he did not seek to realize it in such a programmatic and explicit manner. From this point of view, a paradox which renders the connection even more interesting is that while Shakespeare—the voice of the British Empire—adopted as its artistic medium a dramatic genre that was accessible to and indeed accessed by the vast majority of the English population of his time (or at least by the people of London), Joyce—the British colonial subject in exile—chose to write "difficult" works that only an educated and devoted élite would be able to tackle.

Of course, for any critic engaged in following Shakespeare's thread in Joyce's art, *Hamlet* is a "must." The tragedy constitutes both a challenge and a problem: as archtext for *Ulysses* it stands second only to Homer's *Odyssey,* and it looms so large on the horizon that Joyceans have found it (and still find it) difficult to "think Shakespearean" without also (or almost exclusively) "thinking Hamletian." Yet in this collection some essays manage to avoid the Danish prince's encumbering shadow and instead explore some virgin Shakespearean ground, from cultural, structural, and thematic points of view.

Thus Valérie Bénéjam focuses on the complex theatricality of the "Cyclops" episode, a theatricality that emerges in Joyce whenever he is interpreting complex political situations. This he chooses to do without the support of a univocal, reliable master narrative, a process that becomes more extreme when the politics of Irish nationalism enter the stage. Bénéjam examines Joyce's use of *Troilus and Cressida* in "Cyclops," a chapter dominated by a problematic orality, and she shows how the in-between narratorial stance of the Nameless One is related to, and most probably inspired by, the theatrical pose and position of Thersites in Shakespeare's only Homeric rewriting.

Traces of *Troilus and Cressida* are found in *Ulysses* by Dieter Fuchs, who wonders at the (intended) marginality of references to the only Shakespearean play that accounts for structural analogy, given the Homeric archtext, but that also, in Fuchs's reading, inspired Joyce's artistic recycling of the Great Chain of Being, classically represented in the famous "degree" speech delivered by Ulysses, Leopold Bloom's Shakespearean parallel character.

In my essay I focus on a rereading of *Othello* in the light of *Ulysses*. It is a textual/cultural investigation inspired by the many similarities that the two protagonists share: Othello and Bloom are both outsiders whose alterity is considered with mistrust by the Christian Venetians and the Catholic Dubliners who represent their host communities. Both the Venetian Moor and the Dublin Jew are victims of real or imaginary adulterous plots committed by male members of those same communities; convergences and divergences between the two texts lead to unanticipated textual understanding and interpretation.

Alerted by an unexpected and sudden quote from the first act of *The Tempest* that swirls in Richard's mind in *Exiles*, Giuseppina Restivo finds unexplored parallels between Richard and Prospero, two bookish intellectuals who, just as if they were playwrights and directors of their own texts, are endowed with a semimagical mental power that they use to control and direct the other characters' actions, decisions, and moral emotions in an attempt to redress history.

Yet *Hamlet* is for Joyce's studies *the* Shakespearean inevitability. There can be no doubt that the Hamlet theory is a central moment in Joyce's maturation as an artist, and there is good ground to claim that his 1912/13 lost lectures in Trieste must have been the starting point for the reflections that took their final form in "Scylla and Charybdis." Joyce's critical handling of *Hamlet* implies a thoughtful and complex relationship with Europe and European culture, as the essays of John McCourt, Vike Plock, and Richard Brown lucidly reveal.

McCourt reflects on the cultural ambience in which Joyce extended and elaborated his relationship with Hamlet during his preparation for his Trieste 1912 lectures and saw in the Adriatic city—with its many Shakespearean performances, its cinematic culture and its vibrant intellectual life—a necessarily inspirational location to create his European Shakespeare, in stark opposition to Edward Dowden's typically imperialist celebration of the Bard's hyper-Englishness.

Vike Plock contemplates the cultural perimeter of the Shakespeare-Goethe-Joyce triangle and identifies in it the traces of an "aggressive discord and competition" with the reception of Shakespeare's plays among the European intelligentsia—a reception that had been dominated by Goethe's own vision of *Hamlet* in *Wilhelm Meister*—as the object of contention. The real agon in "Scylla and Charybdis," Plock's asserts, is not so much between Shakespeare and Joyce as between Goethe and Joyce; if Shakespeare is "the happy hunting ground" (*U* 239) of this tricky contest, *Wilhelm Meister* is the hunting text of the whole chapter.

Richard Brown considers Stephen's Hamlet theory as a pivotal moment of Joyce's self-modernizing process during the Trieste years, a process that was compounded by many weighty European cultural forces. Stephen's vision of Shakespeare, who (very much like Bloom himself) is busy walking the city and engaged in the everyday activity of going to work and shopping, brings him very close to an early twentieth-century urban modernity, while Marinetti's Futurism provided the Irish writer with some of the intellectual tools Stephen employs in his tense acrobatic journey through Shakespeare's art in "Scylla and Charybdis."

Hamlet's shadow can nevertheless cast itself in unpredictable shapes and forms, away from the character of Hamlet and from Stephen and nearer to Bloom. Sam Slote reflects on the fact that the Hamlet theory represents Stephen's swan's song, since after "Scylla and Charybdis" Stephen's presence in the novel is drastically downsized. Slote detects in the Hamlet theory a crypto-presence of none other than Leopold Bloom, the figure in the carpet of Stephen's theory of art, of the artist-creator, and of Shakespeare, creator of all, "Father of thousands." Because the artist is every man and every man is potentially an artist, Stephen's theory of Shakespeare is also a theory of Bloom, the undisputed Everyman of Joyce's masterpiece and one who knows that which is still outside Stephen's spiritual scope, the care for the other, the love for alterity, the meaning of that "word known to all men."

Finally, Vincent Cheng's and Paul Fagan's essays tackle the spiky presence of *Hamlet* in *Finnegans Wake* from two very different and "dialogic" perspectives. Cheng convincingly reasserts his belief that Shakespeare—the man and the creator of worlds—is the major matrix of the *Wake*, with *Hamlet* in a central position, given that Joyce's text alludes to the Danish tragedy more often than to any other play, with parallels more precise and more frequent than for any other Shakespeare text. Fagan, on the other hand, problematizes Cheng's cornerstone contribution by challenging the very notion of the matrix text model. Working from the perspective of linguistics, Fagan claims that the language of the *Wake* could and should be considered "English" since it is "syntactically and semantically predictable" and it is "a creative and comically exaggerated form of the possibilities of the English language system." Because of this, the need to find and refer back to a matrix text—such as *Hamlet*—to give meaning to an otherwise unclear sequence of words is not as urgent as it has been traditionally considered and may actually restrict understanding of the *Wake*'s polysemantic possibilities.

I would like to conclude this introduction by observing how nowadays these two imposing figures of world literature are often associated by critics, almost *en passant*, as if it had become a cliché, or just normal, to consider them together side by side. One of the most illustrative examples is a very recent review of the 2007 *Oxford Companion to James Joyce* (edited by Richard Brown) by Onno Kosters. The reviewer concludes his piece with these words: "Much like Shakespeare before him, Joyce has become even more important for the survival and export of Western literary and cultural studies than as a writer studied for the sake of his written word. Exporting Joyce (to New Zealand, to Japan) is the new, dare I say postcolonial game of re-colonizing the former pockets of refreshing resistance to Western culture dominance in ways that in themselves deserve companions too. Exporting Joyce guarantees the survival of the Joyce industry" (Kosters 2010, 77).

The colonized Irish subject in exile James Joyce and the master voice of the British Empire William Shakespeare are now oddly united in a colonizing enterprise of non-Western worlds. It is therefore as if Joyce, with his written word and all the words written by others about him, was doing to others, the non-Western Others, what once had been done to him and his once conscienceless race. One wonders what Joyce would have to say about this ironic twist of hermeneutical efforts: yet more evidence that proves the J/S nexus is a universe whose definite borders will always remain a work in progress.

I would like to express my deepest gratitude to each of the contributors for their generous cooperation and enduring patience throughout the entire editing process. I would like to extend special thanks to Jim MacKillop, editor of the Syracuse University Press Irish Studies series, for believing in this project from the very beginning, and to Jennika Baines, again of Syracuse, for her help, support, and advice during the various stages of this volume's preparation. I am also indebted to Fabio Polidori for his invaluable help during the final editing process. I would also like to thank John McCourt, as always ready to encourage and support any academic (and indeed human) enterprise that I decide to undertake. Thanks to Liam and Eoin for being Liam and Eoin. Finally I wish to express my gratitude to Marcello, for his presence, aid, and unyielding patience.

Abbreviations

Throughout this volume, references to Joyce's publications are to the editions shown here (unless otherwise specified) and are abbreviated as listed below, with quotations noted by arabic page and line number. Quotations from Shakespeare plays are cited with roman numerals (e.g., IV, i, 1; signifying act 4, scene 1, line 1).

D	*Dubliners*. 1996. Edited by Robert Scholes and A. Walton Litz. London: Penguin.
E	*Poems and Exiles*. 1992. Edited by J. C. C. Mays. New York: Penguin.
GJ	*Giacomo Joyce*. 1968. Edited by Richard Ellmann. London: Faber & Faber.
FW	*Finnegans Wake*. 1959. New York: Viking Press.
JJA	*The James Joyce Archive*. 1977–79. 63 vols., edited by Michael Groden, Hans Walter Gabler, A. Walton Litz and Danis Rose. New York: Garland.
JJII	*James Joyce*, new and rev. ed. 1982. Ellmann, Richard. New York: Oxford Univ. Press.
JJQ	*James Joyce Quarterly*. 1963–. Univ. of Tulsa.
LI, LII, LIII	*Letters of James Joyce*. 1966. Vol. I, edited by Stuart Gilbert. Vols. II and III, edited by Richard Ellmann. New York: Viking.
OCPW	*Occasional, Critical and Political Writings*. 2000. Edited by Kevin Barry. Oxford: Oxford Univ. Press.
P	*A Portrait of the Artist as a Young Man*. 1964. New York: Viking.
SH	*Stephen Hero*. 1963. New York: New Directions.
U	*Ulysses*. (1922) 1993. Edited by Jeri Johnson. Oxford: Oxford Univ. Press.

Joyce/Shakespeare

1

Shakespeare's Theater and the Critique of Mythmaking Historiography

The Case of "Cyclops"

VALÉRIE BÉNÉJAM

Under the ironic title "Shakespeare Explained," the Dublin *Daily Express* dated November 19, 1903, carried James Joyce's scathing review of a book by A. S. Canning, *Shakespeare Studied in Eight Plays*. The young Joyce was ruthless in his thrashing: "[i]t is not easy to discover in the book any matter for praise," he wrote in his opening (OCPW 97). Not only is the work "very long" and "expensive," it offers but "meagre, obvious, and commonplace" interpretations, together with misquotations and naïvetés (OCPW 97). Determined not to take his object seriously, Joyce closed with a devastating anticlimax: "even the pages are wrongly numbered" (OCPW 98). Reading the review, we are not even told what were the eight plays selected by Canning for his study (only *Julius Cæsar* and *Richard III* are explicitly mentioned), except that the choice is deemed "haphazard."[1] However, thanks to the one citation from Canning that Joyce chooses to quote (or rather to misquote, as I will soon reveal), we can surmise that

---

1. Canning's (2004) chapters actually study in turn: *Troilus and Cressida, Timon of Athens, Julius Cæsar, Antony and Cleopatra, Richard III, Henry VIII, King Lear,* and *A Midsummer Night's Dream.*

Troilus and Cressida was also part of the selection. Indeed, it is the only play in the canon that could correspond to the following description: "His noble comrade fully rivals Achilles in wisdom as in valour. Both are supposed to utter their philosophic speeches during the siege of Troy, which they are conducting with the most energetic ardour. They evidently turn aside from their grand object for a brief space to utter words of profound wisdom" (Canning 2004, 6).[2] Joyce complains about the superficiality of such a reading, denouncing the same pandering to the taste of what he had elsewhere called "the rabblement,"[3] and which here appears under the term "base multitude": "[h]ere is no psychological complexity, no cross-purpose, no interweaving of motives such as might perplex the base multitude. Such a one is a 'noble character', such a one a 'villain'; such a passage is 'grand', 'eloquent', or 'poetic'" (OCPW 97). In Joyce's view, Canning has clearly not "explained" Shakespeare, or rather he has made it so "plain" that it no longer resembles the Shakespeare Joyce knows.

I have chosen to open the chapter with this review because it gives us to read, in Joyce's own words, what he probably valued most in Shakespeare's theater: "complexity," "cross purposes," perplexing "interweaving of motives," and the undermining of ready-made opinions about noble or villainous characters (in stark contrast with Canning's own use of clichés such as "most energetic ardor," "grand object," and "words of profound wisdom"). Why Joyce should have selected this precise sentence as the epitome of Canning's lack of penetration is quite transparent to anyone familiar with *Troilus and Cressida*: "energetic ardour" is definitely not what the wavering Achilles displays while conducting the siege of Troy, and it does not take a very developed sense of irony to discover that the bulk of the Greek heroes' speeches comprises in fact few "words of profound wisdom."[4] That such irony should have totally escaped Canning

---

2. This is the quotation as it appeared in Joyce's "Shakespeare Explained" (OCPW 97).

3. See "The Day of the Rabblement" (1901) (OCPW 50–52).

4. Richard Brown, who envisages *Troilus and Cressida* in relation to Joyce's *Ulysses*, says of the play: "Shakespeare's Greeks frequently appear in a less than heroic posture. Achilles 'in his tent / Lies mocking our designs' (I, iii, 145–46) and 'Ajax is grown

must have particularly annoyed Joyce. In fact, he was so irritated as to forget one character's name in the passage he quoted and, retrospectively, the slip is a remarkable one coming from Joyce: Canning's original sentence actually starts with, "[h]is noble comrade *Ulysses* fully rivals Achilles in wisdom and valour" (Canning 2004, 6; emphasis added). The here absent heroic name would of course reappear quite prominently in the Joycean œuvre nearly twenty years later and, I will argue, offer Joyce the opportunity to illustrate his own, remarkably modern, reading of Shakespeare's *Troilus and Cressida.*

In light of this early review, I would like to examine the use a more mature Joyce would later make of *Troilus and Cressida* in the "Cyclops" chapter of *Ulysses.* First, however, a few contextualizing detours will be necessary, to consider how the young Joyce, the one who thought so highly of Shakespeare and so little of Canning's simplistic interpretation, negotiated his own potential career as a dramatist, and did so possibly in relation to the Shakespearean canon. From an exchange of letters with the famous London critic and translator of Ibsen, William Archer, we know that in the summer months of 1900 Joyce wrote a play, which at the time he considered his first major literary achievement. At least this is what can be assumed by the title of the work: "'A Brilliant Career' / drama in 4 acts / — To — / My own Soul I / dedicate the first / true work of my / life."[5] William Archer sent the play back with a polite letter. But in spite of this setback, becoming a dramatist seems to have been one of Joyce's first ambitions, and scholars usually cite Ibsen's influence as

---

self-willed' (I, iii, 198). Nestor and Agamemnon, though more responsible, are ineffectual and even Ulysses, whose speech on the necessity of order is the most frequently quoted part of the play, seems either too philosophic or else too conniving to be a hero in the ideal sense" (Brown 1999, 347).

5. The play itself has disappeared. We know its title because William Archer copied it onto Joyce's letter (*LII* 7n5). See more about this episode in Richard Ellmann's biography (*JJII* 78–80), as well as Peter Costello's (1992, 168–69). Costello, however, makes a telling mistake by providing a slightly different title for the play—"*My* [rather than *A*] *Brilliant Career,*" no doubt making explicit the young Joyce's hopes for the work and its author.

primordial. Indeed, in his youthful essay "Drama and Life," Joyce seems to prize the realistic productions by the Norwegian playwright far above the classical Shakespearean corpus. Richard Brown, however, has offered a thought-provoking analysis of this essay, noting how the terms in which Joyce praises Shakespeare's plays ("Shakespeare was above all a literary artist"; his art is "literature in drama," [*OCPW* 23]) seem to fit his own later works, announcing how Joyce's debt to Shakespeare would transpire in his dialogic literary writing (Brown 1997, 95).[6] Furthering Brown's point about "Drama and Life," I would also argue that, although he might have wanted to keep his distance with the very symbol of English literature—with the "chap that," as Mulligan would provokingly put it in "Scylla and Charybdis," "writes like Synge"[7]—the young Joyce must have nevertheless recognized the dramatic potential in Shakespeare's plays. Indeed, it is to one of the most famous and theatrical of Shakespearean creations that he eventually reverts when attempting to define the very "spirit" of drama, who "is, one might guess, somewhat of an elfish nature, a nixie, a very Ariel" (*OCPW* 25). Ariel is both the tool and the embodiment of Prospero's magic and of his control over the plot and stage effects in *The Tempest*, the play itself functioning as a self-referential *mise en abyme* reflecting on Shakespeare's own theatrical control and mastery at the end of his career. In spite of Joyce's surface criticism of Shakespeare, it is Ariel, eventually, who becomes Joyce's final choice of a metaphor for the spirit of drama. And beyond those youthful and somehow involuntary tributes paid to the great English playwright, there is little doubt that the young Joyce's dismissal of Shakespeare would later abate, together with the youthful, polemical tone of "Drama and Life." When Frank Budgen put to him

---

6. In this and another later article (Brown 1999), Brown offers a unique study of Joyce's reflection on the Shakespearean corpus and of his awareness of the European reception of Shakespeare, as well as an evaluation of his use of Shakespeare in the context of World War I Zürich.

7. As Mulligan joins the discussion of Shakespeare in "Scylla and Charybdis," his reaction hints at the ambivalent position a young Irish writer could have regarding the chief representative of English literary supremacy: "Shakespeare? . . . I seem to know the name. . . . To be sure, . . . The chap that writes like Synge" (*U* 190).

the oft-quoted question of the desert-island book, Joyce's only hesitation was between Dante and Shakespeare, and in the end, "[t]he Englishman is richer and would get my vote" (Budgen 1972, 184). I would argue that Joyce probably also came to see that theater could be of use in the development of his fiction, and that Shakespeare's influence was not necessarily opposed to the specific realism he wished to develop.

As a young man, however, Joyce seemed to value Ibsen's realism in drama. Following very closely Yeats's efforts to launch a national theater for Ireland, he was disappointed when, in his view, Yeats betrayed Ibsen's model of dramatic realism for one of dramatic idealism. Refusing a modern, urban setting for representing Ireland and holding on to a rural, nostalgic, and parochial vision of the country were choices that Joyce could not abide. In the end, although he recognized the dramatic possibilities for a theatrical rendering of Ireland, he must have considered the audience was not ready for such stage productions, while he was not prepared for the sort of compromise Yeats had made with his own theater.[8] Instead, Joyce succeeded in incorporating theatricality into nontheatrical writing: the dramatic potential of Dublin conversations is a constant feature of his work, and one that he did not abandon with his theatrical ambitions. The influence of theater can be felt throughout his work, from the first minimalist dramatic epiphanies to the dramatic construction of the Christmas dinner scene in A Portrait of the Artist as a Young Man, via the dialogical narrative technique of "Ivy Day in the Committee Room," not to mention the bold formal experiments of the later works: the "Circe" episode in Ulysses or the "Mutt and Jute" section of Finnegans Wake. Theater, and particularly dramatic scripts, provided him with a model for writing conversations, suggesting the strength of orality and the power of its ephemeral utterance, while retaining the printed book's invitation to browse back and forth, and the reflexive potential of second reading.[9]

8. For lack of space, I am putting things broadly here; Forkner (2000) provides a detailed study of this question.

9. See my own article on the subject, where I develop this point particularly in reference to the epiphanies and to Dubliners (Bénéjam 2008).

It is revealing that, in *Dubliners* as well as in *A Portrait*, Joyce's dramatic narrative technique is at its most extreme when broaching political questions and the sensitive topic of Irish nationalism. Both in "Ivy Day" and in the Christmas dinner scene, it is the mode chosen to present the debate over Parnell's downfall and what Joyce considered his betrayal by the Irish: with very little narratorial intervention—or, in the case of *A Portrait*, a child-narrator who chiefly voices interrogations and perplexity, and in the process conveys most effectively the tensions of the scene—Joyce clearly refuses to pass explicit judgment. As readers of Joyce's nonfiction writings realize, it is not that he had no judgment to pass. On the contrary, he probably thought his message more efficiently transmitted by allowing all the partisans to express themselves unfettered. Indeed, we know exactly what was Joyce's strong, polemical position about the tragic end of Parnell's political career and life: "[I]t redounds to the honor of his fellow-countrymen that they . . . did not throw him to the English wolves: they tore him apart themselves" (*OCPW* 196).[10] It is Emer Nolan who has remarked most perceptively that Joyce had been "unable to articulate in its full complexity" the "divided consciousness of the colonial subject" in his writings about Ireland, and that he had only succeeded in doing so in his fiction (Nolan 1995, 130).[11] This chapter argues that, if theatricality often played a central part in Joyce's articulation of the problematic political history of Ireland, it is the Shakespearean model of "psychological complexity," "cross-purpose," and "interweaving of motives" (*OCPW* 97) that was the decisive inspiration for the dialogical, dramatic presentation of Irish nationalism and Irish history.

That subtlety and ambivalence, double entendre and complexity, are the hallmarks of Shakespearean theater is now undoubtedly a cliché, and it would be rather awkward, here or anywhere, to stereotypically expatiate on Shakespeare's debunking of stereotypes. For clarity in this chapter,

---

10. From "L'ombra di Parnell" (published in *Il Piccolo della Sera*, May 16, 1912), translated by Conor Deane as "The Shade of Parnell."

11. Also quoted in Derek Attridge and Marjorie Howes's illuminating introduction to *Semicolonial Joyce* (Attridge and Howes 2000, 2).

however, I wish to briefly revive this stereotypical issue within the context of Shakespeare's histories and of the twentieth-century critical debates they spurred. The War of the Roses that had opposed the two famous branches of the Plantagenet family became both a widely developed interest of the Tudor era and one of the most perfected tools of its political propaganda: according to this view, when the Earl of Richmond won the day at Bosworth, he not only freed England of the cruelest tyrant and reconciled the white rose and the red, but also installed an era of peace and economic growth to replace and repair years of civil war that had pitted father against son, brother against brother. After God sent this long period of strife and pain to pay for the sin of a deposed and murdered king (Richard II), culminating with the scourge of Richard III, England was to be finally restored to splendor and glory under the guiding hand of the Tudor dynasty. One can almost hear the trumpet flourish and resounding drums. Indeed, the Elizabethans' knowledge of this recent history was so widespread, its interpretation so generally—or at least officially—accepted, and its dénouement such a necessity that Shakespeare could write his two tetralogies backward, like George Lucas's *Star Wars*, beginning with the end (the three parts of *Henry VI* and *Richard III*), and ending with the beginning (*Richard II*, the two parts of *Henry IV*, and *Henry V*), Agincourt providing a perfectly glorious conclusion. At least this is the story, or historical narrative, that was fed to generations of English literature students, following E. M. Tillyard's study of "the Elizabethan world picture" in the 1940s.[12] The New Historicism of the 1980s, spearheaded by Stephen Greenblatt, introduced more subtle views of the permeability between historical context and literary production. Eventually, scholars would come to question Shakespeare's straightforward adherence to the Tudor propaganda.[13] Although there is no question that dissenting views could not openly be voiced, let alone staged or printed, in Shakespeare's

12. See Tillyard ([1944] 1966 and [1942] 1972).

13. About the histories, see particularly Holderness's *Shakespeare: The Histories* (2000) as well as his edition of the New Casebook Series about Shakespeare's histories (Holderness 1992). Reading side by side the two successive collections of the Casebook Series and New Casebook Series is generally a good illustration of this critical shift.

time, hints of doubts or questioning may be discerned in the texts thanks to precise contextualization, together with the presentation of much more objective historical interpretations than Tillyard had originally presented.

A significant illustration of Greenblatt's critique may be found in his interpretation of the staging of *Richard II* on the eve of the Essex rebellion (Greenblatt 1982b).[14] On February 7, 1601, the day before the Earl of Essex's abortive *coup*, a group of supporters paid the Chamberlain's Men to revive the play at the Globe. Although the actors were never really threatened in the ensuing repression, one of the shareholders for the company was summoned and had to answer for their good faith in the matter.[15] This particular staging may thus be considered an indicator of the potential political subversion inherent to the play, in support of which critics often quote Elizabeth's own 1601 remark to William Lambard: "I am Richard II. Know ye not that?" (Forker 2002, 5). Indeed, beyond its central topic of a sovereign's deposition and murder, *Richard II* is a telling example of political double entendre and equivocation, a feature noticeable even in its use of historical sources: while Hall's history, the vehicle for the official view of Richard's deposition as leading to the internecine warfare of the following years, was Shakespeare's general inspiration for the play, editors have noted that more specific verbal links may be found between the play and Holinshed's densely packed pages concerning the end of Richard's reign.[16] In Holinshed's chronicles, contradictory testimonies are archived and juxtaposed, offering a complex and multivocal confrontation of opposite views, a surprisingly modern historical approach that seems the very

14. A reissue of Greenblatt 1982a.

15. See Forker's introduction to the play (Forker 2002, 10).

16. Hall and Holinshed were the two major historical sources for Shakespeare's two tetralogies: Edward Hall's *The Union of the Noble and Illustre Families of Lancastre and York* was first published in 1542, Raphael Holinshed's *The Chronicles of England, Scotland, and Ireland* in 1577. Shakespeare used the second edition of 1587. Holinshed was mainly an editor for the work of several other contributors, who worked as compilers, linking primary sources into consistent narratives, but quoting, paraphrasing, and copying freely, with the explicit methodological aim of not leaving anything aside (see Forker's introduction to the sources of the play [Forker 2002, 124–38]).

model retained by Shakespeare for the structure of his play. When read closely, *Richard II* presents fairly both Richard and Bolingbroke's views, and only weak productions will make a caricature of one (an effeminate Richard or a boorish, fascistic Bolingbroke), ruining the poise and tension of the play.[17] In fact, one of the most famous productions of *Richard II*, directed by John Barton for the Royal Shakespeare Company in 1973, achieved an interesting balance between the two antagonistic parts by interchanging the two actors every night (Richard Pasco and Ian Richardson). The play ran for two hundred performances, and the critics who returned noted that both actors had refined their conceptions of each role, further developing the dynamic interaction between the two and underscoring the ambivalent double message conveyed by the play. While the two opposite poles of the play's historical interpretation could still be summed up as "Richard was an incompetent king who had to be deposed" and "yet it was a sin to depose and kill him," it became impossible to decide between those two competing truths. The replacement of a classical either/or alternative logic with a both/and inclusive logic is indeed necessary to an exhaustive and subtle interpretation of the play. Such predilection for the synchronous expression of antithetical ideologies, sometimes at the very microcosmic level of one character, or even at the microscopic level of a few words, is, as I will presently show, at the very heart of Shakespeare's influence on Joyce's dialogic writing.

The subtlety and equivocation in *Richard II* is perhaps best expressed in the internal doubts of the main character, as he self-questioningly reflects on his own impossible identity as both a legitimate and usurped king. When Bolingbroke senses his doubts in act 4, he puts the question to him bluntly: "Are you contented to resign the crown?" (IV, i, 200). This is followed by Richard's famous abdication speech, as he ritualistically gives up all the symbols of his pomp and power. But the first words in answer to his cousin's question encapsulate all the ambivalence of his position: "Ay, no. No, ay," says Richard (IV, i, 201). The punctuation of these

17. I am referring particularly to Giles's 1978 BBC recording, with Derek Jacobi in the title role.

four syllables differs according to the editions, but most importantly the spelling itself varies, as the 1623 Folio carries "I, no; no, I." Indeed, the phrase plays on double entendre, with the possible variation on "I" and first-person personal pronoun, or "ay" as "yes."[18] In parallel, we can also hear the verb "to know" in Richard's negation, so that the simple wavering between a positive and an affirmative statements (ay, no; no, ay) becomes a negation of Richard's true nature (I, no; no, I), as well as a questioning of his self-knowledge in relation to his both royal and no-longer-royal nature (I know no I, or no longer know what I am). The potential polysemy of these four words brings to mind a very similar equivocation and wordplay in Joyce's "Circe." Just before letting go of his male identity, and a few pages before he is turned into a "charming soubrette" (U 502), Bloom is confronted with Bella's talking fan asking him, "Have you forgotten me?" (U 495), and the answer the fan is given bears striking resemblance to Richard II's response to Bolingbroke: "Nes. Yo," says Bloom (U 495). Next to the obvious wavering between "yes" and "no," no longer expressed in alternation but in a reversal of first letters, Joyce also conveys Bloom's doubts about his identity: we can hear the Spanish *es yo* (this is I), but also a slightly elided *no es yo* (this is not I). And taken together, the two words express the Latin *nescio* (I do not know), thus condensing in just two syllables all the ambiguities that were also present in the Shakespearean text. That such punning and double entendre is reinforced by theatricality is self-evident: because it is spoken word, and not only permanently written—or rather permanently re-edited—text, Shakespeare's line potentially carries its series of significations independently from editorial choices. Each spectator is free to select his or her own interpretation, possibly to retain them all and experience the full complexity of their nonbinary logic, which so potently condenses the troubled nature of the main character and the complex political situation. Similarly, because the "Circe"

18. The first editions (original quarto and 1623 Folio) use the spelling "I," but this is characteristic of Elizabethan orthography and refers to both meanings. For full information, see the commentary and textual notes in Forker's edition (particularly Forker 2002, 399).

episode is presented as a theatrical script, albeit one impossible to stage, it encourages the oral rendition and aural perception of its words, which best render the full array of these words' meanings.[19]

The potentially polysemous play on orality and text brings me back to the "Cyclops" episode in *Ulysses*, in which the conflict between written and spoken words is concentrated in the narrative struggle between the nameless narrator, with his undeniably spoken tone, and the competing passages of gigantism, offering parodies of written styles and documents. Complicating the relation between the two, the passages of gigantism often bear some essential connection with oral speech, either as precise transcriptions or accounts of spoken material, or as texts destined to be uttered aloud: they are minutes of parliamentary debates or of political organization meetings, nineteenth-century transcriptions of orally trans-mitted legends, newspaper coverage of public events, accounts of verse recitation, legal trial records, prayers, etc.[20] Conversely, in spite of his "easy colloquial flow" (Budgen 1972, 156), Joyce's Nameless One seems to be offering a silent narration, fixed, printed, and only accessible to the readers of *Ulysses*, since no one in Barney Kiernan ever seems aware of his devas-tating, disparaging railing. Although it suggests orality and seems an invi-tation to be read aloud, we are bound to realize that the Nameless One's words are not only offered anonymously; they are in fact never spoken out loud, at least not in any identifiable context other than our own reading.

The "locus and time of the I-narration" in "Cyclops" may in fact turn into a real narratological quandary, especially if we care to retain a realistic setting for the narration. Nevertheless, I would not follow David Hayman's conclusion that the narration takes place "drinks later in an unnamed pub" (Hayman 1974, 263–65). Without getting into the details of Hay-man's demonstration, I do not find that the hypothesis of a dual time and place for the episode makes sense within the tight spatial and temporal

19. The influence of Shakespeare's polysemous theatrical text will evidently be con-tinued into *Finnegans Wake* with its constant play on orality and aurality.

20. For the precise identification of the passages of parody in "Cyclops," see pages 312–81 of Gifford's annotated volume (1998).

organization of the book, nor that the clues pointing to this duality, and particularly to another pub, are clear enough within the episode itself. More importantly, I do not believe that Joyce, at this point in his composition of *Ulysses*, still required a plausible source or localization for his experimental narrative voices. On the other hand, I wish to show here that the in-between narratorial stance of Joyce's Nameless One is extremely close to—and most probably inspired by—the theatrical pose and position of Shakespeare's Thersites in *Troilus and Cressida*. Indeed, the "Cyclops" narrator has often been related to this character, and particularly to a specific performance of the play given at the Pfauentheater in Zürich in the spring of 1916, with Wilhelm Karsten in the role.[21] In *James Joyce and the Making of Ulysses*, Frank Budgen mentions Joyce's admiration for the actor's performance and makes the link with the "Cyclops" narrator explicit: "Himself a snarling Thersites, he liberates the Thersites in us" (Budgen 1972, 158 and 171). Similarly, in his biography, Ellmann writes in a footnote that "[a]ccording to Stanislaus Joyce, the idea for Thersites as principal narrator of this episode came to his brother while watching a German performance of Shakespeare's *Troilus and Cressida* in Zürich" (*JJII* 459). Finally, referring to Karsten's part years later in a letter to Budgen, Joyce termed it "[a] wonderful creation—a parallel part to Cyclops 'I.'"[22] Although we cannot know exactly what Karsten did with the part, we may surmise how Shakespeare's dramatic construction of the character might have inspired Joyce into calling them "parallel part[s]."

Such parallelism is perhaps best understood if we consider how the character of Thersites mediates between the represented world of the play and the representing world of its production and performance, what the Shakespearean critic Robert Weimann calls *locus* and *platea*.[23] Inspired by

21. See Richard Brown's mention of the April 17 *Neue Zürcher Zeitung* review of this production, as well as his contextualization of Joyce's interest in the play as a rewriting of Homer's *Iliad* in the complex situation of wartime Zürich (Brown 1999, 345).

22. Letter to Frank Budgen, September 10, 1933 (LI 337).

23. The following analysis is inspired by the work of Robert Weimann (1978, particularly 227–32; and 2000, particularly the third chapter, "Pen and Voice: Versions of Doubleness," 54–78).

such theatrical conventions as the Vice or the Prologue, Thersites is a creation that plays on the distinction between *locus* and *platea*, or to put it in more modern terms, allows for the breaking of what twentieth-century dramatists and theorists of the theater later called the fourth-wall convention of realism: presumably situated in a downstage position, Thersites often addresses the audience directly in a series of comments spoken in asides whose status may be confusing. Most importantly, he seems to do so from an almost extradramatic perspective, commenting on the representation sometimes in the language of a professional performer, invoking moral issues, spurring or sarcastically cheering the action as it goes on. Such multiple perspective is particularly evident in the scene of Cressida's infidelity with Diomed (V, ii), in which can be distinguished three levels of (re) presentation: the performed event in which Cressida betrays Troilus with Diomed in front of Calchas's tent, a second level in which Ulysses and Troilus witness the scene and comment upon it from within the represented world of the play, and finally a third level, that of Thersites's *presentation* of the scene, in which the player remains unobserved and is not overheard by the other characters, a level which does not seem to be lost, so to speak, in the *representation*. It is possible to see how such a dramatic combination of presence on site and distance from the action was transplanted by Joyce into his narrative creation of the Nameless One. First of all, the situation itself may have inspired Joyce: the central theme of infidelity, combined with a cuckold character aware of his plight (Bloom is both Ulysses by correspondence and Troilus in situation), corresponds to Bloom's central concern over Molly's adultery in *Ulysses*. And like Thersites, who sees the world in terms of lechery and cuts down to size the Homeric material accordingly ("All the argument is a whore and a cuckold" [II, iii, 74–75]), the malicious narrator of "Cyclops" has an uncanny understanding of the adulterous situation Bloom finds himself into. He retells Bloom's official version ("She's singing, yes. I think it will be a success too. He's an excellent man to organise. Excellent" [U 306]) in his own picturesque and exposing lingo, a modern Irish version of Thersites's jeering and insults: "Hoho begob says I to myself says I. That explains the milk in the cocoanut and absence of hair on the animal's chest. Blazes doing the tootle on the flute. Concert tour. [. . .] That's the bucko that'll organise her, take my tip" (U 306).

It is in the narrative technique, however, more than in the style or themes, that Joyce's debt to Shakespeare is most remarkable. The numerous moments in *Troilus and Cressida* when Thersites either speaks in asides or is left alone at the end of a scene to comment and rile upon what has just taken place once the main Homeric heroes have left the stage recall the occasions when Joyce's narrator produces a retort that is obviously unheard by the character who triggered it. "Who wants your opinion? Let us drink our pints in peace. Gob, we won't be let even do that much itself" (*U* 308) is the unspoken answer to J. J.'s "In my opinion an action might lie"; and more symptomatically "Talking about new Ireland he ought to go and get a new dog so he ought" (*U* 292) is one of the numerous reactions to the citizen's nationalistic zeal that remain prudently silenced.[24] Indeed, this narrator seems to inhabit a specific narrative space, which is not so much double (as Hayman termed it) as defying a logic of noncontradiction, and in which he is both within and without the narrated pub scene, at once an intradiegetic and an extradiegetic narrator (to use Gérard Genette's [1972] categories), both present at Barney Kiernan's and unheard by the characters whose words and jest he is nevertheless reporting and commenting upon in present tense. This double, contradictory space is obviously inherited from Shakespeare's play between *locus* and *platea* as Joyce saw it at work with Thersites. The Nameless One is the narrative inheritor of the plebeian intermediaries, like Thersites, but also like Apemantus in *Timon of Athens*, like the gravediggers in *Hamlet*, through which Shakespeare voiced skeptical and debunking commentaries that offered alternatives to the main, official view of things.[25] Through them, readers and spectators become aware that

24. Indeed, although Joyce turned into a narrative technique the typically dramatic creation of Thersites's position, the character he produced is obviously a lot less outspoken than his Shakespearean counterpart, and he never rails at the Irish heroes to their faces. Nor does he get threatened or beaten up as Thersites is by Achilles, Patroclus, or Ajax. It is Bloom instead who inherits this function of opposition to the main accepted discourse in "Cyclops," and who suffers violent reactions in consequence.

25. Although the case of *Hamlet* is a more complex one: as Weimann well shows, Hamlet himself is an intermediary character, one whose values, ideas, and attitudes are radically different from the other characters (Weimann 1978, 231–32). Many of the

the values held by the main characters are relative to their particular position in the action, just like the counterperspectives offered by the intermediaries are relative to their own counterpositions. As Weimann pertinently puts it, "This basic recognition of the relationship between character and circumstance, like so much else in Shakespeare, is a profoundly original observation that must be seen in connection with the dramatist's awareness of the tensions between society and the individual, the general, and the particular, from which an essential element of Shakespeare's universality derived" (Weimann 1978, 228). No doubt Joyce would have preferred that understanding of Shakespeare to Canning's explanation.

Having examined the spatial and dramatic particularities of Thersites, and what Joyce made of them stylistically and narratively, I would like to return to the question of history. In a study of "Joyce at Work on 'Cyclops'," Michael Groden (2007) notes that "[t]he possibility that a specific incident from this period [the Zürich performance of *Troilus and Cressida*] inspired Joyce to create the narrator is especially interesting in light of his sudden introduction of the figure [of the narrator] in the National Library of Ireland's draft," thus connecting most closely the theatrical experience of a particularly efficient dramatic character with Joyce's creation of an equally efficient narrative voice (235). Indeed, the revelation brought by genetic study that, contrary to the feeling we have while reading "Cyclops," the narrator's voice actually came second in the composition of the episode, and the passages of gigantism first (219),[26] may be further explained by the connection to Shakespeare, theatricality, and historiography.

As Richard Brown has shown, *Troilus* presented Joyce with a rewriting of Homer's *Iliad*, one that could easily be interpreted as deeply antimilitaristic within the historical context of wartime Zürich.[27] It offered

---

references to Hamlet in "Scylla and Charybdis" may in fact be understood from this perspective.

26. But see also Groden's chapter on "The Middle Stage: 'Cyclops'" (Groden 1977, 115–65).

27. "We might say that, by all but omitting the war and by turning the love tragedy inside out, *Ulysses* also makes a modern comedy out of one of Shakespeare's most

him Shakespeare's take on the Odysseus hero and on his sensible perspective in wartime, one that bore obvious parallels to Bloom's attitude in the "Cyclops" episode. Additionally, the crescendo of chaotic violence at the end of *Troilus* can be compared to the final eruption of aggression and hostility at the end of Joyce's chapter. The stylistic similarities are also remarkable: like the Nameless One, Shakespeare's Thersites presents the audience with a colloquial language—underlined by the prose in which it is written, in stark contrast with the verse used by most of the other Homeric warriors surrounding him, just like the colloquial narration in "Cyclops" is pitted against the parodic passages of gigantism. In addition, Thersites's mocking and jeering are most often expressed through insults and obscene puns (letting us hear the "jakes" in "Ajax"), and definitive debunking of his fellow warriors' heroic natures. However, in *Troilus*, this effect is not simply one of mock-epic burlesque, and may actually be related to the same kind of underlying political critique to be observed in the more obviously historical plays. *Troilus and Cressida* does not broach Plantagenet history, but it does bear some relation to the political propaganda under Elizabeth's reign through its handling of the Homeric matter of the fall of Troy. In the late Middle Ages, the English started elaborating the *translatio imperii* fantasy, a fictional genealogy invented to give the infant nation an appearance of antiquity: in the thirteenth century, Geoffrey of Monmouth told the story of a Trojan called Brut, the grandson of Æneas and grandsire of King Arthur, who had colonized England.[28] Together with

---

bitterly tragic plays. / *Ulysses* in this guise may furthermore emerge as a more directly political work in the sense of its being—like a production of *Troilus and Cressida* in wartime Zürich—an anti-war work but also in the sense that it, like *Troilus and Cressida*, may be seen as a profound work of cultural synthesis or 'translation' in which the constructed parallelisms between Shakespeare and Homer suggest resonances and repercussions of linkage that go deep into European cultural history, suggestively linking Homeric and Virgilian as well as English and European traditions of representing the Trojan war, thus imagining a pan-European and pacific epic vision on an ambitious scale" (Brown 1999, 351).

28. The Arthurian legend would be the other major fictional narrative of national origins in the Tudor era.

Hall's univocal interpretation of the War of the Roses, this ancient myth of dynastic legitimation, later comforted by Spenser in *The Faerie Queene*, served to solidify the Tudor monarchy's claim to the throne.[29] The myth was continued for many years, and when Dryden revised *Troilus and Cressida* in 1679, the preface by R. Duke concluded: "our great Charles being sung by you, / Old Troy shall grow less famous than the new."[30] Through the mythical "translation of empire," seventeenth-century London would inherit the cultural energies passed from Troy. However, as most readers—apart perhaps from Canning—realize, Shakespeare's *Troilus and Cressida* does not so much reinforce this official view as it undermines its very foundation. Matthew Greenfield notes how "[t]he play shows the Troy myth being produced through a series of falsifications," and it "is not a history but a sceptical analysis of history-making, an emptying out or undoing of the work of the chronicles" (Greenfield 2000, 187).[31] Questionably heroic behavior may be observed in all characters, and Cressida is far from being the only unreliable figure in the play: even Hector eventually debases epic battle into selfish bloodlust, when in the last act he hunts down an unknown warrior in sumptuous armor "for [his] hide" (V, vi, 31). In return for this breach of the heroic code, the Worthy will immediately be slaughtered by Achilles's Myrmidons who have found him disarmed (V, viii). The falsifying process of history-making can be observed at work just a few lines after Hector's fall, as Achilles advises his soldiers: "On, Myrmidons, and cry you all amain / 'Achilles hath the mighty Hector slain'" (V, viii, 13–14). The contrast between the cowardly deed of the group and the officially heroic version that idealizes Achilles as an individual is stark. The scene offers an obvious critical rewriting of the well-known Homeric version of the fight between the two legendary warriors, thus

29. See Greenfield's analysis (2000, particularly 184–87).

30. R. Duke, prefatory poem to *Troilus and Cressida*, edited by John Dryden (London, 1679), 31. Quoted in Greenfield (2000, 185).

31. On the subject, see also Douglas Cole: "[*Troilus and Cressida*] seeks to move its audience through a series of shocks of recognition toward a skepticism about the process of myth-making itself, and hence to an urgent and anxious re-examination of its own myths of personal and social order" (Cole 1980, 78).

implicitly questioning the very process of historical mythmaking. Achilles's spoken words will remain the chosen interpretation of the event, to be written down for posterity by Homer. However, Shakespeare's critique of the legendary Homeric version does not begin in act 5 with the murder of Hector by the Myrmidons. This is just the culmination of the chaotic war scenes closing the play. Appearing in act 2 and holding the stage and the audience's attention, Shakespeare's main vehicle for the debunking of all heroic deeds and values in the play is certainly the character of Thersites, much developed from his role in Homer's *Iliad*, or rather in Chapman's *Iliad* where commentators usually agree that Shakespeare found him.[32] One of his great additions to Chaucer's version of the *Troilus and Cressida* myth was in bringing to the fore the railing Thersites, the deformed, snarling warrior who jeers at all the others and famously exclaims: "Lechery, lechery, still wars and lechery! Nothing else holds fashion" (V, iii, 193–95). His devastating quips and insults continuously balance any temptation we would have to see, like Canning, nothing but nobility and heroism in the play. Ulysses himself, a far more reliable, if just as jeering, figure, will comment about Menelaus's cuckoldry: "O deadly gall, and theme of all our scorns! / For which we lose our heads to gild his horns" (IV, v, 30–31). In openly criticizing the Homeric legend and exposing it as a beautified version of a much more complex and ugly history, Shakespeare presented a covert critique of the very process of nationalistic mythmaking that used the Homeric version to idealize London as a New Troy.

The parallel between London's New Troy and Homer's Old Troy immediately brings to mind the opening of "Cyclops" and the otherwise unexplained nickname of the very first character mentioned by the narrator: "I was just passing the time of day with old Troy of the D. M. P." (*U* 280). In the context of *Troilus and Cressida*'s influence on the episode, the reference takes on another dimension: while Shakespeare covertly debunks

---

32. For the sources of *Troilus and Cressida*, I am indebted to Kenneth Palmer's introduction of the 1989 Arden edition, which I use here for all references (Palmer 1989, 1–93; and particularly for Thersites: 35). I have also occasionally used the third series of the Arden Shakespeare edition (Bevington 1998).

the *translatio imperii* mythical narrative of British origin, Joyce's attack on the Irish nationalists' attempt at recreating a new Ireland from a mythic old one is perceptible both through the Nameless One's narration and through the ironic passages of gigantism. Thus, the mock-heroic description of the citizen in the "Cyclops" episode (U 284–85), which culminates in a delirious list of Irish heroes—including "Patrick W. Shakespeare" himself (U 285)—is also an attack on the very process of nationalist myth-making. In a more oral vein, the narrator will offer long enumerations that undermine all the mythical episodes of Irish nationalism, presenting them as a long list of clichés, generally introduced by gerunds, giving us the impression of an endless, worthless enumeration: "So of course the citizen was only waiting for the wink of the word and he starts gassing out of him about the invincibles and the old guard and the men of sixtyseven and who fears to speak of ninetyeight and Joe with him about all the fellows that were hanged, drawn and transported for the cause by drumhead courtmartial and a new Ireland and new this, that and the other" (U 292). In such awkward periods, the narrator's style impedes the very fluidity of the oral conversation that it is supposed to render by producing a long, mostly unpunctuated sentence, which in effect is impossible to utter as it is written. This invasive narrator is quite distant from Joyce's narrative habits, and his unfair, biased treatment of his material is the equivalent of Thersites's insults and interruptions of Shakespeare's Greek heroes. The only fluidity achieved in "Cyclops" is that of the reader's perusal of the sentence, producing an acceleration that can only further undermine the political content of the intended message. Besides, the Nameless One constantly interrupts the other characters' conversation in the pub: when he does not do so with silent but mean-spirited jibes, it is with the perpetual reminder of his narrative presence, as he constantly specifies "says Joe," "says the Citizen," and even "says I." Such invasive narrative habits are so unlike Joyce's usual mode of narration, particularly in contrast to the previous episode of "Sirens," where exchanges tend to be left to develop their own dynamics irrespectively of whether readers know who is speaking or not, that we are bound to notice the change when we come to "Cyclops." Joyce's narrator is therefore an overwhelming narrator, who in effect presents us with an attempt at constructing a master narrative at the very moment when the event is taking place (like Achilles's version of Hector's murder), except that, like Thersites's counterperspective, his version is not the only one available, and it is the very critique of history-making as mythmaking that Joyce allows us to witness.

In other words, to complement his critique of the historiographical discourse of the Anglo-Irish revival, which he was already developing in the passages of gigantism, Joyce may, when he went to see *Troilus and Cressida* at the Pfauentheater, have hit on another dramatic technique that had proven its efficacy in undermining a powerful historical myth, the British fictional narrative of national origins and Trojan descent as inevitably leading to the Tudor rule.[33] Joyce would construct his own narrative of "old Troy of the D.M.P." (*U* 280), after Shakespeare's critique of the Tudor "New Troy." And in the end, the very contest for narrative supremacy that readers get to witness in "Cyclops," the parodic passages of gigantism vying with the downsizing nameless narrator's report, produces a textual comic drama as efficient as a performance of *Troilus and Cressida*. As Joyce realized and knew how to incorporate into his narrative, Shakespearean theatricality will capture the very "spirit of drama," both as aesthetic effect and as historiographical critique.

33. On the subject of Joyce's reaction to the romanticized version of Irish history, see analyses by Watson (1987) and Gibson (2002) (as well as Groden 2007, 230–31).

2

"He Puts Bohemia on the Seacoast and Makes Ulysses Quote Aristotle"

Shakespearean Gaps and the Early Modern Method of Analogy and Correspondence in Joyce's Ulysses

DIETER FUCHS

In James Joyce's *Ulysses*, a scrupulously realist representation of everyday life is blended with the structural design of Homer's *Odyssey* to compensate for the early twentieth-century experience of loss of sense and continuity with archetypal patterns of order and meaning. Although the characters of *Ulysses* remain ignorant of this aspect as far as their figural awareness is concerned, their deeds correspond to an intertextual framework of myths and archetypes that guides their lives by means of analogy and correspondence. What they do is meaningful in terms of the corresponding patterns of the "mythical method" of *Ulysses* (Eliot 1923), although they consider themselves as insignificant agents thrown into a seemingly chaotic world.

As can be seen from Joyce's explanation of some of these interrelating clusters of meaning in the Linati Schema and the Gorman-Gilbert Plan (Ellmann 1972, appendix), the structural framework of *Ulysses* not only echoes the medieval method of the church fathers who ordered and categorized the world in an encyclopedic manner comparable to Joyce's lists (Eco 1989, 5–8); it also reflects the early modern belief that heaven, earth, and mankind are held together by an elaborate system of analogies and correspondences known as the Great Chain of Being (Lovejoy [1936] 1948)—the notion of Renaissance man as a microcosmic world *en minia-ture* (mis-)ruled by the four bodily humors and structurally related to the macrocosmic elements of the universe. As will be shown in this chapter, Joyce studied this aspect not only from Ben Jonson's comedy of humors as implied by Ellmann (1982, 120–27), but primarily from Shakespeare, whose *Troilus and Cressida* provides the most famous outline of the early modern, or "Elizabethan World Picture" (Tillyard [1942] 1972),[1] in the "degree" speech cunningly delivered by the Shakespearean character of Ulysses:

> The heavens themselves, the planets, and this centre
> Observe degree, priority, and place,
> Infixture, course, proportion, season, form,
> Office and custom, in all line of order.
> And therefore is the glorious planet Sol
> In noble eminence enthroned and sphered
> Amidst the other, whose med'cinable eye
> Corrects the ill aspects of planets evil,
> And posts like the commandment of a king,
> Sans check, to good and bad. But when the planets
> In evil mixture to disorder wander,
> What plagues and what portents, what mutiny?
> What raging of the sea, shaking of earth?
> Commotion in the winds, frights, changes, horrors
> Divert and crack, rend and deracinate
> The unity and married calm of states
> Quite from their fixture. O, when degree is shaked,
> Which is the ladder to all high designs,
> Then enterprise is sick. How could communities,
> Degrees in schools, and brotherhoods in cities,
> Peaceful commerce from dividable shores,
> The primogenity and due of birth,
> Prerogative of age, crowns, sceptres, laurels,
> But by degree stand in authentic place?

---

1. Of course new historicists such as Greenblatt (1980) and Wilson (1992), and cultural materialists such as Dollimore and Sinfield (1985), have focused on the blind spots inherent in Tillyard's ([1942] 1972) essentialist approach to history since the 1980s.

Take but degree away, untune that string,
And, hark, what discord follows!

(I, iii, 85–110)

Like the early modern world held together by analogy, order, and degree, James Joyce's *Ulysses* is structured by a complex chain of correspondences. As is pointed out in the Gorman-Gilbert plan, the set of analogies immediately relevant for the context of this chapter on *Ulysses* and Joyce's early modern method is to be found in the "Scylla and Charybdis" episode, which fashions an analogical link between the personae of Odysseus and Shakespeare:

> *Correspondences:* The Rock—Aristotle, Dogma, Stratford: The Whirlpool—Plato, Mysticism, London: **Ulysses**—Socrates, Jesus, **Shakespeare**. (Gorman-Gilbert plan; my emphases)[2]

Although the characters of Ulysses and Shakespeare have, (ana)logically speaking, nothing in common, Joyce's *Ulysses* presents them as counterparts by means of analogy. To shed light on this carefully fashioned corresponding pattern based on Renaissance thinking, this chapter will focus on four aspects: the character of Ulysses from Shakespeare's *Troilus and Cressida* as a variant of the Odysseus archetype and a prototype for Joyce's early modern method; the "Odyssean Shakespeare" fashioned by Victorian and Edwardian psychoanalytical and pseudobiographical readings of *Hamlet* and the *Sonnets*; Joyce's tongue-in-cheek presentation of Shakespeare's Last Will as an "Odyssean" document; Sir Philip Sidney's *Astrophil and Stella* as an unknown source for Joyce's rewriting of the Odysseus myth via Shakespeare.

Let us first look at Shakespeare's Ulysses from *Troilus and Cressida* as a variant of the Odysseus archetype and a prototype for Joyce's ironic indirection. Whereas Linati and Gorman-Gilbert offer an extratextual

---

2. Quoted from Ellmann (1972) "Appendix: The Linati and Gorman-Gilbert Schemas Compared."

explanation, Joyce's early modern method of the ordering of the world in terms of analogy and correspondence remains entirely unexplained within the text of *Ulysses*—an aspect that may be called Joyce's "art of the gap," or ironic indirection. This technique can be observed not only from the structural performance rather than textual presence of the early modern world picture summarized by the Ulysses figure from Shakespeare's *Troilus and Cressida*, but, most of all, from the absence of clearly identifiable textual clues to the Homeric *Odyssey* as the central set of analogies at work in *Ulysses*: whereas the Homeric episodes to which the eighteen chapters of *Ulysses* correspond—"Telemachus," "Nestor," "Proteus," and so on—are listed in the schemata, they are omitted in the merely numerological chapter titles. Likewise there is method in the circumstance that the name of the Homeric Odysseus only appears in the unexplained title of *Ulysses*, but not in the body of the text, which refers only to non-Odyssean Ulysses figures—such as Ulysses Browne, the Austrian eighteenth-century Fieldmarshall with a Hibernian pedigree (*U* 316), and Ulysses Grant, the eighteenth president of the United States (*U* 708)—rather than to the Homeric archetype. These gaps and silences can be observed not only as far as the ancient source text of Homer's *Odyssey* is concerned but also with regard to Joyce's allusions to post-Homeric rewritings of the Odysseus theme, such as Dante's *Divine Comedy* (1952), Shakespeare's *Troilus and Cressida*, and Tennyson's (1986) dramatic Ulysses-monologue (cf. Stanford 1963).

Even if—in contrast to the adaptations by Dante and Tennyson—the Shakespearean Ulysses from *Troilus and Cressida* is explicitly mentioned in "Scylla and Charybdis," this aspect confirms rather than subverts Joyce's "art of the gap" mentioned above: when John Eglinton says that Shakespeare "makes Ulysses quote Aristotle" (*U* 203), the textual presence of Ulysses turns out to be an intertextual absence based on this character's faulty memory, owing to the fact that it is Hector and not Ulysses who (anachronistically) mentions the Stagyrite philosopher in *Troilus and Cressida* (II, ii, 165).[3] By thus presenting the Shakespearean Ulysses as an absently present persona,

---

3. Cf. Gifford and Seidman (1988), 248 [entry 9.995–96].

Joyce's "art of the gap" becomes, structurally speaking, a Trojan horse—an apparently empty shell of a signifier filled with signifieds manipulated by Odyssean cunning and wit, which has to be interpreted with the utmost caution. Such teasing of the reader must be considered as the quite serious background to Joyce's ironic statement that "The demand that I make of my reader, is that he should devote his whole life to reading my works" (Ellmann 1982, 703).

The absently present Odysseus figure from Shakespeare's *Troilus and Cressida,* however, does not merely function as an example of Joyce's art of ironic indirection welded with the early modern belief in analogy. As the Shakespearean Ulysses is fashioned as a master ironist who delivers his already-quoted speech on degree as a trick to make war-weary Achilles return to battle—and who thus subverts, and even violates, the ordering principle of the Elizabethan World Picture (Tillyard [1942] 1972) by its tongue-in-cheek affirmation for intrigue's sake—*Troilus and Cressida* may be also considered as the decisive inspirational source for Joyce's early modern method of the gap.[4] As Shakespeare stresses the ambivalence and the unreliability of the Homeric archetype, his rewriting of Ulysses in *Troilus and Cressida* foreshadows Joyce's trickster-like application of the early modern system of degree, analogy, and correspondence and provides the epistemological background for the aspect that we shall examine

4. According to Garber (2005), *Troilus and Cressida* may be considered as a model for Joyce's *Ulysses* owing to the fact that Shakespeare rewrites the Homeric *Iliad* with the same demystifying spirit as Joyce refashions the *Odyssey.* As in Joyce's *Ulysses*—where the characters function as "debased, " or demythologized versions of their mythical counterparts—"we see Shakespeare's Greeks quarrelling among themselves like peevish schoolboys. Instead of going to battle, Achilles and Patroclus improvise comic imitations of the Greek leaders for their own amusement. . . . [Thus] the audience is confronted with a tremendous loss of idealism, with a debased ideal" (Garber 2005, 538).

As mentioned by Laura Pelaschiar in an informal discussion of this aspect, "another element Joyce and Shakespeare have in common is that they both choose the theme of betrayal and female infidelity as central: in *Troilus and Cressida* Helen's betrayal of Menelaus is doubled (and debased) by Cressida's betrayal of Troilus; in *Ulysses,* Stephen's Shakespeare theory doubles Molly as an unfaithful Penelope with the characters of Anne Hathaway and Penelope Rich."

in the next section of this chapter: the tongue-in-cheek fashioning of a "Shakespearean" Odysseus in Stephen's theory presented in "Scylla and Charybdis."

The second aspect to be discussed in this chapter focuses on the "Odyssean Shakespeare" fashioned by Victorian and Edwardian psychoanalytical and pseudobiographical readings of *Hamlet* and the *Sonnets*. As in the case of the Shakespearean Ulysses from *Troilus and Cressida*—which as a variant of the Odysseus archetype is only presented as an absently present piece of manipulated information—Joyce's fashioning of William Shakespeare as an "Odyssean" persona turns out to be ironically forged: quite obviously there is no analogically sound connection between the Homeric Odysseus and William Shakespeare, although such a link is sophistically pushed forward in Stephen's weird theory presented in "Scylla and Charybdis." In mockery of nineteenth-century biographical criticism, Stephen's approach fashions Shakespeare as an Odysseus-like person who left his wife Anne Hathaway as "a Penelope stayathome" (U 193) for "twenty years" (U 193) and who—in parody of Ulysses blessed with a faithful spouse—suffered under Anne's shrewish disposition as a cuckold: "But all those twenty years what do you suppose poor Penelope in Stratford was doing behind the diamond panes?" (U 193) "Sweet Ann [sic passim!] I take it, was hot in the blood" (U 194).

One need not be overscrupulous to realize immediately that Stephen's pseudo-Freudian "Portrait of the Artist as a Sexually Frustrated Man"—who lived in the pre-Freudian age of the four bodily humors—must be considered as a great juggler's trick, a tongue-in-cheek system of forged analogies and correspondences that ironically intermingles the Bard's life and work, claiming, for instance, that Shakespeare wrote *Hamlet* in order to communicate with his deceased son Hamnet as his own absently present ghost in the playhouse to tell him that "you are the dispossessed son: I am the murdered father: your mother is the guilty queen, Ann Shakespeare, born Hathaway" (U 181):

> —The play begins. A player comes on under the shadow, made up in the castoff mail of a court buck, a wellset man with a bass voice. It is

the ghost, the king, a king and no king, and the player is Shakespeare who has studied *Hamlet* all the years of his life which were not vanity in order to play the part of the spectre. He speaks the words to Burbage, the young player who stands before him beyond the rack of cerecloth, calling him by a name:

Hamlet I am thy father's spirit

Bidding him list. To a son he speaks, the son of his soul, the prince, young Hamlet and to the son of his body, Hamnet Shakespeare, who has died in Stratford that his namesake may live for ever. (*U* 181)

When asked whether he believes his theory, Stephen "promptly" replies that he does not (*U* 205). Absurd as it may be in scholarly terms, however, Stephen's tongue-in-cheek approach to the life of William Shakespeare via *Hamlet* corresponds with the Ulysses theme presented by Homer insofar as the archetypal topics of fatherhood, filial obligation, usurpation, revenge, and the challenged family triad are concerned.

In contrast to these very general analogies echoed in *Hamlet*—whose Freudian tongue-in-cheek application was inspired by Joyce's reading of Ernest Jones's study of *The Problem of Hamlet and the Oedipus Complex*[5]—Shakespeare's *Sonnets* offer a more specific link between Shakespeare and Odysseus. Presenting a fair young aristocrat torn between the love of the middle-aged poet-speaker and that of the seasoned lady who (amongst other affairs) has sex with his "fatherly" mentor, the *Sonnets* weld the "Oedipal" constellation archetypically inscribed in *Hamlet* with a topical allusion to the Odysseus myth via nineteenth-century biographical Shakespeare criticism: as explained by Gifford and Seidman, Stephen's reading of the *Sonnets* as a key to the Bard's life echoes a scholarly tradition that presents the lyrical persona as the empirical "Shakespeare in love" with the Elizabethan gentlewoman Penelope Rich as a namesake of the Homeric "Penelope," so that the lyrical I becomes, structurally speaking, an early modern Odysseus:

5. Ellmann points out that Joyce owned the German translation of "the earliest version of Ernest Jones's celebrated psychoanalytic theory, *The Problem of* Hamlet [sic!] *and the Oedipus Complex*, then just [1911] translated into German" (1977, 54).

The principal exponent of this view was the English poet-scholar Gerald Massey, whose *Shakespeare's Sonnets Never Before Interpreted* (London, 1866) presented a tangled argument to prove that Penelope Rich was the object of Pembroke's love and that Shakespeare wrote many of the sonnets not from his own point of view but as dramatic communications in an elaborate four-way love intrigue between Pembroke, Lady Penelope, Southampton, and one Elizabeth Vernon. Other writers elaborated Massey's fictions into different kinds of liaisons between Shakespeare and Lady Penelope, none of them with any known basis in fact. (Gifford and Seidman 1988, 230)[6]

In ironic contrast to the Odysseus myth and the chastity implied by her Homeric first name, however, "Penelope Rich" (*U* 142) as Massey's real-life counterpart of the Dark Lady has become known principally as an adulteress who had an extramarital love affair and successfully obtained a divorce from her cuckold husband.[7] By letting Stephen refer to "lady Penelope Rich, a clean quality woman . . . suited for a player" (*U* 193; i.e., for "Shakespeare" the theater-man who documents his unfortunate love to that lady in *Sonnets*), James Joyce's *Ulysses* not only presents Penelope Rich as Massey's promiscuous lady of the *Sonnets* and thus parodies the Petrarchan convention of an unattainably chaste woman wooed by her Neoplatonic poet-lover; it primarily offers a corresponding link between Leopold Bloom as Joyce's modern counterpart of the Homeric Ulysses and Shakespeare via the modern Penelope Molly, who—like her early modern double Penelope Rich—turns out to be not as chaste as her Homeric correlative.

When Stephen, like the elaborators of Massey's theory mentioned in the already quoted entry in Gifford and Seidman, speculates that

6. Whereas Joyce refers in greater detail to many other theories and fictions of the *Sonnets* as a key to Shakespeare's life—such as George Bernard Shaw's *The Dark Lady of the Sonnets* (1914) (*U* 188), Frank Harris's *The Man Shakespeare and His Tragic Life-Story* (1909) (*U* 188), and Oscar Wilde's *Portrait of Mr. W. H.* ([1921] 2003) (*U* 190) (cf. also Gifford and Seidman's [1988] entries on these text passages)—he remains notably brief in alluding to Massey's speculation on Penelope Rich. Such brevity may be considered another clue to Joyce's "art of the gap" or ironic indirection.

7. Cf. Gifford and Seidman (1988), 153 [entry 7.1040].

Shakespeare himself rather than his patron, the Earl of Pembroke, "is the spurned lover in the sonnets" (*U* 194) "where there is Will in overplus" (*U* 201), however, it is not only Penelope Rich but also Anne Hathaway, the Bard's allegedly shrewish (*U* 194) and hot-blooded (*U* 194) wife, who is presented as a potential candidate of the Dark Lady. In partial allusion to the anti-Petrarchan description of the Lady presented in Sonnet 130 ("My mistress' eyes are nothing like the sun"), Anne is not only featured as "a boldfaced . . . wench" (*U* 183) and "the ugliest doxy in all Warwickshire to lie withal" (*U* 183). She is also fashioned as a Circe-like witch who bereaves her Shakespearean lover of his will (in various ways, cf. Sonnet 135: "Whoever hath her wish, thou hast thy Will") and assigns him the position of her slave: "He was chosen, it seems to me. If others have their will Ann hath a way" (*U* 183).[8]

Like Anne Hathaway (the "poor Penelope in Stratford," *U* 193) and Penelope Rich as "real-life" prototypes for the unfaithful Lady, Joyce's Dublin Penelope, Molly Bloom, betrays her spouse Leopold, who is thus transformed into the "Shakespearean Odysseus" presented as the speaker of the *Sonnets* by Massey and his followers. This parallelism is not only revealed when the Dublin Ulysses Leopold Bloom gazes into a mirror and perceives the horned face of William Shakespeare rather than his own (*U* 528) and when "ravenhaired" (*U* 306) Molly—whose eyes are "as darkly bright as loves own star" (*U* 725)—resembles the Dark Lady whose "eyes are nothing like the sun" and whose hair is compared to "black wires" (Sonnet 130; 1 and 4). It also surfaces when—in allusion to the lyrical I of the *Sonnets*—"Old Bloom" blessed with "a touch of the artist" (*U* 225) is featured as an aged poet betrayed by his Lady and his young friend, when he refers to Molly and Blazes Boylan as "dark lady and fair man" (*U* 72),[9] and when—being far from satisfied with her current lover—Molly

---

8. Cf. Gifford and Seidman (1988), 209 [entry 9.256–57].

9. With regard to Joyce's appropriation of the triangular constellation of Petrarchan love, this article profits from Burnham's excellent treatment of this topic in her article entitled "'Dark Lady and Fair Man': The Love Triangle in Shakespeare's Sonnets and Ulysses" (1990). Other important, albeit more general, treatments of Joyce and Shakespeare include Cheng (1984) and Schutte (1957).

fantasizes about seducing Bloom's son-like protégé Stephen Dedalus in her nightly reverie presented in the "Penelope" episode:

> I could look at him all day long curly head and his shoulders his finger up for you to listen theres real beauty and poetry for you I often felt I wanted to kiss him all over . . . Im sure itll be grand if I can only get in with a handsome young poet at my age Ill throw them the 1st thing in the morning . . . and I can teach him the other part Ill make him feel all over him till he half faints under me then hell write about me lover and mistress publicly. (*U* 725–26)

Let us now proceed to the third aspect to be looked at in this chapter: Joyce's tongue-in-cheek presentation of Shakespeare's Last Will as an "Odyssean" document. When, as already mentioned, Joyce refers to Anne Hathaway in terms of "If others have their will Ann hath a way" (*U* 183), he welds the intertextual background of Sonnet 135 punning on the Shakespearean persona's will ("Whoever hath her wish, thou hast thy Will") with the Bard's Last Will according to which the "swan of Avon" (*U* 180) bequeathed "his Secondbest Bed" (*U* 195) to his wife as his "swansong" (*U* 194). Although the true meaning of Shakespeare's Will is most probably going to remain a riddle unsolved for ages yet to come, Joyce's analogical "art of the gap" offers a plausible explanation of this enigma for the meaning making process at work within the scope of *Ulysses*: by letting Eglinton remark that "Antiquity mentions famous beds" (*U* 195), Joyce forges a corresponding link between Shakespeare's "Secondbest Bed" (*U* 195) and the most famous bed of the ancient world which is, without doubt, the bed prominently featured in the Homeric episode of the return of Ulysses. When Odysseus and his wife are reunited after their twenty years' separation, Penelope does not immediately recognize her sea-changed husband and laconically offers to command her servant to move the marriage bed (i.e., the best bed the household has to offer) outside of her bridal chamber to accommodate the allegedly strange visitor:

> "Strange man,
> if man you are . . . This is no pride on my part

nor scorn for you—not even wonder, merely.
I know so well how you—how he—appeared
boarding the ship for Troy. But all the same . . .

Make up this bed for him, Eurýkleia.
Place it outside the bedchamber my lord
built with his own hands. Pile the big bed
with fleeces, rugs, and purest linen."

(Homer 1982, XXIII, 197–205)

What looks like a ritualized (and thus unmotivated) gesture of ancient
Greek hospitality at first sight, however, turns out to be a knack to know a
knave: Penelope tests the identity of the newly arrived stranger owing to
the fact that only the true Odysseus knows that the bed—which he built
on the stump of an olive tree—cannot be moved. As a secret shared by the
two spouses only, the knowledge about the unique mechanism of the marriage bed leads up to the anagnorisis of prudent Penelope and her witty
husband Odysseus:

With this she tried him to the breaking point,
and he turned on her in a flash raging.

"Woman, by heaven you've stung me now!
Who dared to move my bed?
No builder had the skill for that—unless
a god came down to turn the trick. No mortal
in his best days could budge it with a crowbar.
There is our pact and pledge, our secret sign,
built into that bed—my handiwork
and no one else's!

                    An old trunk of olive
grew like a pillar on the building plot,
and I laid out our bedroom round that tree,
lined up the stone walls, built the walls and roof,
    gave it a doorway and smooth-fitting doors.

Then I lopped off the silvery leaves and branches,
hewed and shaped that stump from the roots up
into a bedpost, drilled it, let it serve
as model for the rest. I planned them all,
inlaid them all with silver, gold and ivory,
and stretched a bed between—a pliant web
of oxhide thongs dyed crimson.

> There's our sign!
I know no more. Could someone else's hand
have sawn that trunk and dragged the frame away?"

Their secret! As she heard it told, her knees
grew tremulous and weak, her heart failed her.
With eyes brimming tears she ran to him,
throwing her arms around his neck, and kissed him.

                              (Homer 1982, XXIII, 206–34)

In contrast to the "Secondbest Bed" (*U* 195), William Shakespeare bequeaths to his Anne Hathaway—who, in Stephen's opinion, like Penelope Rich as the Dark Lady of the *Sonnets*, committed adultery "behind the diamond panes" (*U* 193) of her bedroom windows as "a Penelope stayathome" (*U* 193)—single-bedded Odysseus recognizes Penelope's faithfulness when he returns back home and finds the bed unmoved after his twenty years' absence. Whereas the Homeric Odysseus considers the unmoved marriage bed as a proof of his wife's constancy, his Joycean counterpart Leopold Bloom has to realize that Molly—the not so chaste Penelope from Dublin—has (probably with the help of Boylan) moved the furniture around their house when he returns home late at night on June 16, 1904:

A sofa upholstered in prune plush had been translocated from opposite the door to the ingleside near the compactly furled Union Jack . . . : the blue and white checker inlaid majolicatopped table had been placed opposite the door in the place vacated by the prune plush sofa: the walnut sideboard . . . had been moved from its position besides the door to a more advantageous but more perilous position in front of the door: two chairs had been moved from right and left of the ingleside to the position originally occupied by the blue and white checker inlaid majolica-topped table. (*U* 658)[10]

Like *Hamlet* and the *Sonnets*, the Last Will—in which William Shakespeare bequeaths his "Secondbest Bed" (*U* 195) to his allegedly adulterous wife—may be thus considered as a part of a carefully fashioned corresponding system based on early modern epistemology, which draws a (mock-heroic) corresponding link between the Bard from Stratford presented in Stephen's theory, the Homeric Ulysses, and Leopold Bloom via Molly, Penelope Rich, and Anne Hathaway: whereas the Homeric Odysseus shares the best marriage bed ever made with the most faithful of all wives, his "Shakespearean" counterpart suffers under the unfaithfulness of his Dark Lady *alias* Penelope Rich *alias* Anne Hathaway, the infidel and hot-blooded, "Penelope stayathome" (*U* 193)—a constellation that recurs in the Bloom family bedroom. Whereas the bed of Odysseus is presented as unmovable, the jingling sound produced by the Bloom marriage bed clearly indicates that this piece of furniture has become a second hand object—a "secondbest bed" whose original stability has become worn out from overuse over the years.

The fourth aspect to be analyzed focuses on Sir Philip Sidney's *Astrophil and Stella* as an unknown source for Joyce's rewriting of the Odysseus myth via "Shakespeare":[11] As far as Joyce's sources for the rewriting of the Odysseus myth are concerned, it has so far been shown that, absurd as it may be in scholarly terms, Gerald Massey's theory on Penelope Rich as the Dark Lady of Shakespeare's *Sonnets* presents a corresponding link between the Homeric Odysseus and what nineteenth-century positivism considered the empirical William Shakespeare.

10. Owing to the fact that, in contrast to the rest of the furniture, the Bloom marriage bed remains unmoved, Joyce's fashioning of Leopold Bloom as a modern counterpart of the Homeric Odysseus and its parody as a pseudo-Odyssean Shakespearean cuckold are simultaneously subverted and contained.

11. Cf. Fuchs 2011.

What has escaped scholarly attention, however, is the fact that—whereas Joyce's "art of the gap" fashions Shakespeare as an early modern Odysseus via Massey's far-fetched theory on Penelope Rich as the Dark Lady of the *Sonnets*—it remains ironically silent about a much more obvious intertext that refers to Penelope Rich in conscious elaboration of the Odysseus myth: Sir Philip Sidney's sonnet cycle *Astrophil and Stella*.[12] Whereas in Shakespeare's *Sonnets* Penelope Rich and the Ulysses theme are only absently present in terms of Massey's speculations, Sidney as a sonneteer alludes to the Elizabethan Gentlewoman as the real-life counterpart of the Lady addressed under the pseudonym "Stella" in a clearly identifiable manner: as Sonnet 37 of *Astrophil and Stella* reveals by the repetitive foregrounding of the word "rich," Stella wooed by the sonneteer's lyrical I, Astrophil, is fashioned as the poetic counterpart of Lady Penelope Rich who—to the disappointment of her admirer Sidney—was married to Sir Robert Rich in 1581:

> My mouth doth water, and my breast doth swell,
> My tongue doth itch, my thoughts in labour be:
> Listen then, Lordings, with good eare to me,
> For of my life I must a riddle tell.
> Towardes Aurora's Court a Nymph doth dwell,
> Rich in all beauties which man's eye can see:
> Beauties so farre from reach of words, that we
> Abase her praise, saying she doth excel:
> Rich in the treasure of deserv'd renowne,
> Rich in the riches of a royall hart,
> Rich in those gifts which give th'eternall crowne;
> Who though most rich in these and everie part,
> Which make the patents of true worldly blisse,
> Hath no misfortune, but that Rich she is.
>
> (Sidney 1962, 37)

12. Gifford and Seidman (1988) comment on Stella as Sidney's poetic representation of Penelope Rich but do not refer to Astrophil as a variant of the Homeric Odysseus: see Gifford and Seidman (1988, 230 [entry 7.1040]).

In contrast to the empirical Lady Rich—who, as already noted, had a love affair and obtained a divorce from her husband—her lyrical persona Stella is not only presented as an unattainably chaste Petrarchan lady. As Sidney features his lyrical self, Astrophil, as the unfortunate suitor of a married woman whose first name corresponds with that of the Homeric Penelope, he also fashions Stella in analogy to the chaste wife of Odysseus—an intertextual allusion that is confirmed by the structural design of Sidney's sonnet cycle as a whole. As *Astrophil and Stella* consists of 108 poems, Sidney's sonnets present Stella *alias* Penelope Rich as a counterpart of the Homeric Penelope who was pursued by 108 suitors during the absence of her husband. Owing to this numerical allusion to the Ulysses myth, every single poem of Sidney's collection of 108 sonnets presents a failed assault on Penelope's fidelity.

In James Joyce's *Ulysses*, Penelope Rich, as a counterpart of her Homeric namesake, is first mentioned in the "Aeolus" episode when the wife of Odysseus is referred to as "poor"[13] and Stephen Dedalus draws an associative link between "Poor Penelope. Penelope Rich" (*U* 142). Young Dedalus thus connects the Homeric Penelope and her less faithful Elizabethan namesakes presented in his theory on the real-life candidates of the Dark Lady of the Shakespearean *Sonnets*: Penelope Rich and Anne Hathaway, the "poor" (*U* 195) "Penelope stayathome" (*U* 193). This correspondence is emphasized when, as already mentioned, the Bard is presented as an early modern Odysseus who leaves Anne Hathaway, spends twenty years of his life away from home, and makes a fortune and falls in unfortunate love with "lady Penelope Rich, a clean quality woman . . . suited for a player" (*U* 193) while his unfaithful but neglected wife—the "poor Penelope in Stratford" (*U* 193)—has "to borrow forty shillings from her father's shepherd" (*U* 194).

Even if Joyce's "art of the gap" attributes this connection to Shakespeare's *Sonnets* in great detail and remains ironically silent about Sidney's

---

13. "ITHACANS VOW PEN IS CHAMP" (*U* 142); "Antisthenes . . . wrote a book in which he took away the palm of beauty from Argive Helen and handed it to poor Penelope" (*U* 142).

Astrophil and Stella as the much more obvious source,[14] it offers a minor intertextual clue to Sidney's sonnet cycle. In allusion to the foregrounding of the word "rich" as a key to Lady Penelope married to Sir Robert Rich in the Sonnet 37 from *Astrophil and Stella,* Joyce presents Shakespeare not only as a horned Odysseus via Massey's theory on the *Sonnets.* He also features him as a counterpart of Robert Rich—the real-life cuckold whom Sidney as a sonneteer fashions as an Odysseus figure richly blessed with his newlywed Penelope: in ironic allusion to Sidney's poem—which states that Penelope is "Rich in the riches of a royall hart" (*Sidney* 1962, 37; 10)—*Ulysses* foregrounds the word "rich" when Stephen Dedalus speculates that, like Robert Rich, Shakespeare "was living richly in royal London" (*U* 194) and "drew a salary equal to that of the lord chancellor of Ireland. His life was rich" (*U* 193).

As can be seen from the ironic distance between Sidney's unattainable muse "Stella" modelled on the faithful wife of Odysseus and her real-life counterpart—the shrewish adulteress who in connection with Massey's theory and Anne Hathaway is presented as the Dark Lady of Shakespeare's *Sonnets*—Penelope Rich thus contributes to the parody of the Homeric Penelope in Joyce's *Ulysses,* which draws a corresponding link between the faithful bridal archetype and a series of unfaithful wives: the early modern adulteress married to Robert Rich *alias* Sidney's poetic muse Stella *alias* Shakespeare's Dark Lady, her counterpart Anne Hathaway *alias* Shakespeare's "poor" (*U* 193) "Penelope stayathome" (*U* 193) and Molly Bloom, the modern Penelope from Dublin.

Sir Philip Sidney's *Astrophil and Stella* as Joyce's pre-Shakespearean source for the rewriting of the Odysseus archetype brings the argument

---

14. As another clue to Joyce's "art of the gap" or ironic indirection, *Ulysses* mentions Sidney's sonnets only in connection with Shakespeare's ("[Shakespeare's] sugared sonnets follow Sidney's" [*U* 196]) and omits the title *Astrophil and Stella.* Comparable to Joyce's teasing of the reader by referring to Ulysses Browne (*U* 316) and Ulysses Grant (*U* 708) rather than to the Homeric archetype, *Ulysses* mentions "Sidney's *Arcadia*" (*U* 203) rather than the intertextually relevant *Astrophil and Stella* and mentions "Sidney Parade" (*U* 285) and a "Mr. Sidney Lee" (*U* 187) rather than the full name of the Elizabethan gentleman-poet.

of this chapter—which focuses on how Joyce fashioned the corresponding tie between the Homeric Odysseus and William Shakespeare as it is presented in Stephen's theory elaborated in the "Scylla and Charybdis" episode—full circle. Having started with an exploration of how the "degree" speech cunningly delivered by the Shakespearean Ulysses from *Troilus and Cressida* sheds light on Joyce's "art of the gap"—the tongue-in-cheek presentation of the early modern method of analogy and correspondence as a Trojan horse—the second part of the chapter focused on how Ernest Jones's psychoanalytic study of the Oedipus complex links *Hamlet* and the *Sonnets* with Homer's *Odyssey* in terms of archetypal constellations such as the challenged family triad, and on how Gerald Massey's pseudobiographical approach to the *Sonnets* shapes Shakespeare as a variant of the Homeric Odysseus via Penelope Rich as the alleged real-life counterpart of the Dark Lady. As a third step, the study proceeded from Massey's biographical reading of the *Sonnets*—"where there is Will in overplus" (*U* 201)—to Shakespeare's Last Will, which offers an ironically forged correspondence between the Bard's "Secondbest Bed" (*U* 195) and the unique bed of the Homeric Odysseus. Last but not least, the fourth section of this case study presented Sir Philip Sidney's *Astrophil and Stella* as an unknown source for Joyce's rewriting of the Odysseus myth via "Shakespeare" to argue that, without Sidney's Ulysses-like Astrophil blended with the background of Massey's theory on the *Sonnets*, there is, analogically speaking, no plausible connection between the Homeric Ulysses and William Shakespeare fashioned as an Odyssean persona. Thus Sidney's rewriting of the Odysseus archetype as an intertextual pattern simultaneously echoed and denied by Joyce's "art of the gap" provides a missing link that allows a tongue-in-cheek exegesis of the corresponding tie between Odysseus and Shakespeare, which finds no analogical explanation when one looks at the Bard and his works as an intertextual source in isolation.

3

"My Story Being Done, / She Gave Me for My Pains a World of Sighs"

Shakespeare's Othello *and Joyce's* Ulysses

LAURA PELASCHIAR

This chapter explores Shakespeare's *Othello* in the light of Joyce's *Ulysses*. This textual/cultural analysis is inspired by the overlapping of two literary silhouettes and motivated by the many similarities that the two protagonists share. Othello and Bloom are both bearers of a cultural alterity that their host communities contemplate with suspicion. They are both also victims of real or imaginary adulterous plots committed by male members of those same communities. The analysis of the emerging common elements and, perhaps more interestingly, of the divergences between Othello and Bloom leads to some rather surprising conclusions, not only as far as Joyce's modern Odysseus is concerned, but even more with regard to the complex character of Othello, the valiant Moor, who emerges in a new light. Were Othello to happen upon that unlikely place which is Bloomusalem, Bloom's fanciful utopia described in "Circe," he would not have it easy. This chapter will try to explain why.

The Shakespeare/Joyce intertextual play is so vast and tentacular as to make any type of systematization a very hard task indeed. In *Ulysses* alone there are hundreds of Shakespearean quotations and allusions: 329, if one went to the trouble of counting those listed in Don Gifford's *Ulysses Annotated*, which inevitably misses quite a few. Joyce very simply plundered the entire Shakespearean canon, even though it is very obviously *Hamlet* that sits comfortably in the lead, with more than one hundred references.

Yet when Joyce decides to make Shakespeare appear on stage—an appropriate term to employ since the Bard's ghost appears in "Circe," the episode structured in dramatic form—he does not speak to his literary critic Stephen Dedalus, as might legitimately be expected of him given the connection established between young Dedalus and Hamlet early on by the text, given that Stephen expounded at length on his Hamlet theory in the "Scylla and Charybdis" episode, and given that the evoking formula pronounced by Lynch, "The mirror up to nature," is taken from *Hamlet*, and Stephen is more equipped than Bloom to recognize the quote and activate the fantasy. Joyce's Shakespeare, instead, chooses to speak to Bloom, using a linguistic pastiche that anticipates the lingua franca of *Finnegans Wake* and referring not to *Hamlet* but to *Othello*. Bloom replies and intertexts with *Macbeth*, and Zoe promptly follows:

LYNCH
>   (*points*) The mirror up to nature. (*He laughs*). Hu hu hu hu hu.

>(*Stephen and Bloom gaze in the mirror. The face of William Shakespeare, beardless, appears there, rigid in facial paralysis, crowned by the reflection of the reindeer antlered hatrack in the hall.*)

SHAKESPEARE
>   (*in dignified ventriloquy*) 'Tis the loud laugh bespeaks the vacant mind. (*to Bloom*) Thou thoughtest as how thou wastest invisible. Gaze. (*he crows with a black capon's laugh.*) Iagogo! How my Oldfellow chokit his Thursdaymomun. Iagogogo!

BLOOM
>   (*smiles yellowly at the three whores*) When will I hear the joke?

ZOE
>   Before you're twice married and once a widower.

(*U* 528–29)

"Circe" is by far the longest and one of the most complex chapters of the book. The complexity is justified by many reasons, one of them being that characters and readers keep fluctuating between two worlds, that of fantasy/hallucination/waking dreams/self-induced visions—a world that Andrew Gibson calls "phantasmagoria" (Gibson 2002, 188)—and that of reality. What is relevant in the economy of the chapter is that both worlds retain for characters and readers alike the same type of *validity*, in that the events which occur in Bloom's and Stephen's fantasies or hallucinations are in terms of their *validity* as experience *au pair* with the events that take place in reality. In this, Joyce is a faithful follower, once again, of Homer and the ancients more than he is of Freud and modern psychology. As E. R. Dodds explains, in his classic study *The Greeks and the Irrational*, for the Greek man has the curious privilege of having right of citizenship to two different worlds that he visits alternatively every day: that of *ypar* (wakening), and that of *onar* (dream). Each of the two has its own logic and its own limitations, but there is absolutely no reason to believe that one is more valid the other. Of course *ypar* offers some advantages— concreteness and continuity, for example—but, Dodds claims, its social possibilities are very restricted since in it we can only meet the people we know. In *onar*, on the other hand, we can approach faraway friends, the dead, the gods. *Onar* is the only experience that can subtract us from the painful and incomprehensible tyranny of time and space (Dodds [1951] 2004, 102–34).

Bloom and Stephen in "Circe" make the most ample and the most flexible use possible of this double citizenship, and in so doing they create that phantasmagoria of faraway friends and dead people (no gods included) that make up 80 percent of the chapter itself. This puts "Circe" into a very close textual as well as epistemological relationship with *Othello*: in *Othello*, fantasy, nonexistent events, imaginary plots, mental fears, and psychic obsessions—the creative powers of the human mind in its destructive version—are also central, where they have an impact on the lives of the characters *as if* they had really happened, with the same disruptive power that reality has on human existence. Fantasy and imagination sit at the core of the plot of *Othello* and are responsible for the tragic evolution of an initially happy marital situation.

William Shakespeare, therefore, is one of the many inhabitants of the "Circe" phantasmagoria. The characters he evokes during his apparition are Iago (Iagogo), Othello (Oldfellow), and Desdemona (Thursdaymomun), the tragedy of *Othello* being his most famous study in male jealousy. In tune with the Bard's words, the obsession that gives origin to this specific vision, which we presume to be Bloom's, is that of Molly's infidelity. The contextual theme is that of adultery. Even the quotes, or rather misquotes, taken from other Shakespearean plays (*Macbeth* in Bloom's exchange with the three whores/witches, and a few lines further down *Hamlet* in Shakespeare's own quote) refer to adultery. And adultery, whether suspected, imagined, remembered, or avoided, as Richard Brown puts it (Brown 1985, 102) is central in Joyce's imagination and to his texts *tout court*.

In a previous Bloomian fantasy, which functions as a prologue to Shakespeare's apparition, Bloom takes part in the adulterous episode between Molly and Boylan in the guise of a servant: he casts himself in the role of Molly's lackey, dressed in uniform, wig, and antlered flunkey, and is busy attending on Boylan, who has just arrived at n. 7 Eccles Street to do his business with Molly.

BOYLAN

> (*Tosses him sixpence.*) Here, to buy yourself a gin and splash. (*He hangs his hat smartly on a peg of Bloom's antlered head.*) Show me in. I have a little private business with your wife, you understand?
>
> (*U* 526)

He is also a passive voyeur, since in the text he watches his wife copulating with Boylan in the company of the other guests: Bloom, Stephen, Lynch, Bella, and the three prostitutes witness Molly's sexual encounter with her lover, they laugh at the scene and are at that point reprimanded by Shakespeare ("Tis the loud laugh bespeaks the vacant mind," *U* 528), who has just appeared in Bella's mirror. After rebuking the onlookers, Shakespeare (a cuckold husband himself, according to Stephen's theory) talks to the betrayed husband: "Thou thoughtest as how thou wastest invisible. Gaze. (*He crows with a black capon's laugh.*) Iagogo! How my Oldfellow chokit his Thursdaymomun. Iagogogo!" (*U* 528).

The fact that Bloom appears in his own mental script as a lackey or a servant in Molly's (and his own) home is an important detail not only because this makes his latent sadomasochism emerge, but also because this directly connects him to the Shakespearean character of Othello. In the same chapter, in fact, but in the course of another fantasy, Bloom had said to Mrs Breen, referring to Molly: "She often said she likes to visit. Slumming. The exotic, you see. Negro servants in livery too if she had money. Othello black brute" (*U* 421). More than once, and with a remarkable isotopic coherence, Bloom connects his own obsessions with and preoccupations about his wife's betrayal to those of the Moor of Venice. The connection is rendered all the more valid since, as we have seen, it is also suggested by the most authoritative of all voices, that of William Shakespeare himself.

It is, indeed, a fascinating connection. After all, Dublin's "wandering jew" and Venice's "erring barbarian" are among the most famous outsiders in Western literature. They are both dislocated subjects, exiles in a racist, strongly xenopobic, and nationalistic community. What's more, they both represent a type of alterity which is *religious* as much as, or even *before*, it is racial. Marjorie Garber identifies race, class, and gender as categories and modes of analysis within which the tensions articulated in *Othello* can and must be interpreted, and most of her own reading of the play is based on them. Yet she is clearly aware of the fact that the Moor's black skin is less central to the dynamics of the play than has been normally assumed. She writes: "Othello is resented by Iago and Roderigo not as much because he is 'black' as because he is a stranger in homogenous Venice. He is, as Roderigo calls him, 'an extravagant and wheeling stranger / Of here and everywhere' (I, i, 137–38)" (Garber 2005, 592). And she is equally aware of the importance of the religious factor when she tries to describe Othello's origins: "He is not a native to Venice, but comes instead, presumably, from northern Africa, where Mauritania (the place of origin of the 'Moors') was located (on the other side of Morocco from where the country Mauritania now lies). . . . Equally important, Moors were conventionally Muslims, not Christians. Arguably, Othello's status as a former non-Christian is as important to the play as his status as a former non-Venetian" (594).

Some interesting critical reflections have re-examined and recovered the importance of the religious framework of the play, a reassessment that in turn may help readdress the balance between the categories invoked and employed by Garber. In *Othello*—exactly as in *Ulysses*—religion and politics are tightly connected and they contribute to build and structure the political discourse of the text. Critics such as Daniel J. Viktus and Julia Reinhard Lupton favor the religious rather than the racial element in Othello's identity and alterity. Viktus reads *Othello* as a "drama of conversion, in particular a conversion to certain forms of faithlessness deeply feared by Shakespeare's audience" (Viktus 1997, 146); in his interpretation, the play reflects the deep religious anxieties of Elizabethan England, which, on the one hand identified the Roman Catholic Church as a manifestation of an almost metaphysical evil, while, on the other, reserving for the Ottoman Turks and their religion a place of honor among the followers of Satan. The historical context is again important. The Ottomans had been pushing in from the East into the Mediterranean for centuries in an attempt to expand into the territories of Western Christianity. In the years preceding the composition of *Othello*, their offensive had become more daring; consequently Protestant propaganda in England had intensified, with the result that religious and political enemies were rolled into one single demonological iconography in which the Pope and the Sultan were associated with Satan and the Antichrist, since both Catholics and Muslims aimed at converting Protestants, a sure way to lead them to damnation (Viktus 1997, 148–50). Julia Reinhard Lupton also stresses the religious dimension of Othello's alterity, claiming that for historical and cultural reasons the Elizabethans perceived such alterity first of all in terms of religious diversity, given that racial diversity was only beginning to emerge then as a cultural discourse. It could be risky, if not totally wrong, to read Othello as a product of a protocolonial culture: "Greenblatt and others," concludes Viktus, "have used a Western imperialist discourse belonging to later centuries, sometimes quite anachronistically, to frame readings of Renaissance texts" (Lupton 1997, 170).

Viktus's theory seems supported by the fact that the Venetian Republic in *Othello* is a synecdoche for Western Christianity as a whole. And

Venice is not here portrayed as an expanding superpower busily invading and colonizing foreign lands (an enterprise in which England had only recently started to engage). The action takes place in Cyprus, not in Terranova or in Guyana or in Virginia, and Cyprus is a piece of Christianity under siege, an outpost of Western civilization that risks being invaded by the Muslims. Within this historical and political context, Othello is also therefore Venice's, and by extension the Christian West's, crusader and their *defensor fidei*.

This religious net of signification allows us to understand another important convergence between Bloom and Othello. Both are, in fact, outsiders who converted to the Christian religion, and it is not at all accidental that the baptism of both characters is mentioned in the texts. Iago talks about it in act 2, scene 3 while he is soliloquizing after convincing Cassio to ask Desdemona to intervene in his favor with the Doge since it would be easy for her "to win the Moor, were it to renounce his baptism, / All seals and symbols of redeemed sin" (333–34). In *Ulysses* Bloom's baptisms are described in great detail in "Ithaca": "Had Bloom and Stephen been baptised, and where and by whom, cleric or layman? Bloom (three times), by the reverend Mr Gilmer Johnston M. A., alone, in the protestant church of Saint Nicholas Without, Coombe, by James O'Conor, Philip Gilligan and James Fitzpatrick, together, under a pump in the village of Swords, and by the reverend Charles Malone C. C., in the church of the Three Patrons, Rathgar. Stephen (once) by the reverend Charles Malone C. C., alone, in the church of the Three Patrons, Rathgar" (*U* 635).

Yet both have rather ambiguously left behind—or at least this is the fear or paranoia that haunts both Dubliners and Venetians alike—an original religion which for Bloom is very clearly the Jewish one, but for Othello is never made explicit. The social danger of this religious ambiguity is clearly perceived and expressed by Dubliners, in "Hades" and in "Cyclops" more specifically, and in Venice by Iago and by Brabantio, who, incapable of accepting his daughter's betrayal, in act 1, scene 2, accuses Othello of having bewitched his daughter by performing black magic on her. He actually goes further than that: in scene 3 of act 1, given the urgency of state business, the duke is eager to dismiss the unpleasant matter of Desdemona's marriage with Othello as quickly as possible; he therefore talks to Brabantio in a series of rhyming couplets full of truisms where he more or less tells the offended father he should accept the situation and put up with it. Brabantio, who is hurt much more than the duke is willing to realize (he will actually die heartbroken before the end of the play), replies by comparing Desdemona's "abduction" at the hands of Othello to the loss of Cyprus at the hands of the Turks. Othello thus becomes the Muslim enemy who conquers and violates a precious Venetian possession.

The ambiguity of faith that characterized Othello's identity is also typical of Leopold Bloom. Although he converted to the Catholic religion, Bloom feels very much a stranger in it: not only does he find its rituals incomprehensible, he does not even believe in them. Nevertheless, like Othello, who is presented very clearly as the defender of the Republic and of its faith, he operates in defense of the political and cultural identity of his community, or rather of the community to which he now belongs, since in Dublin the rumor is widespread that Bloom had given Arthur Griffith some of the most relevant ideas for the articulation of his political agenda. In "Penelope" Molly remembers how Bloom used to "blather on" about the "Land League and Home Rule" and that "the Doyles said he was going to stand for a member of Parliament" (*U* 721). In spite of this military (in Othello's case) and political (in Bloom's case) commitment to communal interest, both Othello and Bloom are regarded with suspicion by the members of the very community they are committed to defend. Their true loyalty is constantly questioned. In this sense it is not accidental that Joyce puts into Mr Deasy's mouth the words "put money in thy purse" with which Iago peppers his long speech at the end of act 1, when he convinces Roderigo to follow him to Cyprus: his is, with the citizen's, the most virulent and intolerant racist and anti-Semitic voice of the text. Deasy is preaching to Stephen with the intention of teaching him how to fare better in life.

> —Because you don't save, Mr Deasy said, pointing his finger. You don't know yet what money is. Money is power. When you have lived as long as I have. I know, I know. *If youth but knew.* But what does Shakespeare say? *Put but money in thy purse.*
> —Iago, Stephen murmured. (*U* 30)

A racist just like Iago, and like Iago (and not like Shakespeare, as Stephen hastens, unheard, to correct) very much into money, Deasy has another characteristic that makes him into a Iago-like figure: he is totally immersed in the sexuophobic misogyny that is typical of patriarchal culture and that Iago is so familiar with. The headmaster is obsessed with women's betrayal and female adultery, to which he assigns a monocausal role in a philosophy of history that he illustrates to Stephen during their encounter in the study. History moves, he says, toward a single telos, the manifestation of God:

> I am happier than you are. We have committed many errors and many sins. A woman brought sin into the world. For a woman who was no better than she should be, Helen, the runway wife of Menelaus, ten years the Greeks made war on Troy. A faithless wife first brought the strangers to our shore here, MacMurrough's wife and her leman, O'Rourke, prince of Breffni. A woman too brought Parnell low. Many errors, many failures but not the one sin. I am a struggler now at the end of my days. But I will fight for the right till the end.
> > *For Ulster will fight*
> > *And Ulster will be right.* (U 35)

In Shakespeare's tragedy, writes Linda Bamber, misogyny and misfortune are very often connected by male protagonists (Bamber 1982, 16). Deasy seems to subscribe to this idea, and it is interesting that his obsession with female unfaithfulness is coupled by Joyce with racism and religious intolerance. Alterity and adultery are in Deasy's mind directly connected.

And yet that very otherness that inspires so much distance in Dublin and in Venice was instrumental, both for Othello and for Bloom, in winning the love of their women and future wives. If one reads carefully through the texts, both protagonists opt for very similar and equally successful seduction strategies, even though there is one (very important) difference. So successful was Othello in defending himself, even if he claimed in the senate to possess no rhetorical skills ("Rude am I in my speech, / and little blest with the set phrase of peace" [I, iii, 81–82]), that he does not hesitate to re-employ these oratorical skills in order to defend himself from Brabantio's accusations in front of the duke and the senators. It is important to remember here that scene 3 of act 1 is entirely Shakespeare's invention and has no counterpart in Giraldi Cinthio's *Gli Hecatommithi*, which is traditionally indicated as the source for *Othello*. It is here that the reader is given to understand that the only magic that the Moor operated upon Desdemona is the magic of language, or even better the magic of storytelling.

> Her father lov'ed me, oft invited me,
> Still question'ed me the story of my life,
> From year to year; the battles, sieges, fortunes,
> That I have pass'd:
> I ran it through, even from my boyish days,
> To the very moment that he bade me tell it.
> Wherein I spake of most disastrous chances,
> Of moving accidents by flood and field;
> Of hair-breadth scapes i' th' imminent deadly breach;
> Of being taken by the insolent foe
> And sold to slavery, of my redemption thence.
>
> (I, iii, 128–38)

And on he goes to mention vast deserts and high mountains, caves, human cannibals and monsters whose heads grew beneath their shoulders. These are the very words that won not only Desdemona's heart, but Brabantio's trust as well. This, and not black magic, is the alchemy used by Othello to bewitch Desdemona. Something Desdemona herself, once she is allowed to enter the scene, confirms.

The archetypal model followed here is obviously that of Odysseus and of the narrations of his own adventures at King Alcinous's court. Like Odysseus, and more than Odysseus, Othello recounts events of *his own* life, stories that happened to him, adventures with one protagonist and one witness only: himself. These are the autobiographical narrations that won Desdemona's heart, and understandably so, as the duke is ready to acknowledge ("I think this tale would win my daughter too"

[I, iii, 171]). The Moor is an egotistically hyperbolic narrator of his own adventurous, exotic, and international life, populated by anthropophagi and human monsters that can only exist in the seductive intent of the conquering Moor.

In "Penelope" Molly admits to having been conquered by a very similar—and yet significantly different—type of rhetoric.

> he excited me I dont know how the first night ever we met when I was living in Rehoboth terrace we stood staring at one another for about 10 minutes as if we met somewhere I suppose on account of my being jewess looking after my mother he used to amuse me the things he said with the half slootering smile on him and all the Doyles said he was going to stand for a member of Parliament O wasnt I the born fool to believe all his blather about home rule and the land league sending me that long strool of a song out of the Huguenots to sing in French to be more classy O beau pays de la Touraine that I never even sang once explaining and rigmaroling about religion and persecution. (U 721)

In evoking her first meeting with her future husband, Molly projects on her own foreign, and more specifically Jewish, looks and thinks that Bloom's attraction to her was connected to his instinctive recognition of the Semitic features she thinks she has inherited from her mother, the Spanish Jewess Lunita Laredo. Bloom speaks to Molly about "home rule and land-league," of the Huguenots, of "religion and persecution," and also about Buddhism and Hinduism (U 721), revealing that international and multiethnic dimension which makes him so unique in a provincially xenophobic Dublin. But while the self-reflexive, narcissistic Othello talks about his own adventurous life, hyperbolically amplifying his story of "most disastrous chances," "moving accidents," and "slavery and redemption" to the point of breaking into fiction and invention ("men with their heads growing beneath their shoulders"), Bloom prefers to dislocate his own traumatic destiny as a marginalized Jew onto historical rather than fictional events that happened to others: those of the Catholic nationalists in Ireland persecuted by Protestants (home rule, land league) and those of the Protestant Huguenots persecuted by Catholics in France. These stories of "religion and persecution," as Molly calls them, very clearly articulate a rhetorical chiasm which, in the specific context of the "Penelope" episode as well as within the wider circle of Irish history, takes on a universalizing nuance that should not escape the attention of the reader. Besides, the fact that Bloom, unlike his Shakespearean predecessor, prefers facts to fiction, is highly significant. It is in the difference of their rhetorical approaches— with Othello revealing himself to be self-centered, self-referential, and fictional while Bloom is allocentric, referential, and historical—that the divergences between the two heroes begin to appear. But before we move on to examine them, it is necessary to mention the last and most obvious common denominator: adultery.

Alterity, adulteration, adultery: Tony Tanner ponders the semantic proximity of these terms in his famous study *Adultery in the Novel, Contract and Transgression* (1979). In a subchapter entitled "The Stranger in the House" (24–26), Tanner connects the theme of adultery—which is present in Western tradition since Homer—to that of alterity and examines the transgressions of marriage contracts in classical literature. He begins with Helen of Troy (a mythological episode mentioned by Mr Deasy) and moves on to Tristran and Iseult, Lancelot and Genevieve, all the way down to Shakespeare's imaginary adulterous plots in *Othello* (which Tanner does not examine in great detail), *Cymbeline*, and *The Winter's Tale*. All the male characters implicated in these "adulterous plots," Tanner claims, have one thing in common: their alterity. They are all aliens of mysterious origin, strangers, to use Tanner's term, in somebody else's house. Examining these situations from an anthropological perspective, Tanner observes that the basic intention of the art of hospitality since ancient times has always been to transform the "stranger" into a "guest" in order to elide the potential threat that the Other always represents for the social order and the balance of the hosting tribe. But hospitality remains an uncertain bet because the ontological danger implicit in the Other is always potentially active (and easy to activate); the process of de-alienation that is the purpose of hospitality can never be said to be complete. Paris, Tristran, Lancelot, and Iachimo are all strangers in the house who break the pact they had symbolically signed with their host by transgressing it (or pretending to transgress it) in the most socially unacceptable way: by desiring and possessing the body of a woman who belongs by contract to another man.

It is significant that in his illuminating synopsis Tanner avoids expanding on *Othello*. This makes sense. Although they are strangers, or semistrangers, in the house, Othello and Bloom are not guilty of committing adultery; instead they are the victims of real or imaginary adulterous plots organized against them by representative male members of the community to which they now belong: Cassio, the perfect courtesan with the good looks and perfect manners, and Blazes Boylan, the supermacho with the quiff. So, both in *Othello* and in *Ulysses*, Tanner's paradigm is not only disappointed: it is literally inverted.

As already indicated, it is the idea of his wife's adultery that makes it possible for Bloom to see in Bella Cohen's mirror a William Shakespeare (with horns) who talks to him about Iago, Othello, and Desdemona. Or rather: he tells him of how "his" (that is, Shakespeare's) Othello ("my Oldfellow") choked "his" (Othello's) Desdemona. Because, come to think about it, the specific episode that Shakespeare mentions in "Circe" is the *killing* of Desdemona by Othello. So, more than adultery here we are actually dealing with uxoricide. And since *this* Shakespeare is but a product of Bloom's unconscious, or preconscious, it follows that in his repressed psychic universe the idea, or even the desire of doing to Molly what Othello did to Desdemona does somehow exists. But it is a repressed wish and Bloom, unlike Othello, does not yield to it. And it is here that the trajectory of Joyce's adulterous plot radically diverts from Shakespeare's imaginary one.

Indeed, the hiatus that separates *Othello* from *Ulysses* is not so much in the distance that separated Othello's high, heroic, and tragic status from Bloom's low, comic, petit bourgeois dimension. It does not even lie in the fact that while Desdemona does not kiss *Lieutenant* Cassio in Cyprus or anywhere else, Molly does kiss in Gibraltar, and under the "Moorish Wall" of all places, *Lieutenant* Jack Joe Harry Mulvey (*U* 732), who gave her a *handkerchief* before leaving Gibraltar and, as the first of a long series of flirts (and possibly lovers), is a prefiguration of Blazes Boylan. The hiatus lies in the opposite reaction that the two protagonists—and hence the two textual strategies, and hence the different cultural systems to which they give voice—choose when they are forced to deal with adultery: it lies in the fact that Othello decides to lay down in his marital bed to choke innocent Desdemona and Bloom enters his own bed to reconcile himself with guilty Molly.

Postcolonial readings of *Othello* usually come to the conclusion that Iago's plot tragically succeeds because Othello has internalized (an unconscious process, therefore) the racism that is immanent in the cultural codes of Venetian society, of which Iago is the most ruthless and outspoken representative. As Alessandro Serpieri (1978) explains, Iago's psychism is but a projection of his own epoch's collective psychism. This racism is so deeply ingrained that even "fair Desdemona" is somehow affected by it: Iago refers to this when, while he is trying to convince Othello of her duplicity, he says, "She did deceive her father, marrying you; / And when she seem'd *to shake and fear your looks,* / she loved them most" (III, iii, 210–13; emphasis added); Desdemona herself hints at her own prejudice against Othello when, in her attempt to persuade Othello of Cassio's good faith and trustworthiness, she says : "Michael Cassio / that came a-wooing with you, and so many times / When I have spoke of you *dispraisingly,* / Hath ta'en your part—to have so much to do / To bring him in?" (III, iii, 71–75). A postcolonial approach would claim Othello has ended up feeling for himself the repulsion that others (including Desdemona at first) feel for him and therefore is condemned to find Iago's fiction very plausible, as Desdemona's adultery is the inevitable consequence of that act of racial adulteration that their union represents. The irretrievable schism between the ideological dogmas of the hegemonic culture that he has adopted and the identitarian "otherness" that he cannot delete, being the stranger in the house, can only lead him to self-destruction; a self-destruction that must be prologued by the elimination of the adulterated—and hence potentially adulterous—Desdemona.

The theory seems to hold. Yet the problem is that Othello does not kill himself after choking Desdemona because of the desperation he feels for the loss of a deeply beloved wife, whose death he laments with powerful words of woe and pain.

> My wife, my wife, my wife; I ha' no wife;
> O, insupportable! O heavy hour!
> Methinks it should be now a huge eclipse

Of sun and moon, and that the affrighted globe
Should yawn at alteration.

(V, ii, 98–102)

For Desdemona's death he invokes huge eclipses of sun and moon and cataclysmic events of global consequence: but no suicide. Because the Moor finishes off his existence only after realizing he has murdered an innocent. Would he have taken his own life had Desdemona (like Molly) been guilty?

Marilyn French, in her gentle feminist reading of *Othello*, claims that "it would be impossible for Iago to seduce Othello if Othello did not already share Iago's value structure. Othello is not dense or blind, he is not the noble savage. He is a male who lives and thrives in a masculine occupation, in a 'masculine' culture the assumptions of which he subscribes to" (French 1981, 212). This masculine culture, French explains, is based on the exercise of power meant as control over others, and over women in the first place; and since the only forms of control over others are "domestication" and "killing," if a female object refuses to be domesticated, then the only alternative is killing. Of the patriarchal culture that articulates his eponymous tragedy, Othello shares not only its sexuophobic misogyny (and this explains the linguistic interchangeability between Iago and Othello upon which so many critics have remarked) but also the religious racism that is integral to the play's net of significations. This is why he is able to order: "Are we turned Turks, and to ourselves do that / Which heaven had forbid the Ottomites / From Christian shame, put by this barbarous brawl" (II, iii, 160–63). It is also why he can compare himself to a "base Indian," and why he mentions the "malignant and turban'd Turk," the "circumcised dog" that he claims to have killed in Aleppo in his famous suicide speech of act 5.

And say besides, that in Aleppo once,
Where a malignant and turban'd Turk
Beat a Venetian, and traduc'd the state,
I took by the throat the circumcised dog,
And smote him thus! [*Stabs himself*]

(V, ii, 355–59)

Encaged within the cultural codes of a hegemonic culture to which he has totally adhered (rather than internalized), Othello cannot coherently bring to fulfillment that "narration of international romance" which his love story with Desdemona represented at the beginning of the play, and thus he betrays that role of "living symbol of Christian universalism" (Lupton 1997, 74) for an excess of zeal toward the "Catholic doctrine of conjugal appropriation of the female body in marriage" (Henke 1990, 2). Othello follows the law of the Old Testament, forgetting that in the New Testament (the Gospel according to John), when the scribes and Pharisees bring to the temple an adulterous woman who, as prescribed by Mosaic law, ought to be stoned, Jesus replies with words of forgiveness:

> And every man went unto his own house. Jesus went unto the mount of Olives. And early in the morning he came again into the temple, and all the people came unto him; and he sat down, and taught them. And the scribes and Pharisees brought unto him a woman taken in adultery; and when they had set her in the midst, They say unto him, Master, this woman was taken in adultery, in the very act. Now Moses in the law commanded us, that such should be stoned: but what sayest thou? This they said, tempting him, that they might have to accuse him. But Jesus stooped down, and with *his* finger wrote on the ground, *as though he heard them not.* So when they continued asking him, he lifted up himself, and said unto them, He that is without sin among you, let him first cast a stone at her. And again he stooped down, and wrote on the ground. And they which heard *it*, being convicted by *their own* conscience, went out one by one, beginning at the eldest, *even* unto the last: and Jesus was left alone, and the woman standing in the midst. When Jesus had lifted up himself, and saw none but the woman, he said unto her, Woman, where are those thine accusers? hath no man condemned thee? She said, No man, Lord. And Jesus said unto her, Neither do I condemn thee: go, and sin no more. (Gospel according to John 7:53–8:11)

Paradoxically, it is Bloom the wandering Jew—twice converted to a Christian religion, and yet totally estranged from it because he is still so deeply rooted in his Jewish culture of origin—who follows the Christian example of the New Testament and does not observe the Mosaic commandment of the Old Testament, which instead is obeyed by Othello, the official defender of the Christian faith. Robert Spoo writes apropos of Molly's adultery and Bloom's reaction to it:

> The theme of the treacherous woman as monocause resounds throughout *Ulysses*, but nowhere more importantly than in the question of Molly's adultery and its effect on Bloom. Is Molly the sole cause of Bloom's marital difficulties? One of the things Bloom comes to terms with in the course of the day is his share of the responsibility for the sundering of their relations.(. . .) A large-scale deconstruction of causality in the Boylan/Molly affair is undertaken in "Ithaca", where Bloom's progress from envy and jealousy to abnegation and equanimity (*U* 17.2154–99; 732.12–733.30) reveals that everyone—Boylan, Molly, Bloom himself— is partly to blame and partly innocent. (Spoo 1989, 451–52)

Light years away from the misogyny of the "inflexibility of the masculine principle" and the consequent "devaluation of the feminine principle" (French 1981, 217) that is typical of Iago's and Othello's male culture, Bloom exhibits behavioral elements that would be classified by that very culture as feminine: he is, after all, described in "Circe" as "a finished example of the new womanly man" (*U* 465) (before performing exhilarating miracles in Christ-like fashion). In "Cyclops" he is attacked by the citizen because he has rejected the principles of "force, hatred, history, all that" (*U* 319) which his Fenian antagonist supports and because his *forma mentis* operates outside the racist and xenophobic ideological framework which Othello did not reject. The new Utopia that Bloom sketches out in "Circe" during one of his visions, is, despite its irresistible comic context, really very close to that ideal of universalism which Othello embodied at the beginning of the play but later failed to live up to.

BLOOM
> I stand for the reform of municipal morals and the plain ten commandments. New worlds for old. Union of all, jew, moslem and gentile. Three acres and a cow for all children of nature. Saloon motor hearses. Compulsory manual labour for all. All parks open

to the public day and night. Electric dishscrubbers. Tubercolosis, lunacy, war and mendicancy must now cease. General amnesty, weekly carnival with masked licence, bonuses for all, esperanto the universal language with universal brotherhood. No more patriotism of barspongers and dropsical impostors. Free money, free rent, free love and a free lay church in a free lay state.

And further down:

BLOOM
Mixed races and mixed marriages.

LENEHAN
What about mixed bathing?

(U 462)

The "Bloomusalem in the Nova Hibernia of the future," which Joyce does not take seriously at all, has the inconsistency and the implausibility of all literary utopias, but unlike other utopias—and perhaps the only one in its genre—it possesses the gift of desirability. And if one were to imagine a fiction located in Bloomusalem in which and Othello and Bloom were accidentally to meet, there is little doubt that the comic, grotesque, and slightly overweight Leopold Bloom could rob valiant Othello if not of the role of epic hero, then at least of his position as absolute protagonist. But this is another story.

4

Joyce's *Exiles* and Shakespeare's *Tempest*

GIUSEPPINA RESTIVO

Joyce's mention of Shakespeare's *Othello* in his notes to his one autobiographical play, *Exiles*, attracts attention not only to the author's sounding of unexplored aspects of jealousy, but also to Shakespeare's constant presence in Joyce's mind. It suggests that Richard's words in the third act of *Exiles*, "I am what I am" (250), following the plain statement "I did not make myself," may well echo Iago's famous "I am not what I am" (I, ii, 65), though with a vengeance. While Iago is proud of his ability to conceal his intentions, to deceive and use his "villainy," Richard—who in a sense "conflates" Othello and Iago in himself—is, on the contrary, proud of his courage to expose his innermost drives, the ambiguous realities of his desires and emotions. But if Joyce had not mentioned *Othello* in his notes (written during the composition of *Exiles* and usually published along with it), the ironical Shakespearean echo in Richard's words would hardly be detectable.

Shakespeare's *Tempest*, in contrast, is not mentioned in the notes, and its context might at first sight seem distant from that of *Exiles*: but an evident quotation from Shakespeare's third act appears shortly before the allusion to Iago's words. It comes at a highly dramatic moment, the night after the protagonist Richard Rowan, a writer mirroring Joyce himself, has pushed his companion Bertha (evoking Nora Barnacle) to meet at night her wooer Robert Hand, a journalist and his best friend (recalling Roberto Prezioso, the editor of the Trieste newspaper *Il Piccolo*). Richard has openly accused Robert of secret dealings (faithfully and constantly

56

reported to him by Bertha), only to leave him alone with Bertha immediately after. In spite of his jealousy, Richard feels no right to detain Bertha from an experience she might value, or to demand from her a faith he has repeatedly betrayed, though not importantly, and constantly self-accusingly. Robert and Bertha must make their own choices. On the one hand, Richard is confident in her restraint; on the other, he ambiguously hopes she will betray him, "compensating" his unfaithfulness or ethical inferiority. At the same time his friend and admirer Beatrice, after an important nine-year intellectual relationship, has just admitted her attraction to him, to no avail, but adding to Bertha's anxiety and to the complexities of the situation Bertha and Richard are living.

After such a testing night, Richard comes home from an early morning walk to the Dublin bay during which he has revolved in his mind the terms of his relations with Bertha, Robert, and Beatrice. On meeting Bertha at home, he suddenly quotes a line from *The Tempest*, which in the Jonathan Cape edition (republished by Granada in Panther Books) appears, with a slight adaptation, as "This isle is full of voices" (*E* 125).[1] In the subsequent Penguin edition it more perfectly reports Shakespeare's verse, "The isle is full of noises" (*E* 244), which is explicitly annotated as an evident quotation. Why this reference to *The Tempest*?

The original Shakespearean passage, contained in Caliban's description of Prospero's "magic island" to Stephano, reveals a strange context where sounds, music, and voices mix together with dreams:

> CALIBAN: Be not afeard, the isle is full of *noises*,
> Sounds, and sweet airs, that give delight and hurt not,
> Sometimes a thousand twangling instruments
> Will hum about mine ears; and sometimes *voices*,
> That if I then had waked after long sleep,
> Will make me sleep again, and then in dreaming
> The clouds methought would open and show riches

---

1. The 1921 Jonathan Cape edition of *Exiles* was republished in 1979 by Granada Publishing/Panther Books, the edition referred to here.

Ready to drop upon me, that when I waked
I cried to dream again.

(III, ii, 132–41)[2]

In both versions of *Exiles* the quotation is evident, as in Shakespeare's passage "noises" and "voices" are connected and even fused: but what relevance can this allusion have to Joyce's themes in the play? What can *Exiles* and *The Tempest* have in common?

Joyce's *Exiles* is obviously related to *Othello* by Richard's jealousy: Joyce's alter ego Richard both fears and seeks Bertha's betrayal, and, though only psychologically, he kills his Bertha/Desdemona in the sense that, as he admits, he kills her innocence. But at the same time, in a less expected way, Richard/Joyce—anticipating Stephen Dedalus in *Ulysses*, who mirrors himself in the intellectual Prince Hamlet—identifies with Shakespeare's other distinguished intellectual prince, Prospero.

The quotation from *The Tempest* is not cursory. Its memory is more deeply embedded than it might at first sight seem in the Joycean setting of tormented couple relationships, apparently distant from the story of wifeless Prospero, concerned mainly with his daughter Miranda's happy marriage and a redressing of his loss of the Milan dukedom. Comparable aspects in the two plays are mostly linked to an overlapping of Richard with Prospero. Five main correspondences are detectable and will be analyzed: like Prospero on his island, Richard is an exile from a usurped country in need of him; at the same time he is, like Prospero, a distinguished intellectual; like Prospero, he is also gifted with a peculiarly strong psychic mind-power over those who deal with him. Moreover, both male protagonists are proud educators who try to use their intellectual superiority to correct/influence human behavior and the course of history. Both act as all-knowing directors on stage, controlling all characters, but their anxiety for control contrasts with a corresponding anthropological anxiety for freedom from all constraints. To this multiple set of correspondences

---

2. *The Tempest* edition used is *The Oxford Shakespeare*, edited by Stephen Orgel (Oxford University Press, 1987).

based on Richard's identification with Prospero as an intellectual, a possible tempting Irish quality of Shakespeare's *Tempest* in Joyce's eyes can be added, which seems to have also stimulated Joyce's quotation, implying a parallel link with Caliban as well.

The aspects connecting Prospero and Richard (whose names might share a similar allusion to "prosperity" or to "richness") extend the impact of *The Tempest* on Joyce's *Exiles* well beyond the space of an occasional quotation. It runs throughout the text, in a continuous indirect comparison, adding to the long underscored complexities of the play, only partly revealed in Joyce's own notes. Delving into this connection can cast new light on both *Exiles* and Joyce's creative process.

The Exiled Intellectual or the Anxiety of Reshaping

Shakespeare's Prospero is both a prince and a scholar of renown, the proud representative of a flourishing *Signoria* of the Italian Renaissance, who for his studies' sake entrusted his brother Antonio with the actual government of his dukedom of Milan, as he explains when revealing his true identity to Miranda:

> my state, as at that time
> Through all the signories it was the first
> And Prospero the prime duke, being so reputed
> In dignity, and for the liberal arts
> Without a parallel; those being all my study,
> The government I cast upon my brother
> And to my state grew stranger, being transported
> And rapt in secret studies.
>
> (I, iii, 70–78)

To him his books have always been more important than his dukedom. Not only does he own that "Me, poor man, my library was dukedom large enough" (I, ii, 109–10), while describing himself as "neglecting worldly ends, all dedicated to closeness and the bettering of my mind" (I, ii, 89–90), but he also continues to obstinately describe his books as "volumes that I prize above my dukedom" (I, ii, 167–68), although this choice has cost him his dukedom, usurped by his brother, and has forced him into a twelve-year-long exile with Miranda on a desert island. Here his magician's powers and books have allowed them to survive and to go back to Milan to redress history.

In *Exiles* Richard Rowan is not, like Prospero, a magician with power over spirits, nor has he lost a dukedom: but he is a daring intellectual, who has lived a self-imposed exile in Italy and has just come back to Dublin and to Ireland, long usurped by the English. He appears constantly concerned with his writing, attached to his books and his study, where he works and even often sleeps. As in Prospero's case, it is his absorbing intellectual quality that has led to his exile; he is not the victim of a usurping brother, but has departed to serve his own intellectual needs, which were suffocated in contemporary Ireland, culturally constrained by its strict Catholic bigotry and Gaelic nationalism.

Forced to take sides as either an Irish propagandist or a "West Briton" (as Gabriel Conroy is labeled by his university colleague Miss Ivors in *The Dead*), Joyce, or his counterfigure Richard, felt the necessity to leave Ireland for a European life abroad, to avoid accepting restricted ideological patterns that would have prevented his far-ranging human exploration to express a new "summa anthropologica." The intellectual self-exile chosen by Richard/Joyce is described in Robert's article "A Distinguished Irishman." Here the journalist distinguishes between the economic exile, in search of bread, and the spiritual exile, like himself, seeking a not less necessary "food of the spirit." A similar need for "spiritual food" has cost Prospero his forced exile.

If Richard repeats some of Prospero's fundamental predicaments, the implied value systems differ, as do the time and space in which the Shakespearean intellectual and his Joycean counterpart are set. Moreover, while Prospero is, throughout *The Tempest*, still in exile, although deviating the course of history with his magical powers, in *Exiles* Richard is already back in Dublin, where he hopes he can contribute to Irish intellectual life and obtain the university post Robert is trying to set up for him. As the title *Exiles* implies, the experience of being exiled is in Joyce's play both a real exclusion from his mother country and a persistent psychic condition, investing all characters at different levels, exiled even from themselves, while trying to get free from the fetters of customary behavior and pretenses.

But the intellectual's exile condition common to Prospero and Richard is completed with other coincidences cumulating on more levels. Prospero's role as a magician, by whose intellect history can be regenerated, is based on the extraordinary power of his mind. In fact Prospero seems to operate on a psychic "hypnotic" basis. The storm he raises in the opening scene, to have his enemies' ship stranded on his island so he can force them to repent for their past ill-doings, is revealed as purely mental. His powerful magic leaves no physical mark, neither on the ship—which had apparently split on the coasts of the island, but has remained intact— nor on its passengers and crew, all unscathed, the former still perfect in the ceremonial clothes they had been wearing at a state marriage in Tunis, whence they were voyaging back to Naples. Similarly, Caliban's punishments for his insubordinations, though perceived physically, show no physical evidence, and the same can be said of the collective punishment Prospero inflicts on his gathered enemies, inducing anguish in them as if they were mad. Prospero's corrections seem communicated and experienced only mentally, though extended by the action of the spirits he can conjure. Ariel's help and ubiquitous presence effectively implement Prospero's pervasive control on the island.

Correspondingly, Joyce's Richard, while not a magician or spirit conjurer, constantly exerts a similar controlling mental influence on all characters related to him. His mind is shown to direct all those around him, or to act as an effective barrier, which exalts his intellectual responsibility, allowing him a unique role, evident throughout the play in everybody's dependence on him and mentioned in some exchanges. In the second act, referring to Bertha, even his rival Robert owns, "You are so strong that you attract me even through her." To Richard's retort, "I am weak," Robert answers, "You are the incarnation of strength" (*E* 189), adding, after Richard's new protests on his hands being weaker than Robert's, that Richard's strength is of another kind. In his own notes to the play, Joyce defines Richard's influence on Bertha as a "mystical" or "spiritual fact," but a real defense that Robert must admit (*E* 345).

As an exile and a distinguished intellectual with unusual mind power, Richard shares important traits with Prospero, the concomitance of which confirms the extended memory of *The Tempest* in Joyce's play, surfacing in the explicit quotation but "spreading" throughout the play: the more so as the aims of the two exiled intellectuals' mind power are in a sense analogous.

The cluster of aspects related to the protagonist's mind power in *Exiles* leads to an ethical reshaping that repeats Prospero's anxious efforts to use his intellectual force to redirect human behavior and correct history, though with no illusion as to easy conversions. In *The Tempest*, while Alonso, the king of Naples, repents, Antonio and Sebastian, the main villains, are forced to give in but appear impervious to Prospero's psychic reshaping. As for Richard's mind power, it promotes a parallel psychic experimentation, since *Exiles* is engaged in an anthropological exploration of new types of relationships, in couples or between friends, that can allow more emotional freedom, less psychological constraint, and a deeper analysis of motivations.

This search, shared by Richard and Robert in their youth, must be pursued against social ties and expectations, but ironically opens to the risks of self-delusion, of an assumed ethical superiority hiding base compromises and uncertainties. Richard finds both noble and ignoble truths in his mind for ambiguously pushing Bertha not to reject Robert's wooing, leading him on to expose himself further.

The sexual complexities of this choice (both hetero- and homosexual, as Robert is attracted by both Bertha and Richard, whom he could in a sense reach through the mediation of Bertha's body) find no reference in Shakespeare's Prospero. Yet Miranda's father is no less ethically polemical toward the society to which he refers.

If his brother's Machiavellian betrayal has been traumatic, Alonso's logic of dynastic marriage, evident in his daughter Claribel's political union with the king of Tunis, is reversed by Prospero, who allows his daughter's and Ferdinand's free choice. This connects with a set of values expressed in the marriage masque he offers the couple.

The masque is not just an elegant spectacle but an ideological manifesto, rejecting the Mars/Venus logic for the couple (Venus and Cupid must be absent) while offering a country background instead of court uses and customs, seen as ethically dangerous and in fact already objected to in Prospero's evaluation of Miranda's better education far away from any court.

This leads to exploration of a further common theme, education, so important in both *Exiles* and *The Tempest*, though in Joyce obviously updated, not without risks, to the complexities of twentieth-century culture and expectations, and at the same time rooted in the author's personal experience, to him the source of real art.

Education and Reinvention

Prospero's pride in Miranda's education is not to be undervalued, nor is Richard's Pygmalion role with Bertha. Describing to Miranda his past as both Duke of Milan and scholar, Prospero states that on the island where they have been exiled for twelve years (but not deprived of volumes from his library that are so important for him) he has taken fond care of her education:

> Here I, thy schoolmaster, made thee more profit
> Than other princes can that have more time
> For vainer hours, and tutors not so careful.
>
> (I, ii, 172–74)

Why this polemical tone in Prospero's words, not only extolling his educational work, the quality of his scholarship and dedication, both better than that of "tutors not so careful" to be found in courts, but actually disowning the court ambience as scarcely an appreciable educational context, where "vainer hours" can spoil a good education? Why, compared with courts, is their desert island to be preferred?

The Milan court appears, indeed, a dangerous place. Here Prospero's brother Antonio, Miranda's uncle—already favored by a more powerful role than allowed by his social position, thanks to Prospero's trust in him for the government of the state—chose to betray both his brother and his country to gain the title of Duke of Milan. Making a political alliance with Alonso, he subjected free Milan to political dependence and to payment of tributes to Naples in order to obtain the aid necessary for a coup d'état and be accepted as the new duke, in spite of Prospero's prestige and popular support. Nor had Antonio hesitated to virtually murder both his brother and niece: he had ordered them to be taken out to sea and abandoned to die there on "a rotten carcase of a butt, not rigged, / nor tackle, sail, nor mast" (I, ii, 146–47). Only Gonzalo's help and Prospero's own magical powers have allowed father and daughter to land on an island and survive. Machiavellian intrigues are the first trait characterizing the court, as Miranda appears to have already learned, though not yet aware of her father's previous position in Milan. In fact, when taught about her past by Prospero, she marvels that Antonio did not have both her father and herself killed immediately on the night he took possession of Milan with the help of a Neapolitan army: she has learned her lessons of history well, and Prospero must explain that his people's love for him had imposed on Antonio a more devious way of getting rid of them.

But it is interesting that while Antonio's dealings with his brother are repeatedly defined as "unnatural," some ethical relativism in state politics has indeed been taught to Miranda. In the chess game scene, she is ready to teach Ferdinand that a prince must take care of the better interests of his country:

> *Prospero discovers Ferdinand and Miranda playing at chess*
> MIRANDA: Sweet lord, you play me false.
> FERDINAND: No, my dearest love,
>   I would not for the world.
> MIRANDA: Yes, for a score of kingdoms you should wrangle,
>   And I would call it fair play.
>
> (V, i, 172–75)

If life at court must be political, it must not become inhuman as in some courts.

Polemical criticism of the court ambience appears then evident in the marriage masque: why should Prospero choose a humble country setting, fields with peasants or "sunburned sickle-men" (IV, i, 134), and nymphs or

naiads rather than a refined spectacular court ceremony and a more elegant, refined court setting, possibly with a rich architectural background,
like the Laurentian Library where Peter Greenaway chose to film *Prospero's
Books*, his version of Shakespeare's *Tempest*, starring Gielgud as Prospero?
In fact, Prospero is not only stigmatizing tragic court intrigues, after all not
a daily practice, but criticizing the court life style itself and its "vain hours":
a criticism later corroborated by a rejection of easy sexual promiscuity, common in courts, and implicit in his recommendations to Prince Ferdinand
not to have sexual intercourse with Miranda before marriage. If the recom-
mendation in the context given is unrealistic, as has been noted, it is still
important as an ideological stance, consistent with Prospero's description
of his education and his avoidance of the court ambience in the masque.

What Prospero is rejecting at several levels is an outlook on life connected to courts, which to him are not obvious seats of superior refine-
ment, as might be expected—especially with reference to a Renaissance
court of prestige like Milan. Rather an ethically negative model, court life
is less desirable than the country lifestyle shown in the masque, so highly
appreciated by Ferdinand, who comments "Let me live here ever, / So rare
a wondered father and a wife / Makes this place paradise" (IV, i, 122–24).

These choices are no coincidence and are perfectly consistent if we
admit that Prospero is taking a stance on a set of values at the core of
his education, innovating as to common expectations and in line with
Ferdinand's choice of Miranda, who is apparently, when they first meet,
a simple maid with no status, though with exceptional qualities and an
exceptional education.

An outlook based on individual achievement, rather than inherited
position and social privilege, here merges with the moral requirements
advocated by what Lawrence Stone has described as "the Country ideology," a current of thought critical of court customs and disseminated
throughout Shakespeare's plays,[3] embraced in particular by Shakespeare's

---

3. For its presence, for instance, in *As You Like It*, see my article "Country Time As
She Likes It" (Restivo 2004). For its presence in *The Merchant of Venice*, see "Shylock and
Equity in Shakespeare's *Merchant of Venice*" (Restivo 2007).

patron, the Earl of Southampton, whose love marriage in 1598, below his social status and against the queen's favor, had cost him a fortune and long exclusion from court and state careers.[4]

Stressing the moral superiority of the country as opposed to the court, the Country ideology linked virtue, honesty, the preferential or "elective couple," with nationalism, individual liberty, Protestant or Puritan values, criticizing court and urban corruption and pointing to the country as both a physical and moral place. It developed a political program in favor of Parliament and against royal absolutism, shared with three further currents of thought identified by Stone: Puritanism, the Common Law and Skepticism, represented by Bacon's philosophy. These ideologies were accompanied by a concomitant "educational revolution" that brought about the growth of a professional class, especially lawyers, and by a degree of social mobility, contributing to the development of what Stone calls the "rising gentry," joined by some aristocrat allies like the Earl of Essex and the Earl of Southampton. At the same time the Country ideology went back to the Roman classics and to Virgil's *Georgics*, sustained at the two universities of Oxford and Cambridge, particularly the latter.[5]

The ideological nature of both the educational background and the "elective couple" choice in *The Tempest* may not have been easy to detect in Joyce's time, as literary criticism was not inclined to stress it. Stone's description of the ideological currents of thought in Shakespeare's time was only to appear in 1972, to be more recently reconfirmed at the end of the twentieth century, after a highly controversial debate concerning the causes of the English Revolution of 1642 as long developing in political opposition since Elizabeth's last years and Shakespeare's age. But, at the same time, Joyce's was a highly personal way of reading Shakespeare,

---

4. See Akrigg (1968). An extended reading of *The Tempest* and its historical background in the light of the contemporary ideological debate, both cultural and political, in the sense here referred to, can be found in my article "The Tempest and History: Pre-enlightenment Outlooks" (Restivo 2010).

5. From Lawrence Stone's perspective the Country ideology evolved into one of the prerequisites of the 1642 revolution, while in the eighteenth century it grew into a real party (Stone 1972).

independent of current criticism (most famously with *Hamlet*), while his own outlook on the couple's emancipation from social constrictions could well be seen to connect with and "adjourn" the polemical stances of *The Tempest*. Joyce's personal choice of a hotel maid as his life companion, below his social middle-class milieu, scandalously against all expectations in his family and among his friends (a "class transgression" repeated in Richard's choices in *Exiles*) was in a sense similar to Southampton's, while "prolonging" for his age the matrimonial, ethical, and educational polemics embedded in *The Tempest*. In any case, Prospero's exalted educational role must have attracted Joyce's attention, as he considered himself a young woman's successful educator.

In *Exiles*, Richard's role with Bertha as an educator is indeed repeatedly exalted by Robert: "She is yours, your work" (*E* 189), and again "You have made her all that she is. A strange and wonderful personality" (*E* 195). To Richard, self-accusingly complaining he has killed "the virginity of her soul," Robert impatiently retorts, "Well lost! What would she be without you?"; and to Richard's answer, "I tried to give her a new life," he confirms, "And you have. A new and rich life" (*E* 196).

Both a proud Pygmalion and a self-ironic critic of the effects of his education, Richard is well aware that his experimental human outlook and innovative attempts carry emotional costs. He is convinced of the necessity of the responsibility he is assuming for a new morality and of the importance of his daring choices to be inherited by the younger generation, represented in the play by his eight-year-old son Archie. This inheritance, however, is openly discussed by Richard and Robert only in a fragment of dialogue now at Cornell (*E* 366), but excluded from the final text. Here the journalist and the writer speculate on Archie's future "type of humanity," uncertain whether he will choose Robert's more careless forms of freedom or Richard's more doubt-tormented way. Archie's attitude is defined by Robert as "creedless, lawless, fearless": a breaking away from the old bonds is seen as a necessary achievement that Richard and Robert are both pursuing.

Richard's has been a lifelong battle against current bourgeois morality and sexuality, started in his youth with Robert, who speaks with some of the overtones of Nietzsche's and D'Annunzio's moral defiance of a youthful and passionate "battle of both our souls, different as they are, against all that is false in them and in the world" (*E* 201). Richard, who has chosen to run away with Bertha and live with her and their son in what to his mother was a condition of sin and shame, but to him is a free union to be constantly reaccepted and not constrained by religion or a contract (just as Joyce had done with Nora Barnacle, whom he married much later, only for economic convenience), has now come to a more problematic awareness of a freedom difficult to define. "To hold you by no bonds, even of love, to be united with you in body and soul in utter nakedness" (*E* 265–66) is Richard's declared choice with Bertha, but, taking a distance from his old friend Robert for a more solitary exploration, he has realized how difficult it is to live up to a fully consistent drive and consciousness. His search has led him to acknowledge inner ambiguities, to live the wounds of doubt and double attitudes, to disclose an inner landscape from which later on Joyce's close friend Samuel Beckett, a generation younger, will in his turn make his own difficult start.

A similar torment of inner contradictions appears evident in Beckett's analogous experiments in his first complete and autobiographical play, *Eleutheria*, which ironically describes young Victor/Beckett in Paris, desperately trying to find his full "freedom," as suggested in the Greek title, by breaking away from all moral and emotional fetters tying him to family and friends, but ending in a helpless crisis. A comparison between the passages on moral freedom in *Exiles* and Beckett's *Eleutheria* would confirm Beckett's inheritance of Joyce's difficult attempts at a moral reshaping of relationships.

But *The Tempest* is also characterized by three striking cries for freedom, verging on rebellion: the Boatswain's against the authority of the king of Naples and the duke of Milan, aboard the ship in the first scene; Ariel's insistent request for freedom from Prospero's service; and Caliban's intrigue with Stephano and Trinculo against Prospero's rule of the island.[6]

A direct line seems to link Prospero to Richard, or Shakespeare to Joyce, in a similar effort to meet the taxing task of redefining changing

---

6. As discussed at length in "The Tempest and History" (Restivo 2010).

moral adaptation, recasting aspects of that "invention of the human" for the western world, which in Harold Bloom's words has been Shakespeare's legacy, to be revisited by each generation and constantly sought or added to in all major literature. Yet, while as an intellectual Richard identifies with Prospero, the words he speaks are Caliban's. Is there another parallel link connecting Joyce and Caliban?

The Irish Isle

The geographical identity of Shakespeare's island in *The Tempest* is difficult to establish, as is Caliban's nature and educability. Caliban speaks the best English in the play, which he has so well learned from Prospero and Miranda; he appreciates music, as a fine gentleman always does in Shakespeare's canon, and has a poetic love for his island and its landscapes; and finally, he contradicts Prospero's opinion of his "ineducability" (due to Caliban's attempt to have sex with Miranda) by appearing ready to repent for scheming against Prospero's life and to be "wise hereafter" "and seek for grace" (V, i, 294–95). By contrast, Antonio and Sebastian appear beyond redemption.

This of course contradicts Prospero's repeated disparagement of Caliban as the son of the wicked witch Sycorax and the devil himself, and as such not receptive to the positive values of education. In fact, educators, even good ones, can be mistaken, as Shakespeare ironically shows in act 5, contrasting, within a few lines, Prospero's disclaiming of Caliban and Caliban's self-correction. Prospero's mistake seems to confirm the necessity of avoiding excessive power in one man, even one of superior qualities like Prospero, who in the play had already wisely renounced his magician's powers, breaking his magic staff and destroying his magic book after achieving his ethical aims and his political task of redressing history. Similarly, Richard, though in full control of the whole range of characters, humbly gives in, leaving others to their choices after he has used his mind power to question problems with them.

But there is more to Caliban's role in *The Tempest* that may have attracted Joyce. Caliban is described by Prospero as "disproportioned in his manners as in his shape" (V, i, 290), yet his physical aspect remains undetermined, except for one surprising detail: he is "freckled" (I, ii, 283), which of course excludes the possibility of his being a black man, as some criticism, especially postcolonial, has tried to make him. Adding to this detail the one physical detail given for his mother Sycorax, described as "blue-eyed"[7] (I, ii, 269), the combination of blue eyes and freckles in the mother/son genealogical line may suggest something very close to Joyce's experience: a human physical typology, possibly associated with red hair, widespread among the Irish. This typology was also well known to at least some of Shakespeare's contemporaries, especially to Shakespeare's patrons, the Earl of Essex and the Earl of Southampton, after their 1599 military expedition to Ireland to fight Tyrone's rebellion. Ireland has indeed been the one case of colonization in Europe, and in Shakespeare's England many considered the Irish as a subhuman "vile race," just as a disappointed Prospero regarded Caliban.

The colonial problem is evoked in *The Tempest* through the allusion to Bermuda, the island reached by Ariel in one of his errands for Prospero, but also the island made famous in 1610 (the year *The Tempest* was written) by William Strachey's *True Reportory of the Wreck and Redemption of Sir Thomas Gates*, a description of the shipwreck in Bermuda of the *Sea Venture*, part of a naval expedition financed by the Virginia Company to sustain the recently established English colony of Jamestown in Virginia. But in 1609 another colonial event was taking place: the *Plantation of Ulster* in Ireland, established under the king's direct control.

James I, whose name was given to the Virginia colony established in 1607, was eager to colonize Ireland in a similar way with a number of Scottish Presbyterians and other religious dissenters, whose emigration to Ireland would have solved the old problem of disorder on the border

---

7. Prospero's description of Sycorax as the "blue-eyed hag" who "was hither brought with child" has embarrassed critics, who have tried to turn the blue eyes of the witch pregnant with Caliban into the supposed "blue eyelids" of a pregnant woman, as usually reported in the play's editions. But the effort to erase this detail appears inconsistent with the straight formulation of the passage, clearly mentioning blue eyes and not eyelids, while it also ignores Caliban's specific freckles (why should they be mentioned?) and pays no attention to the dramatic background of the 1609 Irish Plantation of Ulster.

between Scotland and England. In Ireland, lands were confiscated from the Irish, who were reduced to slavery just like Caliban.

In fact, Shakespeare's allusion to colonialism in *The Tempest* may well be double, both in space and concept. Whereas in Bermuda or in Jamestown the colonial problem was not a problem of relationships with the colonized, but rather of the control of the English colonizers by their mother country (Bermuda was a desert island, and in Jamestown the main problem was the internal organization of the English colony under the appointed authorities), in Ireland the colonizers had enslaved the local population. If in *The Tempest* the boatswain's rebellion in the opening sea storm scene can recall the rebellion of *The Sea Venture* colonizers against their authorities, Caliban's subjugation and rebellion can rather suggest the Irish condition in the new Ulster Plantation.

The Irish connotation of *The Tempest*, generally ignored by criticism, may have appeared to Joyce in two ways: through his knowledge of Irish history and folklore, which he would later use so extensively in *Finnegans Wake*. In fact, if Caliban can well be a colonized Irishman, Ariel can well evoke Irish mythology in his connection with tree trunks (he has been freed from imprisonment in a cloven pine tree by Prospero) and with weather control (in the sea storm scene, raised by him on Prospero's order). An Irish flavor in Shakespeare's play may have stimulated Joyce.

In "Scylla and Charybdis" (U 196), Stephen mentions Caliban as "Patsy Caliban, our American cousin," an obvious allusion to Irish immigration in America, proving that to Joyce Caliban had an Irish quality he himself shared. If as an intellectual Richard acts like a Prospero, at the same time as an Irishman he also identifies with Caliban. In fact, Richard/Joyce speaks some of Caliban's words and, like him, a choice English acquired from strangers. Shakespeare's isle seems to have turned into Joyce's Irish island, full of noises and voices, waiting to be reshaped into his own creative "consciousness of his race": as in Joyce's program in his *Portrait of the Artist as a Young Man*, to flourish through a European or Western rethinking of modernity.

5

Joyce's Shakespeare

A View from Trieste

JOHN MCCOURT

"Ah, there's only one man he's got to get the better of now, and that's
that Shakespeare!"
—Nora Joyce[1]

I expound Shakespeare to docile Trieste: Hamlet, quoth I, who is most
courteous to gentle and simple is rude only to Polonius. Perhaps, an embit-
tered idealist, he can see in the parents of his beloved only grotesque
attempts on the part of nature to produce her image . . . Marked you
that?" (GJ, 10)

For James Joyce, minor poet, failed playwright, getting the better of
William Shakespeare was always going to be a challenge, one with which
he battled throughout his entire writing career and which had a major
impact on his final two novels. His Triestine period turned out to be a
crucial one in the genesis of his understanding of Shakespeare and, in
particular, *Hamlet*. In Trieste, among other things, he delivered a series of
a dozen lectures on *Hamlet* in 1912, which would come to form the core
of Stephen Dedalus's *Hamlet* theory in *Ulysses*. Only some rather scant
notes for these talks remain, which can trigger little more than conjecture
about how Joyce tackled what he later, in *Finnegans Wake*, called "the

1. As recalled by Frank Budgen, according to Clive Hart (1962, 163).

puchypatch of hamlock" by the looming presence that was "Great Shape-sphere" (*FW* 31.23 and 295.04). The texts of these talks would undoubtedly have provided hugely revelatory evidence as to Joyce's growing fascination with Shakespeare's play, which later came to exercise such a fundamental and indeed foundational role in both *Ulysses* and *Finnegans Wake*.

Just a few years after the Shakespeare lectures, in or around 1915, Joyce began the long process of writing the "Scylla and Charybdis" epi-sode of *Ulysses*. By April 9, 1917, he told Ezra Pound that the only episode he had ready to send him was the "Hamlet chapter" (*LI* 101). It was already his habit to refer to the episode in this way, or as the library chapter, rather than by its Homeric name. It was the only episode that he referred to in such a singular way. At the end of 1918, on the last page of the fair copy version of "Scylla and Charybdis," Joyce wrote "New Year's Eve, 1918|End of First Part of *Ulysses*" (Crispi 2004), thus giving the episode a vital struc-tural position within the overall body of his novel. The fact that "Scylla and Charybdis" was Joyce's first completed episode, that he habitually referred to it as the Hamlet chapter, and that it came to occupy a turn-ing point or a point of no return within the overall text (it's the ninth of eighteen episodes), makes manifest the centrality of the *Hamlet* elements in *Ulysses* as a whole. In *Ulysses*, the force of *Hamlet* is felt in how Joyce explores the father-son relationship, themes of paternity and usurpation (literary and real), the subject of betrayal, the connections between a writ-er's biography and his written texts, and the question of belonging for a great "national" writer.

At the episode's core, Stephen puts forth his theory of *Hamlet* for a select audience of Russell, Lyster, Mulligan, and Eglinton at the National Library in Dublin but, as René Girard has commented, the "real ideas of the lecture shine only intermittently, tiny jewels almost invisible in the trampled mud of a pig pen" (Girard 2000, 261). In the face of a barrage of mostly hostile critical comments and platitudes from his four interlocu-tors, and developing the biographical trend of reading works according to their authors' lives but contrary to contemporary popular takes on Shake-speare, Stephen Dedalus identifies the Bard not with Hamlet the prince, but with his father, the murdered king. This is the part that Shakespeare himself played when the tragedy was first performed. Hamlet the prince, on the other hand, is to be identified with young Hamnet Shakespeare, "who has died in Stratford that his namesake may live for ever" (*U* 181).

The theme of betrayal lies at the heart of Stephen's *Hamlet*, and its motivation is to be found in the fact that he believes Shakespeare is a cuckold who transferred his suffering over Anne Hathaway's supposed affairs onto the play's "guilty queen" when turning it into "a French triangle" (*U* 205). Stephen notes that Shakespeare left Hathaway his second-best bed in his will and that "the theme of the false or the usurping or the adulterous brother or all three in one is to Shakespeare, what the poor are not, always with him" (*U* 203). When Shakespeare's face appears in "Circe," the cinematic play within Joyce's novel, it is "crowned by the reflection of the reindeer antlered hatrack in the hall" (*U* 528), by horns, that is, that symbolize the cuckold, in what might be taken for a parodic reflection of Joyce himself, who appears to have attempted to play the role of the cuckold in Trieste in what would indeed have been a French triangle, a bedroom farce involving himself, Nora, and his journalist friend, Roberto Prezioso, and which is later reflected in *Exiles*. A viable alternative to this Irish-Italian triangle might also be sought in the complicated Joyce-Nora-Stanislaus arrangement, which saw them sharing Triestine apartments for several years and where brotherly jealousies more than occasionally arose. Jean Kimball, in fact, sees the Joyce-Stanislaus nexus as the dominant paradigm behind the brother relationships in Joyce's fiction (Kimball 1988, 227), and if this is so it gives added significance to the adulterous brother reading that Joyce provides with regard to Shakespeare.

Hamlet, prince of Denmark, or, as he comes to be named or better misnamed, "camelot prince of dinmurk" (*FW* 143.7), also occupies a vital place in *Finnegans Wake* becoming, as Vincent Cheng, among others, has argued, both "structurally and analogically important": "There are by far more allusions to *Hamlet* than to any other play (Shakespearean or otherwise); and the parallels are more frequent, precise, and insistent: HCE as King Hamlet, Shem as the Prince, Shaun as Laertes-Polonius. References to *Hamlet* are ubiquitous; and, as in the case of *Ulysses*, the themes and motifs in *Hamlet* are structural counterparts to those in *Finnegans Wake*" (Cheng 1984, 6–7).

Although Joyce was undoubtedly well-acquainted with *Hamlet* long before moving to Trieste (having worked on his theory of the play as early as 1904), it was in the Adriatic city that he deepened and developed his understanding of it during the process of preparing his lectures. He did so in an environment in which debate about the Bard was extremely common, with many of Joyce's Triestine acquaintances actively involved. His friend, Silvio Benco, doyen of Trieste's literary journalists, was a longtime Shakespeare devotee (Gruber Benco 1972, 331) and cited the fantastic elements in Shakespeare's *A Midsummer Night's Dream* and *The Tempest* as important sources for his libretto for the opera *Oceana* (1903), written by Antonio Smareglia, longtime neighbor and later friend of Joyce. Italo Svevo, too, nurtured a lifelong Shakespeare passion. *La Coscienza di Zeno* contains an allusion to *Hamlet* that suggests Svevo was well acquainted with the text: "la profetica anima mia" (Svevo 1987, 108), a direct translation of the line from *Hamlet* "O my prophetic soul!" Even as a teenager away at boarding school, Svevo had "spent sleepless nights over Hamlet" until the headmaster, Dr Spier, confiscated his Shakespeare volumes before he could get to *King Lear* (Furbank 1966, 11). But Svevo was unperturbed and, on December 2, 1880, writing under the pseudonym Ettore Samigli, when given the opportunity to publish his first article in the Trieste newspaper *L'Indipendente*, he chose as his topic Shakespeare and concentrated in particular on the character of Shylock. Unlike Svevo but very similarly to Joyce himself, the young Triestine writer Scipio Slataper initially devoted his critical energies more to Henrik Ibsen than to Shakespeare. He wrote his degree thesis in 1912 on the Norwegian writer (and it was published, posthumously, in 1916). But he tired of Ibsen and turned to Shakespeare, complaining of Ibsen's "Lutheran dryness" ("*secchezza luterana*") his inability to cry, to let himself go, to love, all of which he compares unfavorably to the richness, generosity, love of the godlike Shakespeare (Slataper 1944, 216–17).[2] In short, Joyce would have had no

---

2. The original reads: "Ibsen non piange, non s'abbandona, non ama . . . Mondo povero . . . Mondo dedotto e non indotto. Secchezza luterana e non comprensione

shortage of company, quite apart from Stanislaus, with whom to sharpen his ideas on Shakespeare.

To some extent we can reconstruct what Joyce might have said in his lectures "in lingua inglese sull'*Amleto* di G. Shakespeare" (the "G" standing for "Guglielmo," as Joyce persisted in his habit of Italianizing English surnames). Initially invited to give ten lectures at the highly respected Società di Minerva on Via Carducci, 28, Joyce probably gave as many as a dozen, which were open to the public at a cost of ten crowns for the full series (five crowns for members of the Minerva).[3] The fact that Joyce was asked to lecture, as he had earlier been invited to write for *Il Piccolo della Sera*, was proof of how influential Triestine friends, like editor Roberto Prezioso and lawyer Nicolò Vidacovich, gave him a helping hand by engineering high-profile invitations for him (which would, it was hoped, attract potential students for his English language lessons, his bread and butter in this period). Not for the first time, following disappointment away from Trieste, in Dublin and, indeed, in Rome, Joyce's Triestine friends did what they could to enable him to bounce back in his adopted city. The choice to lecture on *Hamlet* was probably Joyce's own, although it might also be presumed that his sponsors advised against the relatively obscure Irish topics that had been the subjects of his earlier lectures and articles in favor of something of more mainstream appeal.

The greater part of Joyce's lectures was philological—a study of Shakespeare's words and their origins. As Joyce put it himself in his letter asking for permission from the "Direzione di Polizia" to give the lecture series, he wished to offer "a verbal commentary and a critical and etymological elucidation" of *Hamlet*.[4] Joyce mostly read and commented on passages from Shakespeare's play for his Italian audience, having provided contextual background to the writer and his times in the opening talks, which drew heavily on Georg Brandes's *William Shakespeare* (1898), Sidney

---

cattolica. Leggendo, e rileggendo, tornando a rileggere Ibsen a un tratto vi prende una smania indicibile: ma! sangue! Riprendete Shakespeare."

3. A copy of the printed ticket to "Amleto di G. Shakespeare" is kept at the Cornell University Library.

4. Letter of November 9, 1912 published in Schneider (2004, 14).

Lee's *A Life of William Shakespeare* (1898), and Frank Harris's *The Man Shakespeare and His Tragic Life-Story* (1909). He would not have pitched his talks "Shakespearian scholars, who are well provided with volumes of research and criticism," but would have sought to render Hamlet "more interesting and intelligible for the general reader," to quote his own scathingly negative 1903 *Daily Express* "Shakespeare Explained" review of A. S. Canning's *Shakespeare Studied in Eight Plays* (OCPW 98). At the same time, it can be presumed that Joyce sought to offer interpretations that were very different from what he termed the "meagre, obvious, and commonplace" observations offered by Canning, devoid of "psychological complexity . . . cross-purpose . . . interweaving of motives such as might perplex the base multitude" (OCPW 98). It can be assumed that many of the perplexing theories elaborated by Stephen in *Ulysses* received their first public outings before what must have been a stoic Triestine audience.

Joyce did not limit himself to English scholarly explication of Shakespeare. Quite the contrary. Indeed, he had already voiced, in his 1907 "Ireland: Island of Saints and Sages" lecture, his dismissal of the provincial nature of much early English Shakespeare analysis, pointing instead to the influence of German scholarship in the strengthening of Shakespeare's reputation: "it cannot be denied that these learned Germans were the first to present Shakespeare as a poet of world-wide significance, before the amazed eyes of his compatriots (who up until then had considered William as a person of secondary importance, a decent devil with a nice bent towards lyric poetry, but perhaps a bit over-fond of English beer)" (OCPW 109). In "Scylla and Charybdis" Thomas Lyster, referring to Goethe's *Wilhelm Meister,* in which *Hamlet* is performed, interprets the play in terms of German Romanticism: "a hesitating soul taking arms against a sea of troubles" (U 176). Elsewhere in the episode references abound to other continental readers of Shakespeare from Mallarmé and Renan, to the extent that, as Richard Brown has argued, it needs to be read in the context of "Joyce's own particularly transient and cosmopolitan cultural situation and particularly to the complex cultural situation of Zürich during the war years" (Brown 1999, 345). But the episode also draws on the equally cosmopolitan environment in Trieste in the decade immediately before this.

Elsewhere, Joyce would further emphasize the European nature of Shakespeare's art. In his essay entitled "Realism and Idealism in English Literature Daniel Defoe—William Blake," he pointed to the number of Shakespeare types that had been imported into stay-at-home Shakespeare's plays from European sources: "A boorish peasant, a courtjester, a half-mad and half-stupid ragamuffin, a gravedigger" (OCPW 164). Joyce also asserted that Shakespeare's great protagonists are almost all of foreign derivation. They all "come from abroad and afar: Othello, a Moorish prince; Shylock, a Venetian Jew; Caesar, a Roman; Hamlet, a Danish prince; Macbeth, a Celtic usurper; Romeo and Juliet, citizens of Verona. Of all the rich gallery, perhaps the only one who can be called English is the fat knight with the monstrous paunch, Sir John Falstaff" (OCPW 164). Shakespeare's hybrid imports provided Joyce with a useful set of prototypes for his Hungarian-Jewish-Irish Bloom and his Spanish-Jewish-Irish Molly in Ulysses. Similarly, if Joyce himself can be seen to have become a Triestinised Irishman, a Giacomo Joyce, it was in part because he had come to see the value of cultural crossover and to appreciate Shakespeare as a foremost example of this: "Shakespeare, with his Titianesque palette, his eloquence, his epileptic passion, and his creative fury, is an Italianized Englishman" (OCPW 164).

Joyce's portrait of a European Shakespeare reads almost as a direct response to contemporary readings of the Bard that were being constructed and to what Felperin has called his "newly allegorized professional career" in the service of "the needs of empire" (especially through readings of the figure of Prospero in The Tempest) (Felperin 1990, 178). These interpretations were being written in England and, perhaps more pointedly, in Dublin by Edward Dowden, professor of English at Trinity College from 1867 to 1913. In his seminal study Shakspere: A Critical Study of His Mind and His Art ([1875] 1880), described as "the most influential Shakespeare biography in the history of literary criticism" (Wallace 2005, 801), in his later, condensed Shakespeare Primer (1877), and in his Introduction to Shakespeare ([1893] 1906) Dowden defined Shakespeare criticism for at least a generation, providing what Joyce calls in Ulysses "The people's William. For terms apply: E. Dowden, Highfield house" (U 196). Dowden read the playwright biographically by studying the works chronologically and took issue with foreign—especially German—readings of Shakespeare, writing, in the course of *Shakspere: A Critical Study of His Mind and His Art*, that "it is somewhat hard upon Shakespeare to suppose that he secreted in each of his dramas a central idea for a German critic to discover" (108). He argued, instead, in *Introduction to Shakespeare*, for the Englishness of the Bard, claiming that Shakespeare expresses "an exultant patriotic pride and an exhilarating consciousness of power" which exudes "the spirit of Protestantism" (44). This was the anticipatory English counterpart to the ludicrous Patrick W. Shakespeare, Irish hero of the "Cyclops" episode (whatever the allusions to Patrick W. Joyce and indeed to Shakespeare's purported Irish background). Unlike Yeats, who, as Andrew Gibson has shown, openly opposed Dowden's reading of Shakespeare (believing he had turned him into an English Benthamite), Joyce was always anxious to disrupt the kinds of binary opposition the imperialist Dowden sought to establish between Irish and English culture and which many Irish writers simply cemented by responding to in kind. Rather than offer a direct retort to Dowden's provocative stances (in an 1865 letter he wrote that he could not "believe that Ireland will produce such a thing [as a Shakespeare] or anything but long-eared asses; . . . the idiotic noises the true Irishman makes from generation to generation are certainly not human, but are part of the irony on humanity of the Aristophanic Spirit who presides over the World-Drama—a chorus of Asses"[5]), Joyce came at the problem from another, wider angle. He was no more taken by Dowden's belief in the inferiority of Irish culture or his exaltation of its English equivalent than he was with Yeats's and the other revivalists' polemical reversal of this. Feeling estranged and rejected by the architects of revivalism and refusing to play on the narrow Ireland-England pitch, Joyce sought instead to accommodate Shakespeare and, in "Oxen of the Sun," all of English literature, on his own even larger personal playing field, that is, within his European Irish epic of *Ulysses*. This was his way to counter Dowden's patronizing attempt to accommodate Irish literature as a minor presence to be tolerated within what he saw as great "English

5. Dowden is quoted by Nathaniel Preston Wallace (2005, 803).

culture" but also to distance himself from any narrow or defensive Irish response by seeking refuge in a greater European canonic tradition where even Shakespeare himself was redimensioned.

It was precisely against narrow, imperialist readings of the ultra-English Shakespeare that Joyce pitched the lectures in Trieste that came to form the core of his Hamlet theory in *Ulysses*. Given that Joyce made his claims for Shakespeare as "an Italianized Englishman" in two further lectures given at the Università Popolare in Trieste, just two months after his *Hamlet* series, there is every reason to believe that Joyce underlined the European contexts of Shakespeare's material and indeed his style in the longer series of lectures. Once again there is an element of Joycean self-fashioning in all this: he was delivering these lectures just as he was also launching into the *Ulysses* project that would eventually be heralded as Ireland's return into the literary culture of Europe. Establishing Shakespeare as a precursor—with Homer and Dante—if only in his own head for the moment, could not, in the long term, be a bad move. In Joyce's view, Shakespeare and the Renaissance lay at the root of the modern age. With the Renaissance, "a sharp, limited and formal mind" was deposed in favor of "a mentality that is facile and wide-ranging . . . restless and somewhat amorphous" (*OCPW* 188). Joyce identifies this new mentality, in this own times, with journalism and cinema, two modern media that exercised a powerful formal influence on *Ulysses*. In Joyce's words: "Shakespeare and Lope de Vega are to a certain extent responsible for modern cinematography. Untiring creative power, heated, strong passion, the intense desire to see and feel, unfettered and prolix curiosity have, after three centuries, degenerated into frenetic sensationalism" (*OCPW* 188).

Following his final lecture, *Il Piccolo* published a highly positive review article, part of which is included here:

> Yesterday evening, Dr James Joyce concluded his series of lectures in English on *Hamlet*. The hall was well attended during all twelve lectures. The English colony appeared to be thinly or not at all represented, so the steady attendance redounded to the credit of the lecturer especially, but also of his Italian audience who have been able to follow a text that was not easy.

As Joyce indicated yesterday, he had purposely refrained from critical or philosophical disquisitions about the play he was reading and interpreting. His first task was to explain the words. His original and slightly bizarre talent changed the nature of his commentary, which might otherwise have been dry, into attractive "causeries." The words, the manners, and the dress of the Elizabethans stirred the lecturer to literary and historical recollections which proved of keen interest to an audience which had been his for so many hours.

Yesterday evening, accepting the duty of closing such a work with a critical synthesis, he read (in English translation) the attack of Voltaire on *Hamlet* and then, suddenly, the eulogy of the same work by Georg Brandes. (JJA 776)[6]

Presumably Joyce would have quoted from Voltaire's famous letter to Bernard Joseph Saurin in which he describes Shakespeare as "a savage . . . who had some imagination. He has written many happy lines; but his pieces can please only at London and in Canada. It is not a good sign for the taste of a nation when that which it admires meets with favor only at home" (Lounsbury 1902, 318). For Voltaire, Shakespeare's art seems to lack a universal appeal and this because it breaks the rules of theater that Voltaire felt were so important and to which he adhered in his own work.

Elsewhere in his *Dissertation sur la tragédie ancienne et moderne*, Voltaire gives a more balanced reading of *Hamlet*, praising, in particular, its use of ghosts (a decisive element, this, for Joyce's appreciation of the play), as John Morley in his *Voltaire* ([1871] 1886), which Joyce may well have read, points out:

Even the famous criticism on *Hamlet* has been a good deal misrepresented. Voltaire is vindicating the employment of the machinery of ghosts, and he dwells on the fitness and fine dramatic effect of the ghost in Shakespeare's play. "I am very far," he goes on to say, "from justifying the tragedy of *Hamlet* in everything: it is a rude and barbarous

6. *Il Piccolo*, February 11, 1913, p.2 (this English translation is taken from *JJII* 776).

piece. . . . Hamlet goes mad in the second act, and his mistress goes mad in the third; the prince slays the father of his mistress, pretending to kill a rat, and the heroine throws herself into the river. They dig her grave on the stage; the grave-diggers jest in a way worthy of them, with skulls in their hands; Hamlet answers their odious grossnesses by extravagances no less disgusting. Meanwhile one of the characters conquers Poland. Hamlet, his mother, and his stepfather drink together on the stage; they sing at table, they wrangle, they fight, they kill; one might suppose such a work to be the fruit of the imagination of a drunken savage. But in the midst of all these rude irregularities, which to this day make the English theatre so absurd and so barbarous, there are to be found in *Hamlet* by a yet greater incongruity sublime strokes worthy of the loftiest geniuses. It seems as if nature had taken a delight in collecting within the brain of Shakespeare all that we can imagine of what is greatest and most powerful, with all that rudeness without wit can contain of what is lowest and most detestable." (133)

The use of ghosts in *Hamlet*, approved of by Voltaire and Joyce, would also loom large in the popular appreciation of Shakespeare being built in these years through theatrical and cinema productions that often put a particular focus on the spectral (and, to recall Joyce's words above, the sensational) and indeed augmented it. In Trieste, Joyce had the opportunity to attend many such Shakespeare performances, such as those at the Teatro Rossetti, which included important productions of *Hamlet* starring Gustavo Salvini, in February 1908, and Ferruccio Garavaglia, in the autumn of 1910. In his unpublished Trieste diary, Stanislaus recorded Joyce's opinions the day after he went to see the Salvini *Hamlet*:

Talking of "Hamlet" today, Jim said that it was full of gross dramatic blunders. I asked him to cite an example. He said that Ophelia's madness took all the force out of Hamlet's simulation, and that her love for her father, whom the audience have seen to be a paltry old imbecile, is a caricature of Hamlet's passion; and the evil in the King's character that accounts for Hamlet's hatred must be supposed for it is not dramatically explained. Salvini acted with energy and intelligence but the rest of the company was wretched. S. acted the piece in six acts and at half past twelve, when Jim came away, it had not yet ended.[7]

If Joyce felt overwhelmed by the sheer length of Salvini's six-act *Hamlet* (interestingly, Maud Ellmann has read both *Ulysses* and *Finnegans Wake* as sixth acts or "extra comic acts to Shakespeare's masterpiece" [Ellmann 2003, 137]), he could have found many far shorter versions competing for his attention at the cinema. By this time, Shakespeare adaptations had become popular in cinemas struggling to assert themselves as something other than places of lowbrow entertainment and which were happy to take whatever cultural plaudits were to be garnered from being associated with the Bard. The very first Shakespeare film, Beerbohm Tree's *King John*, was made as early as 1899 and was followed by at least thirty-six American Shakespeare productions between 1908 and 1913 and many more in Britain and Europe (Pearson and Uricchio 2004, 148). *Hamlet* had first made it on screen in 1900 with Sarah Bernhardt, whom Joyce saw performing in Paris in 1903, cross-dressing to fill the role in the very short, silent *Le Duel d'Hamlet*. In reality this film presented only the sword fight between Hamlet and Laertes, but of course Bernhardt had already played the prince on stage in a full production in 1899. In a letter to the London *Daily Telegraph*, Bernhardt made it clear she wanted no truck with the rather traditional construction of Hamlet as an "effeminate" but described him instead, as "manly and resolute, but nonetheless thoughtful . . . [he] thinks before he acts, a trait indicative of great strength and great spiritual power" (Gay 2002, 164). As Tony Howard has commented, Bernhardt's "version was not just the apotheosis of the traditional female Hamlet [but] heralded its demise" (Howard 2007, 92). Another famous female *Hamlet* film, a Danish one, this time, appeared in 1920 with Asta Nielsen in the title role (directed by Sven Gade and Heinz Schall).

The critical basis for Hamlet being played by a woman was to be found in Edward P. Vining's *The Mystery of Hamlet*, although this text

---

7. Stanislaus Joyce, *Triestine Book of Days*, February 10, 1908. A copy of this documented was consulted at the McFarlin Library, University of Tulsa.

seems to endorse the more traditional view of the effeminate Hamlet which Bernhardt rejected. Vining argued that "Hamlet lacks the energy, the conscious strength, the readiness for action that inhere in the perfect manly character" and claimed that he was "a woman attempting to play a man's part" (Vining 1881, 46). Vining quotes from Carl Rohrbach's 1859 *Shakespeare's Hamlet erläutert*: "He always talks more than is necessary . . . At all events, he can under this mask [of madness] give free play to his tongue, and that, and not the use of his hands, suits him above all things. Were he a whole man and no weakling, and if he would go wisely to work, why does he not at least keep his mouth shut? . . . He is a weakling. When he says, 'Frailty, thy name is woman,' he might have used his own name here" (49).

In short, Hamlet's behavior resembles that of "a gently-nurtured woman, rather than from a fervid young prince glowing with desire to end unequalled wrongs" (Vining 1881, 53), a woman in disguise and very much in love with Horatio:

> The question may be asked, whether Shakespeare, having been compelled by the course and exigencies of the drama to gradually modify his original hero into a man with more and more of the feminine element, may not at last have had the thought dawn upon him that this womanly man might be in very deed a woman, desperately striving to fill a place for which she was by nature unfitted, and, in her failure to do that which it was impossible for her to do, earning an admiration and a pity which no mere weakling, dawdling about his proper task and meanly failing to achieve it, could inspire. (59)

Vining later comments on instances of cross-dressing used by Shakespeare, noting that "a favorite fancy it was of Shakespeare's to allow his heroines to masquerade in male attire" and claiming that he had "an intuitive fondness for placing his characters in the situations most foreign to their natural dispositions, and then allowing their natural peculiarities to show themselves and reveal the real nature of the human being whom he had created, in spite of all disguises and through them all" (60). Victorian Vining's text is full of sexist speculation on Hamlet's femininity, which is located in his melancholy, hysteria, faintness, excessive poetizing, and lack of strength and courage, demerits, these, "that are far more in keeping with a feminine than with a masculine nature" (48). As if all this were not enough, Hamlet, we learn "has a woman's daintiness and sensitiveness to perfumes" (77). Vining was neither the first nor the last to emphasize Hamlet's feminine side, as David Leverenz has pointed out:

> Hamlet is part hysteric as Freud said, and part Puritan in his disgust at contamination and his idealization of his absent father. But he is also, as Goethe was the first to say, part woman. And Goethe was wrong, as Freud was wrong, to assume that "woman" means weakness. To equate women with weak and tainted bodies, words, and feelings while men possess noble reasons and ambitious purpose is to participate in Denmark's disease that divides mind from body, act from feeling, man from woman. (Leverenz 1980, 123)

Vining's was not an original theory, but it was probably the most cogently argued version of it. In *Ulysses*, we find a reference to the female Hamlet hypothesis, when Bloom thinks about this possibility in connection with Rudolph Virag. In "Calypso," he recalls 1865 (the year of his birth) and what is, effectively, the second chronological "fact" in his family history as it is constructed in the novel. Bloom remembers that Rudolph saw Kate Bateman play Hamlet in London that year:

> Mr Bloom stood at the corner, his eyes wandering over the multicoloured hoardings. Cantrell and Cochrane's Ginger Ale (Aromatic). Clery's Summer Sale. No, he's going on straight. Hello. LEAH tonight. Mrs Bandmann Palmer. Like to see her again in that. HAMLET she played last night. Male impersonator. Perhaps he was a woman. Why Ophelia committed suicide. Poor papa! How he used to talk of Kate Bateman in that. Outside the Adelphi in London waited all the afternoon to get in. Year before I was born that was: sixtyfive. (U 73)

If Hamlet were a woman this would, as Bloom suggests, provide a more ample justification of Ophelia's suicide and would neatly answer

Joyce's criticism, posed in Trieste after the Salvani production, that she weakened the overall structure of the tragedy.

While the character of Hamlet has traditionally been most strenuously associated with Stephen Dedalus, the idea that Hamlet was a woman or at least was "womanly" would bolster the arguments to associate him with Bloom. Both protagonists are fatherless and sonless, both are haunted by the ghosts of their dead fathers and are afflicted by similar forms of passivity, frustration, prevarication, and powerlessness, and also united by their having a common artistic bent. All of these common features make it entirely possible that this womanly Hamlet may have been a source for Joyce of his own rather androgynous Bloom, who is presented as a "womanly man" in *Ulysses*, in the text's most obviously theatrical episode, "Circe":

DR DIXON
    (reads a bill of health) Professor Bloom is a finished example of the new womanly man. His moral nature is simple and lovable. Many have found him a dear man, a dear person.

                                           (*U* 465)

If Bernhardt's (or Vining's) female *Hamlet* in some way contributed to the construction of Bloom's vision of the play, other specific *Hamlet* films, along with the infinitely more important text of the play itself, may have influenced Joyce's own writing of *Ulysses*, a text that numerous critics have shown was receptive to the innovative modes of cinema to which Joyce attempted to respond and even sought to replicate in his prose.[8] Many of the early filmmakers turned their hands to Shakespeare adaptations, most often to *Hamlet*. In 1907 George Méliès directed a silent *Hamlet* that was followed by (among others) three separate Italian productions in 1908 by Mario Caserini, Luca Comerio, and Giuseppe De Liguoro, and a French one with Mounet-Sully in 1909. The year 1910 saw a British production of *Hamlet* by William George Barker, a Danish one by August Blom, and a French production made by Henri Desfontaines. In 1913, Cecil M.

---

8. See, most recently, John McCourt (2010) and Thomas Burkdall (2001).

Hepworth's one-hour version appeared with Sir Johnston Forbes-Robertson, the leading Shakespearean actor of his time, in the title role. In short, there was no escaping the ghost of Shakespeare, who appeared through his multitude of characters on stage and screen with alarming regularity.

Caserini's was the first Italian adaptation of the complete work, but was preceded internationally by Méliès's 1907 film. Neither survives today, but it is safe to say that it made use of Méliès's characteristic techniques and tricks, such as the stop-action method, the dissolve, and multiple-exposure or transparency, which was very useful for the screening of ghosts. Although Méliès's *Hamlet*, in which the director himself played the title role, no longer exists, we have a rich description of it, penned by his brother, Gaston:

> The melancholy disposition of the young prince is demonstrated to good advantage in the grave-yard scene where the diggers are interrupted in their weird pastime of joshing among the tombstones by the appearance of Hamlet and his friend. After questioning them he picks up one of the skulls about a newly-dug grave, and is told that it is the skull of a certain Yorick, who was known to Hamlet in his natural life. Hamlet slowly takes up the skull, and his manner strongly indicates, "Alas, poor Yorik, I knew him well!" The following scenes combine to show the high state of dementia of the young prince's mentality. He is seen in his room where he is continually annoyed and excited by apparitions which taunt him in their weirdness and add bitterness to his troubled brain. He attempts to grasp them but in vain, and he falls to brooding. Now is shown the scene in which he meets the ghost of his father and is told to take vengeance on the reigning monarch, his uncle; but not content with this, Hamlet's fates tantalise him further by sending into his presence the ghost of his departed sweetheart, Ophelia. He attempts to embrace her as she throws flowers to him from a garland on her brow, but his efforts are futile; and when he sees the apparition fall to the ground, he, too swoons away, and is thus found by several courtiers. He is raving and storms about in a manner entirely unintelligible to them; but they calm him gradually.[9]

9. Gaston Méliès is cited in Ball (1968, 34–35).

In the hands of filmmakers like Méliès, early cinema (like Shakespeare before it, who would be attacked for his vulgarisms by Ben Jonson) reveled in *trucage,* in optical illusion, in ghosts and the spectral, in spiritualism and transformations, and would often be criticized for these spectacular elements. Yet these were among the core ingredients Joyce would borrow in Trieste and elsewhere as part of the rich cornucopia of elements he needed for *Ulysses.* Cinema tore up the rules of time and space and, by following its lead, helped Joyce produce scenes such as that in "Circe" when Stephen, Bloom and Shakespeare somehow merge into one in the mirror: "*Stephen and Bloom gaze in the mirror. The face of William Shakespeare, beardless, appears there, rigid in facial paralysis, crowned by the reflection of the reindeer antlered hatrack in the hall*" (U 528).

Shakespeare in this image is captured in a "still," frozen or paralyzed—momentarily paralyzing both Stephen and Bloom but not their creator, Joyce, who is, as ever, pulling all the strings not in the least inhibited by having had to spend so much of his creative life being exercised by the hyperpresence of the long-dead Bard, a ghost who would not lie down but demanded to be read, reread, and subsequently rewritten by the Irish author in the pages of his final two novels. Joyce, too, would later press a similarly enabling/paralyzing demand on his own literary followers, and in doing so achieved what he set out to achieve: to take his place, always on his own terms, in the canon beside, among others, his Europeanized Shakespeare, whom he has been so good as to allow to speak only "*in dignified ventriloquy*" (U 528).

6

Made in Germany

Why Goethe's Hamlet *Mattered to Joyce*

VIKE MARTINA PLOCK

HAMLET: Give us the foils.
LAERTES: Come, one for me.
HAMLET: I'll be your foil, Laertes. In mine ignorance
Your skill shall like a star i'th' darkest night
Stick fiery off indeed.

(V, ii, 250–54)[1]

On first glance it must appear counterproductive to suggest that Joyce took any interest in the *Hamlet* interpretation put forward by Johann Wolfgang von Goethe in his 1795–96 theater novel *Wilhelm Meister*. Although "Scylla and Charybdis" opens with the "quaker librarian" (*U* 178) enthusiastically referencing Goethe's take on *Hamlet*, "—And we have, have we not, those priceless pages of *Wilhelm Meister*. A great poet on a great brother poet. A hesitating soul taking arms against a sea of troubles, torn by conflicting doubts, as one sees in real life" (*U* 176), Lyster's mighty attempts to contribute to the ongoing *Hamlet* discussion in the National Library

I would like to thank Anselm Haverkamp who drew my attention to the numerous parallels and textual overlaps that exist between Joyce's and Goethe's *Hamlet* and whose own analysis of Shakespeare's *Hamlet* inspired aspects of my argument.

1. All references to Shakespeare's *Hamlet* will be to the Arden Shakespeare edition edited by Harold Jenkins (1982).

are dismissed as grotesque platitudes by a "sneer[ing]" (*U* 176) Stephen Dedalus. It is therefore tempting to agree with William M. Schutte, who concludes that "Goethe is not on Stephen's select list of heroes" (1957, 33).

Joyce himself, resembling his protagonist Stephen Dedalus in many of his literary tastes and dislikes, remained similarly unimpressed by the achievements of Germany's greatest man of letters, whom he regarded as "*un noioso funzionario* (a boring civil servant)" (Ellmann 1982, 394). Unsurprisingly, the extensive notes for his 1912–13 Triestine *Hamlet* lectures do not contain a single reference to the German writer (Quillian 1975, 7–63).[2] Admittedly, Joyce relied strongly on elements of Goethe's *Faust* when drafting his "Circe" episode, but Goethe's *Theaterroman* appears to have been of comparatively little use to him. Indeed, as Richard Ellmann argues, Joyce incorporated an allusion to *Wilhelm Meister* into the library chapter, "if only to disagree with it" (Ellmann 1977, 51). It looks, therefore, as if a discussion of Goethe's literary influences on Joyce can be conclusively shelved.[3]

In spite of this compelling evidence, a number of Joyce critics have tried to establish links between the German and the Irish author. Richard Ellmann himself acknowledges that Joyce, in self-consciously ornamenting his first novel with the haughty title *Stephen Hero*, "had also in mind *Wilhelm Meister*, where Goethe's hero is embarrassed by his surname (Master) until he has earned the right to it" (Ellmann 1977, 15). In a 1992 article Gerald Gillespie further emphasizes the conceptual similarities between Goethe's *Wilhelm Meister* material and Joyce's preoccupation

---

2. Joyce was also delighted to report to Harriet Shaw Weaver in 1932 that "Jolas is bringing out a *Transition* number which is to be an attack on Goethe (whose centenary it is) and a homage to me" (*LI* 313). For more information on Joyce's complex attitude toward Goethe see also Booker (1995, 111–38).

3. But a rather unsettling passage from a 1932 letter to Frank Budgen also indicates that Joyce was only too familiar with the *Wilhelm Meister* material. Joyce here comments on a "picture of myself and daughter and of Wilhelm Meister" and suggests that there is "something Mignonesque" about Lucia (*LIII* 261). Given Mignon's obvious erotic interest in her adoptive father Wilhelm in Goethe's novel, Joyce's comment might appear problematic, inviting all sorts of speculation about his relationship to Lucia.

with Stephen Dedalus as young artist figure. The protagonist's artistic formation is central to both texts, and in both Goethe's *Wilhelm Meister* and Joyce's *Ulysses* professional and personal maturity hinges on "attaining fatherhood" (292). Moreover, as Gillespie points out, both writers treated their protagonist's juvenile aspirations in "an anticipatory version" (291–92). While Joyce's development of the Dedalus topic is comparable to a sixteen-year-long Odyssey (from *Stephen Hero* in 1904 and *A Portrait* in 1916 to the 1922 publication of *Ulysses*), Goethe's interest in the *Meister* plot took on equally epic qualities. What started in 1775 as *Urtext* in *Wilhelm Meisters theatralische Sendung* (*Wilhelm Meister's Theatrical Mission*) was extensively rewritten and published almost twenty years later as *Wilhelm Meisters Lehrjahre* (*Wilhelm Meister's Apprenticeship*).[4]

Following Gillespie in the attempt to consolidate the thematic and structural affinities between Goethe and Joyce, Barbara Laman (2004) underlines the irony of Stephen's apparent disdain for Lyster's *Hamlet* theory. While she states that Goethe's interpretation was responsible for creating the romantic image of Hamlet as "beautiful ineffectual dreamer who comes to grief against hard facts" (*U* 176), Laman also points out that Stephen's understanding of artistic creation and his subsequent biographical reading of Shakespeare's plays is indebted to a Romantic concept of authorship as "intensely personal" (103). Try as he might, Stephen cannot evade the morose influence of romanticism on his own art. No doubt, Laman's argument sounds compelling, but it fails to acknowledge that paradoxes and incongruities are essential components of Stephen's Shakespeare theory. As I have argued elsewhere, Stephen's new-historicist reading of Shakespeare, accentuating the importance of biography and historical context in an author's creative labor, is undermined by the fact that Stephen's own artistic product, the Shakespeare theory, is assembled from textual quotations (Plock 2010, 85–86). It should therefore not astound us that Stephen's art is both dismissive of and subservient to Romantic inflections.

---

4. Moreover, Goethe would, in 1821, also publish a follow-up novel *Wilhelm Meisters Wanderjahre* (*Wilhelm Meister's Journeymanship*).

In my view the critic who comes closest to accurately describing the relationship between Goethe and Shakespeare is Richard Brown, whose analysis of Joyce's Shakespeare is very alert to the "continental European perspectives" (1999, 339) on *Hamlet* that Stephen has to tackle in "Scylla and Charybdis." Brown rightly points out that Stephen's *Hamlet* needs to diverge from both "the German Romantic and the French Symbolist readings" (354). Keith Booker similarly points out that "Lyster's introduction sets up Wilhelm's reading as a predecessor of the detailed discussion of *Hamlet* that will be delivered by Stephen in the course of the chapter" (1995, 119). In what follows I intend to take up the productive suggestion that the intertextual association between Goethe and Joyce can be best explained as one of aggressive discord and competition. For that reason the first part of my argument might appear self-evident. It was Joyce's aim to challenge, surpass, and negate Goethe's *Hamlet* interpretation, which had, since the publication of *Wilhelm Meister*, dominated the reception of Shakespeare's play in European intellectual circles. Not a seamless incorporation of the textual elements he found in *Wilhelm Meister* but the development of a *Hamlet* theory that could hold its own next to Goethe's was Joyce's primary aim in his attempt on Shakespeare in *Ulysses*. I will therefore argue that Goethe becomes the true opponent in Joyce's literary sparring match that is acted out in "Scylla and Charybdis." For Joyce it is Goethe who is the backdrop for his own intellectual skills to shine "like a star i'th' darkest night." Shakespeare is merely "the happy huntingground" (*U* 239) in the library chapter, used as the figurative floret or rapier in this contest between literary giants. However, while Stephen (and Joyce) aim to counteract Goethe's *Hamlet* theory, *Wilhelm Meister*, like the ghost in Shakespeare's play (I, v, 91), begs to be remembered. In spite of Joyce's reputed statement to the contrary, specific elements of Goethe's novel live on, unacknowledged, as ghostly textual presence in "Scylla and Charybdis." The second part of this chapter will therefore trace *Wilhelm Meister*'s spectral existence in the pages of Joyce's *Ulysses*, and the subsequent reading will unearth specific intertextual resonances among the three texts, *Hamlet*, *Wilhelm Meister*, and *Ulysses*. Such a comparative reading across textual boundaries can uncover how intimately aspects of

Joyce's politics and aesthetics are contingent on the use of Goethe's Shakespearean hypotext.

If Goethe's *Hamlet* interpretation had such immense cultural cache at the time Joyce was writing *Ulysses*, an obvious question would be: which elements of *Wilhelm Meister* created such repercussions in nineteenth-century literary circles? A cursory glance at Goethe's novel reveals it to be an episodic survey of Wilhelm Meister's personal and professional progress. Born into a middle class entrepreneurial family, Wilhelm is, from boyhood, obsessed with the theater and vouches to cultivate his intellect and personality by choosing the career of an actor. Halfway through the novel Wilhelm falls under the spell of Shakespeare's works. While he dons Elizabethan costumes and takes up fencing matches with his appropriately named coactor Laertes that reenact "the duel in which Hamlet and his opponent come to such a tragic end" (Goethe 1995, 132),[5] he also takes on the challenging job of directing a *Hamlet* performance, in which he plays the part of the Danish prince. However, before the planned performance—a quasi "play within a play"—can go ahead, Wilhelm has to adapt Shakespeare's tragedy for the stage, a task that gives him the opportunity to deliver a number of *Hamlet* lectures for the benefit of a docile ensemble.[6] Wilhelm is both Shakespeare and Hamlet, and Goethe's novel, in a masterly fashion that anticipates Stephen's interpretative work in *Ulysses*, confuses the role of author, actor, character, and literary critic. After all, Wilhelm's critical intervention can be regarded as a piece of staged *Hamlet* reception.

Shortly after the first *Hamlet* performance, in which a mysterious stranger, who is oddly reminiscent of Wilhelm's deceased father, plays the role of the ghost, Wilhelm suddenly parts ways with the theater company

5. "Wilhelm und Laertes griffen zu den Rapieren und fingen diesmal in theatralischer Absicht ihre Übungen an. Sie wollten den Zweikampf darstellen, in welchem Hamlet und sein Gegner ein so tragisches Ende nehmen" (Goethe 1998, 223).

6. In *Giacomo Joyce*, Joyce uses exactly this expression, "docile," when describing his lecturing activities in Trieste: "I expound Shakespeare to docile Trieste: Hamlet, quoth I, who is most courteous to gentle and simple is rude only to Polonius" (*GJ* 10).

and unexpectedly leaves the world of the stage. In the second half of the novel, his fate becomes intertwined with the workings of an enigmatic Tower society (*Turmgesellschaft*), a Freemason order, which has specific designs on his education and personal development. It is mostly due to the interventions of the Tower society that Wilhelm is, at the end of Goethe's novel, united, in a rather fortuitous manner, with a considerable fortune, the lady of his choice, and his prodigal son. No doubt Goethe realized and played up the irony inherent in his literary creation: in his novel, "Master Will" becomes Wilhelm Meister ("Wilhelm Master") who is, paradoxically, by no means master of his own will or fate.

However, if Wilhelm lacks agency to control the particulars of his life, his enthusiasm for Shakespeare produces a *Hamlet* theory that proved to be extremely enduring. In Goethe's novel Hamlet is reborn as a sentimental melancholy man devoid of political agency. As Wilhelm states: "In these words, so I believe, lies the key to Hamlet's whole behavior; and it is clear to me what Shakespeare set out to portray: a heavy deed placed on a soul which is not adequate to cope with it. . . . A fine, pure, noble and highly moral person, but devoid of that emotional strength that characterizes a hero, goes to pieces beneath a burden that it can neither support nor cast off" (Goethe 1995, 146).[7] Consequently, "the hero has no plan" although Wilhelm acknowledges that "the play has" (151).[8] And even though it was scorned by modernists such as T. S. Eliot, who insinuated that Goethe "made of Hamlet a Werther" ([1919] 1975, 45), Wilhelm's theory was, as the critic William Diamond pointed out in 1925, "because of Goethe's dominating influence" "accepted and elaborated by August Wilhelm Schlegel, Ludwig Tieck, and other Romanticists in Germany, and by Samuel Taylor Coleridge in England" (90). In the course of the

7. "In diesen Worten, dünkt mich, liegt der Schlüssel zu Hamlets ganzem Betragen, und mir ist deutlich, daß Shakespeare habe schildern wollen: eine große Tat auf eine Seele gelegt, die der Tat nicht gewachsen ist . . . Ein schönes, reines, edles, höchst moralisches Wesen, ohne die sinnliche Stärke, die den Helden macht, geht unter einer Last zugrunde, die es weder tragen noch abwerfen kann" (Goethe 1998, 245–46).

8. "Hier werden wir anders belehrt; der Held hat keinen Plan, aber das Stück ist planvoll" (Goethe 1998, 254).

nineteenth century Goethe's interpretation of Hamlet as a sentimental idealist, in other words, threatened to eclipse Shakespeare's original creation. To a certain point Stephen is right when he claims in "Scylla and Charybdis" that Shakespeare was "made in Germany" "as the champion French polisher of Italian scandals" (*U* 197).

In Joyce's novels Stephen Dedalus consistently rubs shoulders with Goethe. But despite (or probably because of) his incontestable literary importance, the German national poet is (together with Shakespeare) dismissed in *Stephen Hero*, where only Ibsen is fit to classify as "the successor to the first poet of the Europeans" (*SH* 41). In fact, Stephen's scorn for Goethe becomes apparent when one of the Daniels family's "marriageable daughters" (*SH* 42), after some hesitation and urging from another "young man," who was "'doing' the same course," nominates the German as her "favourite poet" (*SH* 43). For Stephen (and for Joyce) Goethe represents, in contrast to the unsettling Norwegian playwright, a safe intellectual choice. Only an exceptionally uninspired mindset would venerate this model of bourgeois artistic tedium and prefer it to the rebellious and virulent energy represented by Ibsen.

But Stephen's and Goethe's paths continue to cross. In *A Portrait* Stephen encounters the bland Donovan, a "fat young man" with a "pallid bloated face" and a "weak wheezing voice" (*P* 211), who happily capitalizes on the rumor that Stephen is "writing some essay about esthetics" to bore the young artist with rather flawed remarks about "Goethe and Lessing," "the classical school and the romantic school and all that" (*P* 212). Even before we turn to *Ulysses* Goethe is therefore positioned by Joyce as Stephen's literary adversary. The giant of German letters has already carved out his artistic territory, and all Stephen seems to be able to do is follow in Goethe's footsteps. Stephen's contempt for the "quaker librarian" in "Scylla and Charybdis" is thus understandable. Once again Stephen's artistic merit will be judged and compared to Goethe's by a "secondbest" (*U* 195) audience. Moreover, since both Donovan's and Lyster's mannerisms and personalities are described as "urbanely" (*P* 229) or "urbane" (*U* 176) respectively, Joyce makes it very clear that these two infuriating encounters with the "idealistic, German, ultraprofound" (*P* 229) school are closely connected in Stephen's mind. It should also be taken into account at this point that the romantic mysticism that developed in the wake of Goethe's *Wilhelm Meister* dominated the artistic mood and atmosphere of the Irish literary revival,[9] another poetic formation to which Stephen remains disinclined in *A Portrait* and *Ulysses*. If Stephen wants to establish a reputation that matches Goethe's, he has to meet and defeat the German poet on his precursor's intellectual terrain. Shakespeare's *Hamlet* is the obvious place to start.

Considering Stephen's antagonistic relationship with Goethe in this manner can therefore help us understand the young artist's efforts in "Scylla and Charybdis." To a certain extent Stephen's Shakespeare theory is nothing but an aesthetic exercise that hopes to match (or displace) the one produced by Goethe's Wilhelm Meister. Not personal conviction but effortless composition and eloquent delivery are what matters most to him. Important is not so much what is said but how well it is put forward. This is why Stephen's *Hamlet* lecture is interspersed with self-reflexive comments such as "Local colour. Work in all you know" (U 180) that serve as prompts while he also expresses annoyance at flaws in his delivery: "Said that" (U 187). It is more than ironic, though, that Stephen, in trying to overcome his predecessor's towering influence and establish himself as an artist who can compete with Goethe, replicates aspects of Wilhelm's style, attitudes, and mannerisms. Like Goethe's hero he creates a subjective *Hamlet* interpretation. Whereas Wilhelm projects his own idealism onto Hamlet, Stephen creates a Shakespearean hero (and a Shakespearean artist) with whom he strongly identifies. Moreover, with his conspicuous "Hamlet hat" (U 47) Stephen, Joyce's ineffectual idealist, also adopts an Elizabethan sartorial style that is similar to Wilhelm Meister's. All this shows that Joyce, in order to distance himself from his literary alter ego, deliberately underlined the inconsistencies and notional imperfections in Stephen's attempts to surpass Goethe. Although Joyce at some point also seemed to have modeled

9. Robert Welch, in discussing James Clarence Mangan's Romanticism, acknowledges that there "were certain spiritual affinities between Ireland and Germany in the early nineteenth century which had to do with the fact that both cultures felt themselves to be under pressure from an imperial threat, in Germany's case that of Napoleon" (1989, 26).

himself on the German poet-critic by delivering his own Shakespeare lectures in Trieste in 1912–13, he had in all likelihood realized, by the time he was writing *Ulysses*, the full absurdity of these juvenile aspirations so that he was able to caricature them mercilessly in Stephen.

Joyce's potential derision for one of his leading acts in *Ulysses* aside, Stephen's self-consciousness as performer raises interesting questions about the library chapter's theatrical elements. Goethe's eighteenth-century novel contained, as we have seen, both a *Hamlet* performance and a critical intervention. Similarly, Joyce's "Scylla and Charybdis" relates a discussion of the *Hamlet* material while it stages aspects of the Shakespearean drama. Attaining literary maturity is thus contingent, in both texts, on orchestrating a *Hamlet* theory that has the potential to be put into theatrical practice. In fact, the structure of Joyce's episode is oddly reminiscent of a staged play. Like "Ivy Day in the Committee Room" it takes place almost entirely within one room, and all of its aspects, apart from Stephen's interior monologue, could be easily dramatized. Apart from the already-mentioned stage directions that are meant to assist Stephen in guiding his way through his performance, the library chapter is one of the episodes in *Ulysses* that contains the most theatrical elements and references. Stephen is, as we have seen, hyperconscious that he is on show in a setting that resembles a stage. Different actors enter and leave. After Lyster has successfully delivered his Goethe discourse to a "sinkapace" (U 176) rhythm at the episode's start, he "corantoe[s] off" (U 176). A few lines later, "Mr Best entered, tall, young, mild, light" (U 178), while A.E. is "due at the *Homestead*" (U 184) and leaves the library before Stephen has been given the chance to elaborate on his *Hamlet* theory. The "[p]ortals of discovery" then open to readmit the "quaker librarian" (U 182) until Bloom's request for a back issue of the *Freeman's Journal* removes him once more from the scene. Pirouetting his "galliard" (U 192), Lyster leaves the stage again.

Other textual details further underpin the episode's structural reliance on a theater play. Anticipating the visual layout of "Circe," "Scylla and Charybdis" suddenly changes its design and is temporarily transformed into a theater script midway through the episode (U 200–1). Likewise, Mulligan's entrance that interrupts Stephen's *Hamlet* exposition at a crucial moment is greeted with the expression *"Entr'acte"* (U

189). Indeed, Mulligan's appearance on the imaginary stage has dramatic consequences for Stephen's own performance. If he had any chances of favorably impressing his audience, Mulligan's arrival after this assumed interval between the acts erodes Stephen's confidence as an actor. From this moment onward, Stephen is "battling against hopelessness" (U 198), and he reluctantly relinquishes the director's seat. It is now "Puck Mulligan" (U 207) who runs the show with his wit, his jests, and his own "play for the mummers" (U 208). In the second part of the episode it is Mulligan who is spotlighted, who receives an invitation to George Moore's soirée (U 206), and who ruthlessly outshines Stephen as lead actor in and executive producer of the staged theatrical.

Meanwhile, the abundance of these theatrical elements and references in "Scylla and Charybdis" invites speculation on what is actually performed in the library. My suggestion would be that what we see (or read) is a version of Shakespeare's *Hamlet* drama. Like Wilhelm Meister, Stephen naturally lays claim to the role of the young Danish prince. Bloom, a possible father figure to Stephen, lingers as "a bowing dark figure" (U 192) in the episode's background and is reminiscent of the ghost of Old Hamlet. Elsewhere Joyce's chapter, through Mr. Best's intervention, self-consciously advertises a *Hamlet* performance on a theater bill:

HAMLET

ou

LE DISTRAIT

PIÈCE DE SHAKESPEARE

(U 179)

Individual characters can thus be dressed in "Scylla and Charybdis" to fit the *Hamlet* template. Mr. Best might make a good Horatio, while Lyster seems predestined to impersonate Polonius. However, using Goethe's *Wilhelm Meister* as a mediator between *Hamlet* and *Ulysses* illustrates that it is, above all, one scene from Shakespeare's drama that can be regarded as an important intertext in "Scylla and Charybdis." As Wilhelm explains, from boyhood on he has distinguished himself by "a passionate determination to turn any novel that I read, any story that I heard from my teachers, into a play" (Goethe 1995, 13).[10] But his infatuation with theatrical adaptations takes a curious turn: Wilhelm, Goethe's sentimentalist, has a liking for the sensational and the melodramatic. His youthful theatrical exploits have the tendency to leap "over exposition and development" and hurry "to the much more interesting fifth act," which means that he composes "a few plays from the ending and working back to the beginning" (13–14).[11] The structure of Goethe's novel emulates its protagonist's liking for the dramatic by containing Wilhelm's theatrical experiences in its first five books. Before the novel moves on to focus on Wilhelm's involvement with the Tower society, its provisional denouement occurs after the reader witnesses the first *Hamlet* performance, a drunken revelry, and a melodramatically staged death at the end of book five.

A similar sense of a temporary ending pervades "Scylla and Charybdis." Allegedly, Joyce thought at some point throughout the writing process of "an *Entr'acte* for Ulysses in middle of book after 9th episode" that was to function "like a pause in the action of a play" (LI 149). It is most likely that the "Entr'acte" Joyce refers to here is "Wandering Rocks," which succeeds the episode in the library. "Scylla and Charybdis" thus appears as the climax of the novel's first part. And indeed, the library chapter resembles a quasi-midpoint of the Homeric narrative Joyce was writing, structurally segregating the first and second part of the novel. It is 2:00 p.m. by the time the chapter opens, and we are halfway through Bloomsday. But "Scylla and Charybdis" is also the last chapter that focuses specifically on Stephen Dedalus. After we see him leave the library with his escort Mulligan, Joyce's text loses sight of him. With the opening of "Wandering Rocks," Stephen blends into the background and becomes just one of the many Dubliners who roam the streets of the Hibernian

---

10. "Meiner Leidenschaft, jeden Roman, den ich las, jede Geschichte, die man mich lehrte, in einem Schauspiel darzustellen, konnte selbst der unbiegsamste Stoff nicht widerstehen" (Goethe 1998, 29–30).

11. "Wenn uns in der Schule die Weltgeschichte vorgetragen wurde, zeichnete ich mir sorgfältig aus, wo einer auf eine besondere Weise erstochen oder vergiftet wurde, und meine Einbildungskraft sah über Exposition und Verwicklung hinweg und eilte dem interessanten fünften Akte zu" (Goethe 1998, 30).

metropolis. And while he no doubt appears in later chapters, episodes such as "Eumaeus" and "Ithaca" focus increasingly on Leopold Bloom's experiences as social and cultural outcast. After his last dramatic performance in the library chapter, Stephen's role is no longer a major one. Likewise, Joyce critics such as Karen Lawrence have argued that "Wandering Rocks" (and "Sirens") marks the first significant departure from the novel's initial style and novelistic form with which readers have become familiar (Lawrence 1981, 80). So Leopold Bloom and the *Ulyssean* style both eclipse Stephen in the novel's second half.

But before he leaves the novel's footlights Stephen attempts to stage, like Wilhelm Meister before him, his own final act. For that reason "Scylla and Charybdis" adopts selected aspects of the duel scene between Hamlet and Laertes in Shakespeare's play. Stephen even announces his own dramatic finale by referring to himself repeatedly as "Lapwing" (*U* 202–3)—the expression used by Horatio for Osric (V, ii, 183), the much-mocked courtier who greets Hamlet on his return to Denmark and delivers the request to "play with Laertes" (V, ii, 195) in a duel that will take both Hamlet's and Laertes' lives. Other key stage requisites that feature prominently in the "bloodboltered shambles in act five" (*U* 180) are also taken into consideration in "Scylla and Charybdis." The "napkin" (V, ii, 291), with which Gertrude offers to wipe Hamlet's face during the duel, resurfaces as Stephen's "Handkerchief" (*U* 202) in the library chapter. And even the reference to Falstaff's sneak-cup (*U* 198) in Stephen's thoughts about Eglinton and Eglinton's father can equally well be read as allusion to Claudius's fatal cup (V, ii, 269). More significant, though, are Stephen's intense reflections on weaponry and arms. He thinks of a "woman's invisible weapon" (*U* 188), his "sword" (*U* 202), and denotes his hat and ash plant as "casque and sword" (*U* 184) that are supposed to shield him in the subsequent battle of wits. Furthermore, the above-mentioned references to the handkerchief and the sword occur in close proximity to the "Lapwing" allusion. Together they form a cluster of *Hamlet* quotations that makes explicit the correspondence between Shakespeare's duel scene and Joyce's library chapter. Naturally, in "Scylla and Charybdis" the armed combat between Laertes and Hamlet is translated into an intellectual dispute. Stephen therefore urges himself to use precise, exact, and well-defined expressions, his "dagger definitions"

(*U* 178). Earlier that day, in "Telemachus," the chapter that also contains numerous *Hamlet* allusions, Stephen had already envisioned an intellectual competition between Buck Mulligan and himself in terms reminiscent of an armed combat: "Parried again. He fears the lancet of my art as I fear that of his. The cold steel pen" (*U* 7). "Scylla and Charybdis" then stages the aggressive and dramatic grand finale to Stephen's intellectual efforts and ambitions that are similar to Wilhelm's attempts to revolutionize the German theater scene with his production of Shakespeare's play. In *Ulysses*, sword play becomes word play.

However, much more remains to be said about the parallels between Joyce's *Ulysses* and Goethe's *Wilhelm Meister*. Up to this point my analysis has concentrated exclusively on establishing similarities between the central characters' individual circumstances, personality, and disposition—and the similarities are certainly striking. The comparative reading of *Ulysses*, *Wilhelm Meister*, and *Hamlet* illustrates that Stephen is modeling himself, to a certain extent, on Goethe's protagonist. He is projecting his own personal situation onto the Renaissance playwright and creates and impersonates a version of Shakespeare's dramatic hero whose temperament and attitudes closely resemble his own. But the triangular reading of Shakespeare's *Hamlet*, Goethe's *Wilhelm Meister*, and Joyce's *Ulysses* also provides an excellent opportunity to consider a completely different set of textual overlaps. Indeed, a lot can be said about the political resonances in all three texts, and once again Goethe's *Wilhelm Meister* can be used as a starting point to go backward and forward to *Hamlet* and *Ulysses*. As we shall see, the analysis of these intertextual dynamics can indicate that, in all three cases, the protagonist's personal drama steals the limelight from the political events that lead a noisy existence in the texts' margins and off-sides.

It is commonly known that Shakespeare's *Hamlet* stages a political succession drama. The usurper Claudius has dethroned both Hamlet senior and junior through his murderous attempt and his opportune union with the queen. This political and domestic treachery now seems to propel Hamlet's paralytic condition and the play's cataclysmic developments. In *Wilhelm Meister*'s words: "His right to the crown was not hereditary, but his father's long life had strengthened the claims of an only son and his hopes of assuming the crown. But now he sees himself, despite virtual promises, excluded, perhaps for ever, by his uncle," and this is "how his mind first takes on a melancholy cast" (Goethe 1995, 145).[12] In Joyce's *Ulysses*, Stephen Dedalus, in analogy to the Shakespearean model, feels similarly usurped (*U* 23) by Mulligan in his hopes for stardom in the Irish literary scene, and critics such as Vincent Cheng have convincingly linked Stephen's personal frustrations to the country's complex state as a British colony and its frustrated attempts to secure home rule (Cheng 1995, 160). But it is, in fact, precisely because of Goethe's *Wilhelm Meister* and because of Wilhelm's *Hamlet* interpretation, that this conflation of the personal and the political in Shakespeare's *Hamlet* and in Joyce's *Ulysses* obtains more ammunition and conceptual precision.

Goethe's novel indicates that Wilhelm's biggest challenge in adapting *Hamlet* for the stage is creating a balance between the "*internal* relationship between the personages and the events" and the "*external* circumstances affecting the characters," among which Wilhelm lists "the troubles in Norway, the war with young Fortinbras, the ambassadorial mission to the old uncle, the settlement of the dispute, young Fortinbras's march into Poland, and his return at the end of the play" (Goethe 1995, 178). Wilhelm eventually proposes to simplify the play's external (political) elements by focusing on "the troubles in Norway" as a "single motivation" for the play's "*internal* relationship between the personages and the events" (178): "After the death of Hamlet senior, the recently conquered Norwegians become restless" and threaten the Danish invaders with an uprising.[13] This scenario, then, is according to Wilhelm the incentive for all that is to fol-

---

12. "Das Recht zur Krone war nicht erblich, und doch hätte ein längeres Leben seines Vaters die Ansprüche seines einzigen Sohnes mehr befestigt und die Hoffnung zur Krone gesichert. Dagegen sieht er sich nun durch seinen Oheim, ungeachtet scheinbarer Versprechungen, vielleicht auf immer ausgeschlossen . . . Hier nimmt sein Gemüt die erste traurige Richtung" (Goethe 1998, 244).

13. "Zu diesen äußern Verhältnissen zähle ich die Unruhen in Norwegen, den Krieg mit dem jungen Fortinbras, die Gesandtschaft an den alten Oheim, den geschlichteten Zwist, den Zug des jungen Fortinbras nach Polen und seine Rückkehr am Ende. . . . Nach dem Tode des alten Hamlet werden die ersteroberten Norweger unruhig" (Goethe 1998, 296–97).

low. Although he decides to blue-pencil young Fortinbras in his version of the play, Wilhelm's *Hamlet* theory rewrites the domestic drama at the Danish court (with all its Oedipal nuances) and turns it into a political dispute between neighboring countries, in which the conquered Norwegians aggressively strive for Home Rule. In other words, it is through Wilhelm's critical intervention that *Hamlet* acquires an explicit colonial twist.[14]

Of course, given *Wilhelm Meister's* historico-political location in eighteenth-century Germany, it is only to be expected that Goethe's hero expresses a strong interest in the latently perceptible political affairs in Shakespeare's *Hamlet*. With its references to the American War of Independence (Goethe 1995, 156, 264) Goethe's novel, set in the time of the French Revolution, is bookended by two democratic insurgencies that radically changed the modern political landscape. Moreover, at the end of the eighteenth century Germany itself did not exist as a geographically defined nation-state but was made up of smaller provinces and imperial free cities with constantly shifting territorial boundaries. National identity and unity had to be artificially created. In this context the establishment of a national theater had immense political significance because it could function as an educational and culturally formative force. This spirit of "national fervor" permeates Goethe's *Theaterroman*, in which the German population is "delighted to indulge poetically in a piece that expressed their own national character and played on their native soil" (Goethe 1995, 70).[15] With a fitting sense of irony, the novel's narrator reveals that

14. The critic Anselm Haverkamp (2006) intriguingly suggests that the Shakespearean *Hamlet* already contains such a "politically conditioned framework that literally hovers at the edge of the family saga" (2006, 182). In his anamorphic reading of the play, "the story of Hamlet appears instantly transformed and displaced into a quite different story: that of the Norwegian conquest of Denmark made possible under the pretext of an invasion of Poland. It is in this capacity that Fortinbras comes up at the beginning and is seen crossing through Denmark on his Polish expedition, just in time to put himself in place and assume power in Denmark" (180).

15. "Jedermann war von dem Feuer des edelsten Nationalgeistes entzündet. Wie sehr gefiel es dieser deutschen Gesellschaft, sich ihrem Charakter gemäß auf eignem Grund und Boden poetisch zu ergötzen" (Goethe 1998, 125).

Wilhelm "saw in himself the great actor, the founder of a future National Theater that he heard various people pining for" (16–17).[16]

Cultural politics similarly intrude on the scene in the National Library. With references to a "Gaptoothed Kathleen" and "her four beautiful green fields, the stranger in her house" (*U* 177) at the beginning of the chapter, Joyce explicitly references turn-of-the-century Irish nationalist sentiments—and Yeats's iconic 1902 play *Cathleen ni Houlihan* in particular. Indeed, in the library chapter Stephen's private performance is threatened to be marginalized by the activities of the Irish literary revival that is eagerly awaiting the production of a "national epic" (*U* 185) and "a figure which the world will set beside Saxon Shakespeare's Hamlet" (*U* 177). While Stephen needs to position himself in relation to the literary fashions of his time, his refusal to "do the Yeats touch" (*U* 208) and to satisfy the revivalist demand for authentic Irish materials has, in all likelihood, dealt a death blow to his professional progress in Dublin. Crucially, like Goethe's Wilhelm Meister, who chooses *Hamlet* for his directorial debut in the face of emergent nationalist cultural politics, Stephen's swan song, the Shakespeare performance, refuses to engage with topics and themes close to his audience's hearts. Artistically, Wilhelm and Stephen appear to be at odds with their cultural surroundings. In both cases, however, the choice to take on Shakespeare, a foreign literary giant, suggests another overlap in Goethe's and Joyce's aesthetic tastes and preferences.

Although Shakespeare's dramatic heroes were widely celebrated in Goethe's Germany as embodiments of the subject theory advocated by the *Sturm und Drang* (Storm and Stress), Shakespeare's *Hamlet* nevertheless remained a foreign import, an alien cultural authority that jarred with the resurgent nationalism pervading Germany at the turn of the eighteenth century. This is why the prominence of England's national poet in

---

16. "Seine Bestimmung zum Theater war ihm nunmehr klar; das hohe Ziel, das er sich vorgestreckt sah, schien ihm näher, . . . und in selbstgefälliger Bescheidenheit erblickte er in sich den trefflichen Schauspieler, den Schöpfer eines künftigen National-theaters, nach dem er so vielfältig hatte seufzen hören" (Goethe 1998, 35).

Wilhelm Meister points to Goethe's complex stance toward the nationalist cultural politics advocated in his time by the romantics. Contrary to contemporary trends, Goethe wrote a novel that preferred cultural plurality over nationalist homogeneity and exclusivity. A quick look at Goethe's late work confirms that his literary interests continued to be outward facing and that he was interested in literary renewal only if it contained distinctive international components. Although Edward Said critically reviewed Goethe's 1819 *West-Östlicher Divan* (*West-Eastern Divan*) in *Orientalism* because it assumes "a kind of intellectual *authority* over the Orient within Western Culture" (2003, 19), this lyric cycle with its inclusion of Oriental literary cultures determinedly pioneered the "genesis of *Weltliteratur*" (world literature) (Einboden 2005, 240) as a form of intercultural dialogue.

Goethe's energetic vote for cultural pluralism at the time of the nation state's emergence makes the German poet-novelist an even more likely model and rival figure for Joyce. For not only does Stephen reject and lampoon the parochialism of the Irish literary revival in "Scylla and Charybdis" in a manner reminiscent of Joyce, who called "such people as Gogarty and Yeats and Colm the blacklegs of literature" (LII 187), but Joyce's own leaning toward an aesthetic and intellectual internationalism that would move beyond the domestic squabbles of his compatriots also situates the two writers in the same academic force field. Only *Finnegans Wake* could be the adequate answer to Goethe's cosmopolitanism and the geopolitically conscious cultural vision propagated in *West-Östlicher Divan*.

Thomas Carlyle, who translated *Wilhelm Meister* into English in 1824, thought of Goethe as "the only living model of a great writer" (quoted in Howe 1930, 95), while Georg Lukács nominated *Wilhelm Meister* a century later as the "most important product of the literary transition from the eighteenth to the nineteenth century" (1968, 50). One way or another Joyce had to come to terms with the lionized German writer, his reputation, and his works. In *Stephen Hero* and *A Portrait* Goethe was used as whetstone to produce Stephen's antagonistic literary aesthetics. By the time Joyce was writing *Ulysses*, it was above all Goethe's artistic entanglement with another writer, Shakespeare, that attracted Joyce's critical attention. It was on this specific intellectual ground that Joyce challenged and hoped to defeat his literary rival. "Scylla and Charybdis," set in the dusty and solemn confines of the National Library of Ireland, produces this clash of intellectual energies: an alternative version of "the battle of the books" that allowed Joyce to stage, with the help of Shakespeare's *Hamlet*, his own (very tumultuous) literary succession drama.

7

Joyce's "Single Act" Shakespeare

RICHARD BROWN

The appearance of Shakespeare in the "Scylla and Charybdis" episode of *Ulysses* can be read in terms of the dynamic and complex process of Joyce's self-modernization that was taking place throughout the long period between the 1904 setting of *Ulysses* and its composition. This process included his residence in Trieste and the lectures on Shakespeare that he gave there, as well as the many other traces of intellectual modernity that were at work and can be registered as modernizing intellectual influences of the time.

It might at first seem odd to think of Stephen's (or for that matter Joyce's) choice of the eminently canonical Shakespeare for the subject of his impromptu lunchtime lecture-cum-performance in the National Library as especially modern or modernistic, but Joyce's own interest in Shakespeare was closely congruent with the progress of his intellectual self-modernization, and I want to argue that it makes good sense to do so. Indeed, this may allow us to place the episode between two of the most prominent, if ultimately contrasting, avatars of modernity: F. T. Marinetti and Walter Benjamin. I want to suggest some things that Stephen's theory has in common with Futurist theater and some things that go beyond that, revisiting what is modern about its "algebra" and its concentration on a "single act," albeit in a wide variety of senses.

In the wake of the one hundredth anniversary of Marinetti's first *Futurist Manifesto* (1909) it is timely to begin with the hints which that document and other elements of Futurism can give us toward understanding Joyce's sense of modernity and the modernity of Stephen's version of

107

Shakespeare. No doubt this Shakespeare can valuably be understood in relation to a wide variety of traditions, including those of more and less popular and highbrow English Shakespearean criticism and performance, the debates around English literature that emerged from Irish revivalism, and contemporary French and Germanic versions of Shakespeare to name but a few. Yet, as Rebecca L. Walkowitz has formulated it in *Cosmopolitan Style: Modernism Beyond the Nation*, Joyce's "triviality" is cosmopolitan inasmuch as it disrupts the "cheerful decorum" of national traditions, and (though Walkowitz herself neither discusses Joyce's Shakespeare in detail nor invokes Marinetti) it may help to ground the "triviality" and cosmopolitanism of both Stephen and Joyce's engagement with Shakespeare in the example of Marinettian Futurism, which was eminently "trivial" and highly disruptive of national decorum across Europe in those years (Walkowitz 2006, 55–77).

Shakespeare in Futurist Theater

Marinetti's first *Manifesto* was published in Paris in February 1909 in *Le Figaro* and then in book form (also in French) in Milan as the twelfth volume under the imprint of the poetry magazine *Poesia*, which Marinetti was editing, with the title *Enquête Internationale sur le Vers Libre et Manifeste du Futurisme*. Confirming Joyce's interest, a copy of this book survives in his Trieste personal library (the books are now housed in the Harry Ransom Humanities Research Center in the University of Texas at Austin).[1] The international *"enquête"* on *vers libre* consists in a series of letters in French and Italian from a mixed group of forty-nine friends, supporters, and international experts who included Gabriele D'Annunzio, La Comtesse de Noailles, Silvio Benco, Frances Jammes, Rachilde (who had supported the French publication of Marinetti's fantasy novel *Mafarka*), and Arthur Symons. That, and the references to poetry in the *Manifesto*

---

1. For this and other texts in Joyce's Trieste library see Richard Ellmann (1977). See also Michael Gillespie (1983). The books are now housed at the Harry Ransom Humanities Research Center, University of Texas at Austin.

itself (in amongst its wild tale of the car crash, its celebrations of machines, speed and war, and its iconoclasm about libraries and museums), might suggest that lyric poetry was the main literary genre through which Marinetti's Futurism was set to express itself. However, in the next years Futurist manifestos appeared relating to several of the arts including painting, sculpture, music and noise, architecture, costume, photography, cinema, and even lust. Theater was certainly prominent amongst the Futurists' favored arts, with contributors to the *"enquête"* taking the opportunity to welcome or comment on what was Marinetti's most recent work, the play *Le Roi Bombance*, which had been performed in Paris that year. As Michael Kirby's *Futurist Performance* shows, mixtures and crossovers between the arts were an especially strong part of the Futurist program, and the Futurist *"serate,"* or evenings—which mixed readings, propaganda, music, and performance—provided an ideal form for this. As Carla Marengo Vaglio has explained, one of the earliest of these *serate* took place on January 12, 1910 in the Politeama Rossetti in Joyce's Trieste (Vaglio 2006, 331).

In 1913 Marinetti produced his manifesto celebrating the mixedness of the variety theater (which had some Anglophone impact, being published in the *Daily Mail* in November 1913), and in 1915 in Milan he produced his account of the Futurist "Synthetic Theatre" as it had by then come to be known.

John McCourt, in his study of Joyce's Trieste years *The Years of Bloom*, describes the strength of the Futurist presence in the city, which Marinetti had visited in 1908 and 1910 (McCourt 2000, 154–69). Marinetti called Trieste one of the three "capitals" of Futurism and his *"polveriera* or tinderbox," and among the people with whom he had contacts could be counted Roberto Prezioso and Silvio Benco, both of whom Joyce knew well. Far from making him a cultural exile from modernity, then, because of Futurism, it might be argued that Joyce's residence in Trieste gave him a shortcut to an international style of the modern. Futurism was indeed fashionable in Paris but hardly made it to his native Ireland, unless we read Joyce's own trip to Dublin to open the Volta Theatre in 1909 as a Futurist project. It was also highly controversial in London (being somewhat anti-English), though influential on an avant-garde figure like Wyndham Lewis and on the first really effective champion of Joyce's writing, Ezra Pound.

It might be objected that Joyce's modernity was by no means identical with or even necessarily directly dependent on that of Futurism. It might even be suggested that his own theatrical modernity predated Futurism's, if we judge, for instance, by the closeness of Joyce's early dramatic epiphanies to some of the brief playscripts of the Futurists that are collected in *Futurist Performance*. It would indeed be fascinating to see these performed together in a Futurist style, and this might throw new light on the potential interest of Joyce's dramatic epiphanies as performable fragments in their own right or as part of a collage of similar fragments, as well as being snatches of dialogue that could subsequently be inserted into narrative prose fiction, as several of them were. For that matter the idea of performing "Scylla" itself as a Futurist *serata* has much suggestive promise.

To read through the Futurist manifestos is to be immediately impressed by the range of style elements, recipes, and proposals for modernity that resonate across modernism in all the arts and with Joyce's writing in particular. One could easily imagine a volume of essays exploring the various positive and negative connections between Joyce and the Futurists that are more extensive than any coverage I could attempt in this necessarily focused approach. As one example from the theatrical area, interesting connections might be suggested between the body madness or *fisicofollia* of the Futurist theater and the surreal and chaotic body movements of Joyce's experiments with drama in the "Circe" episode of *Ulysses*. More particularly we might pause to consider the close contemporaneousness between the developing programs of Futurist theater in the years before the First World War and the fact that Joyce chose to lecture in Trieste in 1912–13 on Shakespeare.

What, we should then ask, did the Futurists make of Shakespeare? As one might have expected, the quick answer would seem to be "not much." Shakespearean theater was a prime example of the kind of *"passéism"* against which the Futurists iconoclastically gestured and (to them at least) the very opposite of the variety and dynamism of the popular theater that they chose to applaud. Joyce's closely contemporary decision to lecture on Shakespeare might be at first seen as something of an alternative or even a rebuke to the Futurist agenda, and in this respect it might be seen as awkwardly engaged with its contemporary local contexts in Trieste just as

Stephen's choice of the subject of Shakespeare in *Ulysses* sits awkwardly with some aspects of the revivalist sensibilities of Dublin of 1904. There is, at any rate, a reassuring scholarly seriousness and intellectual ambition about the choice which certainly seems suitably distanced from Futurism in its silliest or most dangerous aspects.

However, as I have tried to suggest elsewhere, it was precisely the generic mixture of Shakespearean drama (as opposed to the "purity" of classical or neoclassical drama) that was coming to appeal to Joyce at the time. Moreover it was in the way Shakespeare was used in late Victorian popular theater and in the comedies of Wilde and Shaw that he saw this aspect of Shakespeare revealed (Brown 1997, 91–113). Joyce included a long quotation from W. S. Gilbert's Shakespearean farce *Rosencrantz and Guildenstern* in his Trieste lecture notes, and he was himself to produce a performance of Shaw's *Dark Lady of the Sonnets* and to write the program notes for it a few years later with the English Players in Zürich. Such an interest, if we can accurately reconstruct it from the notes and fragmentary reports that we have, exposes and subverts the false binary opposition between popular variety and *passéist* theater that the Futurist attack on tradition might invite or require.

The qualities of anarchic comic synthesis, reduction, and concentration that communicate the dynamic energy and chaotic humor of the Futurist performance project (despite its disastrous political outcomes) would surely have appealed to Joyce's sense of humor and sense of modernity, and I propose that echoes of them do seem to provide Stephen with some of the intellectual tools he needs to get him through the hurdle of negotiating Shakespeare in "Scylla."

In the best known Futurist manifestos, Shakespeare is barely mentioned, but the few references that we do find are surely suggestive and significant for Joyce. In 1915, for example, Marinetti declared that "Our Futurist theatre jeers at Shakespeare but pays attention to the gossip of actors" (Kirby 1971, 200). This appears to recommend a disrespectful attitude apparently no less extreme than that which we might have expected, on the one hand, from the anticolonial Irish national project and, on the other hand, from a more recent theater such as that of Pirandello, in which the actors take over from the author as the focus of the theatrical work.

Significantly, the role of "jeering," at least jeering at Stephen, is the one taken on in *Ulysses* by Buck Mulligan, whose Futurist credentials might be suggested by the nature of his theatrical opening to the text, his stated intellectual affiliations with Nietzsche, and perhaps also in his theatrical blasphemy and parody of the Mass.

In "Scylla," it might be argued that Stephen pays attention to the "gossip of actors" in the sense that parts of his theory are based on stories of or about actors concerning Shakespeare's marital infidelity. On the level of narrative structure, such a "gossip of actors" may also be seen in the narrative techniques of interruption by his interlocutors (and by his own interior monologue) that makes Stephen's performance "theatrical" and much less "authorial" in the conventional sense that is usually the case in prose narrative.

In 1913 Marinetti argued for a transformation of the variety theater that is posed against *passéism* but, in practice, his intention was not necessarily to ignore classics so much as creatively subvert them and, in particular, comically condense them: "performing for example all the Greek, French and Italian tragedies, condensed and comically mixed up, in a single evening . . . play a Beethoven symphony backward, beginning with the last note—boil all of Shakespeare down to a single act" (Marinetti 1910, 129). With the benefit of hindsight this idea of doing *all* tragedy in a single night might sound likely to produce a very long and confusing evening's theater, and there may not be all that much future in playing Beethoven backwards. However, the reduction of "all of Shakespeare" to "a single act" has had a considerable popular currency, most recently in the comedy of the so-called "Reduced Shakespeare Company" (which was founded by Daniel Singer in California in 1981, and which performed in London and elsewhere for many years). It was also fundamental to the 1998 film *Shakespeare in Love* (directed by John Madden, written, appropriately enough, by Marc Norman and Tom Stoppard), which mixed trivia from Shakespeare's life and works into a comic romance. These texts surely resemble "Scylla and Charybdis" in these respects.

An aesthetic of comic reduction, however respectful, mocking, or otherwise, is at work throughout "Scylla" in intermittently serious and playful ways. Stephen's theory, in its entirety, can be seen as an extraordinary work of comic condensation, remarkably synthesizing a huge range of Shakespeare's plots and characters from plays and poems throughout his career with key scattered facts about his life as they have come down to us. It might be said that Joyce's episode—with its defined location, partly new cast of characters, and complex interaction through dialogue—resembles the "single act" of a play into which "all of Shakespeare" is compacted. Indeed, for that matter, it ambitiously purports to contain a whole history of human thought in its neat structural opposition between the whirling Charybdis of Platonic idealism and the rock-like Scylla of Aristotelian fact.

According to Stephen, Shakespeare's plays can themselves be seen as condensations of a variety of different source materials, worthy of "synthetic theatre" at its most synthetic. Admittedly he employs a quasi-Shakespearean word, rather than a Marinettian one, to define this process of condensation, saying of the Edmund subplot of *King Lear* that it is "lifted out of Sidney's *Arcadia* and spatchcocked onto a Celtic legend older than history" (*U* 203). A spatch-cock (according to its first use in Grose's *Dictionary of the Vulgar Tongue*, 1785) is a chicken hurriedly killed and cooked (i.e., done with dispatch), hence something "spatchcocked" is quickly inserted or sandwiched together. This bold culinary metaphor might have something in common with the extreme combinations of elements that were proposed in Marinetti's subsequent *Futurist Cookbook*.

Seen as comic condensation, almost all of Stephen's thoughts, whether about single plays or characters or positions from the wider history of thought, have the kind of pithy compactness that had inspired Haines, at the start of the day, to make a "collection" of his "sayings" (*U* 16). Stephen calls such thoughts his "dagger definitions" (*U* 178): a phrase that seems appropriate enough for the Shakespearean subject matter of "Scylla" as well as for some of the more memorable formulations in it. Almost as compacted are the contributions of the others present in the scene and the summaries of the thoughts of critics and writers with which the episode is crammed, though by comparison with Stephen at his sharpest, even these can seem long-winded at times. In part this is an effect of the quick-fire witty dialogue. It is also the impression produced by the suggestively Freudian tendency to condense in Joyce's way of narrating interior monologue in a syntax of abbreviated thought associations.

To take an example, when Eglinton wishes to question Stephen's sketch of the biographical context for the late plays that he has made by reference to the "apocryphal" play *Pericles*, he comes out with a wordy accusation about the "leaning of the sophists towards the bypaths of the apocrypha" (*U* 187). Stephen's lightning-quick association ("Good Bacon: gone musty" [*U* 187]) at once comically condenses and subtly mocks Eglinton's comment, inasmuch as it apparently identifies it as a half-quotation of one or other example of the "distempers" of learning from Francis Bacon's *Advancement of Learning* (1605). Though often annotated as recalling Bacon's passage critiquing extremes of novelty and antiquity adopted by vain reasoners, this also recalls Bacon's critique of "unprofitable subtility or curiosity," which is especially relevant here since Bacon himself invokes there the myth of Scylla.[2] Linked to that association is the suggestion that (at least in Stephen's unspoken thought) Eglinton's comment backfires on him as (no doubt recalling his full Irish bacon breakfast) Stephen makes the analogy with fresh food gone stale. Stephen's knowledge that Shakespeare's father was a butcher is no doubt lurking in the associative mixture here, too.

Stephen's next thought leaps to the theory that Shakespeare's works were not actually written by Shakespeare but by Francis Bacon. This was an idea extravagantly proposed by the American novelist Delia Bacon in 1857 and subsequently by politician Ignatius Donnelly. Stephen thinks: "Shakespeare [:] Bacon's wild oats" (*U* 187). The text does not actually print a colon here but I have presumed to insert one to clarify the abbreviated thought. Stephen's quick association offers the theory that Shakespeare's plays were an output of Francis Bacon's wild youth, which these Baconians had proposed (almost as if to provide their own example of one of Bacon's "distempers"). In only four words, then, Stephen dramatically condenses the Baconian authorship controversy and demonstrates in turn how this approach might itself be considered to synthesize all of

---

2. Jeri Johnson, in *"Ulysses": The 1922 Text*, 840, follows Gifford. The respective passages can be found in *Francis Bacon: The Major Works* edited by Brian Vickers (Bacon 2002, 140–41).

Shakespeare to a single thought if not a single act. He jokily critiques this process at the same time as performing it.

His punning thought seems at least potentially to ambitiously balance two hugely significant and contrasting intellectual traditions that emerged from the seventeenth century: Bacon's scientific, enlightenment, rationalist kind of thought on the one hand, and Shakespeare's playful, punning, linguistic theatricality on the other. At its best, such playful language can say much more with a good deal fewer words than the deliberately expanded forms of reasoning we associate with enlightenment rationalism. Much academic scholarship and criticism is more a Baconian "advancement of learning" than Shakespearean poetry in this respect, but Stephen is more of a Shakespearean than a Baconian in the condensed character of his thoughts. In these four words, then, a debate between the partly complementary and partly competing discourses of rationality and the aesthetic is also comically contained.

The strongest example of a "jeering" as well as a "synthesized" Futurist Shakespeare can be found in "Scylla" when Mulligan offers his farcical miniature play, which is set out as a supposed playbill, and this may somewhat recall the experimental typography popular in Futurism. It appears at the end of the episode as if in a comic reduction of what has gone before:

EVERYMAN HIS OWN WIFE

or

A HONEYMOON IN THE HAND

(A NATIONAL IMMORALITY IN THREE ORGASMS)

BY

BALLOCKY MULLIGAN

(U 208)

Here, Mulligan's "jeering," or, to use Joyce's word, "mocking," is aimed primarily at Stephen. If we were to read Joyce's episode as wittingly or unwittingly Futurist, it would make sense to think of this jeering element in the figure of Mulligan as an attempt to make Stephen's comic reduction of Shakespeare all the more trivial in its tone and intent. Mulligan's minifarce promises to "boil all of Shakespeare" into a single act in the theatrical sense, but its mockery also plays on the "sole act" in a sexual sense and may even look forward to Bloom's solitary sexual act in the "Nausicaa" episode to come. Marinetti's Italian is *"un solo atto,"* and in Italian, as in English, the word *act* can mean an action in the world as well as the structural division of a theatrical work, as the context demands.

In the course of the episode Stephen has in fact imagined a Shakespeare engaged in a range of sexual acts by no means all of which are solitary in Mulligan's sense. He imagines the biographical Shakespeare in the process of visiting Gerard the herbalist in Fetter Lane: "In a rosary of Fetter lane of Gerard, herbalist, he walks, greyedauburn. An azuredharebell like her veins. Lids of Juno's eyes, violets" (*U* 193). The presumed sight of Gerard's herbs apparently encourages a fragment of Shakespeare's own interior monologue in which flower references from the later plays *Cymbeline* and *The Winter's Tale* are combined. Stephen's thoughts here consist in a series of minutely imagined hypotheses about a potential moment in Shakespeare's inner life, informed by biography and by the highly compacted readings of scenes from *The Rape of Lucrece* and from *Cymbeline* that we have been given a few pages earlier.

Shakespeare muses over Anne Hathaway's betrayal: "Afar, in reek of lust and squalor, hands are laid on whiteness" (*U* 193). When challenged by Buck Mulligan to name her suspected partner, he rapidly attempts a highly condensed double-betrayal-and-homosexual-love-triangle hypothesis (based mainly on the *Sonnets*, though recalling his earlier reading of the poem "Venus and Adonis"), according to which Shakespeare, having first been betrayed by Anne Hathaway in Stratford with person or persons unknown, is then betrayed in London by the "court wanton" Mary Fitton and his own male lover or "dearmylove," the young man (*U* 193).

A Single Act

Whilst Stephen's construction of Shakespeare's inner life is extraordinary, the imagination of his outer life at this moment may be thought to be just as significant. Shakespeare's life in London is condensed into the "single act" of walking in the city. This single act provides the historical and geographical specificity of the theory and its ramifications may take us beyond Futurism to other vital aspects of Joyce's encounter with modernism and modernity.

Stephen imagines Shakespeare as a resident of London during the period of the performance of *Hamlet*, walking through the city, from his only known address there at that time. He walks across and along the bank of the Thames on his way to work at the Globe Theatre in Southwark. In miniaturist Futurist style we see him as an actor-manager rather than as an author, about to perform the role of the ghost. Beyond the Futurist theater program, which animates the gossip of the actors, we see the audience: "Canvasclimbers who sailed with Drake" chewing sausages among the "groundlings" (*U* 180). In the later paragraph we see him once again, this time walking on the North side of the Thames, Fetter Lane being close to his only known address in London at the time, lodging with the Huguenot Christopher Mountjoy in Silver Street. Stephen's imaginative hypothesis is based on the idea that the possible actions of Shakespeare, like those of anyone else, would have to be bounded by the physical circumstances of time and space. He thinks: "He walks. One life is all. One body. Do. But do" (*U* 193).

Shakespeare is "One body," a unitary subject who is located in real physical time and space. In this respect he might be contrasted with Stephen himself, whose identity as would-be poet and critic is still "Protean" and whose theory has frequently invoked more complex notions of selfhood. At one point his quasi-Shakespearean interior dialogue puzzles over the nature of identity in connection to his indebtedness to George Russell (*U* 182), seeming to propose that identity is not unitary or stable—at least since Heraclitus. As if to prove this Protean vision in terms of Shakespearean drama, he himself appears at one point in costume as Hamlet ("My casque and sword" [*U* 184]), at another playing "Cordelia. *Cordoglio*. Lir's loneliest daughter" (*U* 185), and at another moment playing the poisoner Claudius as he is represented in the dumb show in *Hamlet's* play-within-the-play ("And in the porches of their ears I pour" [*U* 188]). Stephen's theory depends on the idea that Shakespeare as author and actor can temporarily occupy a huge range of identities, that he is "myriadminded" as Best's quotation from Coleridge (*U* 197) suggests, or "all in all" (*U* 204). Yet, in the "single act" of walking in the city, Stephen's Shakespeare becomes historically real and, in that, Joyce's episode speaks to the experience of modernity that he was determined to capture in his own fiction in ways that go beyond Futurist gestures of comic condensation and speak to modernity in a different sense.

Among the strongest critics of Marinettian Futurism is cultural theorist Walter Benjamin, according to whom Marinetti's aestheticization of war led to fascist militarism (Benjamin 1973, 243–44).[3] Paradoxically, this part of Stephen's embodiment of Shakespeare in a single act seems more relevant to the work of Benjamin and others who have frequently reflected on the ways in which modernity is experienced, often in their attention to the writing of Baudelaire.

In Michel Foucault, for example, Baudelaire is invoked in order to explain modernity as an attitude that "consists in recapturing something eternal that is not beyond the present instant, nor behind it, but within it" (Foucault 1984, 39–42). The discovery of modernity in the present requires a recognition of its reality that is a complex quest for that element of poetry in everyday experience through which it can be made heroic, however ironically, and in which the subject can engage in a process of trying to "invent himself." Foucault's reading of Baudelaire's "Painter of Modern Life" and "On the Heroism of Modern Life" built on the work of Walter Benjamin, whose rich and complex readings of Baudelaire's perceptions of modernity date back to the 1930s and focus on Baudelaire's representations of the experiences of modern everyday life, above all on the experiences of walking in the city that fill the poems, the essay on Constantin Guys, and the translation of Poe's short story "The Man in the Crowd" (Benjamin 1973, 157–202). There are many important aspects of Benjamin's reading of Baudelaire that are less directly relevant to the present argument, since much of it rests on a perception of the crowd and of individuals that might not quite fit with Stephen's vision of Shakespeare. However, one deep congruence might be explored through the two different German words for experience—*Erfahrung* and *Erlebnis*—which Benjamin invoked to define the modern moment.

---

3. Benjamin (1973) takes issue with Futurism in this way.

These might broadly be glossed as experience of a routine and familiar type as against experience as a kind of novelty lived and perceived through an alert consciousness, as he puts it "in the sphere of a certain hour in one's life" (165). I would argue that Stephen's vision of Shakespeare suddenly embodied in the act of walking in the urban space of London has a similar function in his work to these symptomatic moments of modernity in Foucault and Benjamin's readings of Baudelaire. The mere mention of his body defined in this temporal and material space and engaged in the everyday activities of walking to work and shopping not only historicizes Shakespeare in the Renaissance but also brings him up to date in what is recognizable as an early twentieth-century urban modernity. It is a moment in which the *Erfahrung* of Shakespeare's life becomes an *Erlebnis* for both him and Stephen.

Such an interest in the modern experience of lived everyday urban life can be found in many thinkers in the modernizing tradition of the late nineteenth century who were directly known to Joyce. The complex contemporary ideas and experiences of cultural modernity that accompany the development of Joyce's image of Stephen from the Ibsenite figure of *Stephen Hero* to the aesthete of *A Portrait,* and ultimately to the Shakespearean theorist that he has become by the time of *Ulysses,* are also the years during which Joyce discovers and develops the contrasting and complementary figure of Leopold Bloom. These are years during which James and Nora became parents. Joyce became involved in such symptomatically modernizing experiences as the 1909 Volta cinema project, and the composition of his letters to Nora during his separation from her that winter. They are the years when he read Freud's Leonardo essay, *The Psychopathology of Everyday Life,* Ernest Jones on *Hamlet,* and Nietzsche. The significance of everyday life to Freud's *Psychopathology of Everyday Life* hardly needs to be stated. Freud's great 1900 work disrupts the borders between pathological and normal behaviors in such phenomena as slips of the tongue and pen and ordinary behavioral mistakes, and in so doing finds new ways of tracing the significance of the everyday. *The Joyful Wisdom* (as it is titled in Thomas Common's early contemporary translation) was another text in Joyce's library, and in it there is one highly relevant passage where Nietzsche makes his call "to the industrious" for a recognition of the "conditions of ordinary existence," including material, physical things as "work," "food," and the "dialectic of marriage and friendship" that he says have been ignored by philosophy hitherto.

Such key texts centrally define modernity for us in their elevation of the importance of the material of ordinary life for literature. Yet Joyce, who achieved an artistic embodiment of so many of their ideas, rarely refers to them in these terms. It is, by contrast, one of the features of Joyce's sense of the Renaissance that he saw it as "modern" in this way. Whereas Benjamin looks back to the nineteenth century and Foucault to both the nineteenth century and to Kant and the Enlightenment, Joyce seems to find the roots of modernity in the Renaissance.

This is apparent in his brief 1912 examination essay on "The Universal Literary Influence of the Renaissance" (*OCPW* 187–90). Here we have one of his rare accounts of early twentieth-century modernity written in terms that a Benjaminian critic might recognize in his "brief list of what we can see on the street of a large modern city" and in his claim that "the trumpeted progress of this century consists for the most part of a tangle of machines whose aim is simply to gather fast and furiously the scattered elements of profit and knowledge" (*OCPW* 187). A similar element in his view of modernity is expressed when he credits Shakespeare and Lope de Vega as being "to a certain extent" responsible for modern cinematography. Joyce's essay defines the modernity of the Renaissance in terms that are comparable to those which Benjamin uses to define the "loss of aura" of the art work in twentieth-century modernity, calling it a secularizing break with "scholastic absolutism"—one whose influence "as far as literature is concerned" is to have "placed the journalist in the monk's chair" (*OCPW* 188).

In *The Work of Art in the Age of Mechanical Reproduction* Benjamin also discusses the modern phenomenon of the newspaper, and he, like Joyce, comments on the practice of publishing letters to the editor, which democratizes the medium of print. Joyce has his poet Stephen compose poetry on the torn off edge of one such letter while he goes further still than Benjamin in centralizing the daily newspaper as the medium of secular modernity. In the Renaissance, Joyce argues, "art was dying of its own formal perfection" (*OCPW* 189), and he writes (again closely conflating

Renaissance and twentieth-century modernity), "If the Renaissance did nothing else, it did much in creating within ourselves and our art a sense of pity for every being that lives and hopes and dies and deludes itself. In this at least we excel the ancients: in this the popular journalist is greater than the theologian" (*OCPW* 190).

While there might be perfectly sound historical reasons for locating a sense of modernity in the Renaissance, there is also the apparent likelihood that in Joyce's case much thinking about modern life accompanied and was driven by his extensive reading about Shakespeare for his teaching leading up to the Trieste *Hamlet* lectures in 1912–13. Both ultimately played into Stephen's theory, which he was to compose four years later, and into his changing sense of artistic priorities for *Ulysses*.

The Shakespeare reading, as we have increasingly known since the 1950s, included a variety of contemporary critical and biographical sources, such as Sidney Lee, Georg Brandes, and Frank Harris, many of which, along with Wilde and Shaw, are mentioned in the "Scylla and Charybdis" episode itself. At the risk of stating the obvious, I think it is worth repeating that this material consists mostly in reading about Shakespeare's life and historical contexts rather than in the kind of literary critical discussion of the play from a variety of differing intellectual perspectives that a modern critic might recognize. It is reading that is both nascently materialist and psychoanalytic inasmuch as it links the plays with the life and social context.

Looking at the surviving collection of transcribed quotations on which Joyce apparently based one or more of his Trieste Shakespeare lectures, one is struck by the obvious fact that most of them do not concern Shakespeare or *Hamlet* directly but rather offer contextual insights into the everyday life of an Elizabethan England that Joyce presumably felt it especially appropriate for him to explain to his audience, and which also define a concept of everyday life. Of the sixty or so transcribed passages, more than thirty derive from extracts quoted in what was probably one of the most useful source texts for the study of that "every day life" and that is the well-known anthology called *Life in Shakespeare's England*, which was produced by John Dover Wilson in 1911. The choice of these passages seems to connect directly to and confirm the contemporary report of the lectures given by

Joyce's Triestine editor, supposed sexual rival, and possible contact with Futurism, Roberto Prezioso, who refers to "the Elizabethan words, fashions and traditions" used by the lecturer (McCourt 2000, 192).

That Joyce had depended on Dover Wilson for the lectures is clear, though (perhaps to avoid the anachronism) in those parts of the "Scylla" episode where Stephen paints the "local colour" of the contemporary social context, Joyce has him follow the wording of the critic who could be described as Stephen's favorite, Brandes.[4] Many of the emphases suggested by the linking of the biographical and the contextual in Dover Wilson indicate his continuing influence too. For the London years, the longest section, Dover Wilson selects material on the commercial and criminal activities of the London streets, and on London's temptations, including passages on drink and tobacco, dress and fashion, and the plague, and then sections on books and authors, on theaters, and on the court that are historical but speak to the modern reader as well. For the last years of Shakespeare's life he gives passages on the house and home, on rogues and vagabonds, and finally on sea voyages and adventures, and he concludes the book with an extract from Nicholas Breton describing various scenes and activities appropriate to the various hours of an Elizabethan day. Many of these elements, and especially the last one, could easily be thought to have influenced Stephen's thoughts about Shakespeare and also the everyday material and hourly structure that Joyce was to use in *Ulysses*.

Proving by Algebra

A final aspect of Stephen's theory of Shakespeare that may strike us by its modernity, whether specifically Futuristic or not, is the quasi-scientific idea that the "proof" of the theory will be done "by algebra" (*U* 18). It is easy enough to overlook this term as an irrelevant bit of Mulligan's mockery, and no Joyce critics as far as I am aware have tried to argue that it might be more than this. Yet the "algebraic" element in the theory may

---

4. Gifford and Seidman (1988) frequently cite references from Brandes.

further reinforce our sense of the modernity of its materializing combination of Shakespearean biography, the Renaissance, and modernity.

Notes that Joyce produced out of his extensive reading do survive and include two brief lists of dates relating to Shakespeare's life, plays, and historical contexts that are certainly of interest as materials used in the construction of his lectures. They may also offer connections to the episode. The first, at Cornell, is only five pages long, and its content suggests the Italian lectures: the birth of Shakespeare is tied to the death of Michelangelo (*JJA* 3:153), his playing of the ghost in *Hamlet* is noted (*JJA* 3:155), and Joyce lists the Italianate sources "Boccaccio: Ariosto: Bandello: Massuccio: Staparola [*sic*]" (*JJA* 3:157), the last being a slip for Giovanni Francesco Straparola, the author of *Le Piacevoli Notti* (*Facetious Nights*) tales that influenced Shakespeare, through Richard Tarlton, for the plotting of *The Merry Wives of Windsor*. Though collected with material relating to the lectures, connections between the life and the plays that were to feed into the thinking for *Ulysses* already appear here, for example, in the suggestion that *King John*, with its depiction of the death of Prince Henry, might have been a "literary monument to memory of son" (*JJA* 3:157). Shakespeare's son Hamnet had died at eleven in 1596, possibly around the time of that play's composition, since it was first mentioned in 1598.

The second list, of "Shakespeare Dates," collected with the notes for "Scylla" (*JJA* 12:323–48) has a full page for each of the years from 1593 to 1613 and shows still more of the kind of concentrated connection between dates and plays that sits behind Stephen's thinking in "Scylla." Early in the composition of *A Portrait of the Artist*, Joyce had announced a modernistic narrative technique built on a sense of the past as what he called "a continuous succession of presents," and this historiographical strategy is apparently also at work here. Joyce, for example, at certain dates such as 1593, 1596, 1601, and 1613 (*JJA* 12:333) pauses to note down the respective ages of Shakespeare's parents "J.S." and "M.A." (John Shakespeare and Mary Arden), his wife "A.H." (Anne Hathaway), his siblings "G.S.," "R.S.," "E.S." (Gilbert, Richard, and Edmund), and his children "H.S.," "J.S.," and "S.S." (Hamnet, Judith, and Susanna).

The exercise has a meticulous microchronological interest in immediate family circumstances, and it is striking that the initial letter name coding and numerical dating constitute something we might indeed want to call an "algebraic" system. I would suggest that Joyce's own practice here offers the explanation for the use of that word in Mulligan's jokey announcement of Stephen's forthcoming proof by "algebra" of his theory in "Telemachus."

Meanwhile, the algebra itself may be more than a mere shorthand. When put in the context of Joyce's reading of Freud and his experimentation with the transcription of dreams also recorded in notebooks at this time (*JJA* 3:185–87), it might strongly suggest the formulaic insistence on the psychodynamics of immediate family circumstances that is central to Freudian psychology. Stephen's theory of Shakespeare overlaps with Joyce's known reading of Freud, and indeed his thinking may specifically connect at key points with Freud's 1909 essay subsequently entitled "Family Romances," with its elements of substitute parents, feelings of resentment, sibling rivalry, the incertitude of paternity, and its glimpse of the imaginativeness of "comparatively highly gifted people" (Freud 1977, 219–25).

Key dates had a special importance for Joyce. In these notes he especially seems to emphasize events of the years around the first performance of *Hamlet* (1602), which become crucial to Stephen's thinking in the episode. These include the death of Shakespeare's father (1601), the death of Elizabeth and accession of James I (1603), and the Gunpowder Plot (1605). The year 1601, with its coalescence of influences and productions, was a key date for Stephen's favored Shakespearean biographer-critic Georg Brandes. For Brandes it is the likely year of his composition of *Hamlet* (Brandes 1911, 341), but in "Scylla" the apparition of Shakespeare's body in London takes place when *Hamlet* is already in production, and so a year during the performance of the play seems to provide a more likely date.

We cannot be sure that Joyce had an exact date in mind, but it is more than a little tempting to think that Stephen's materialization of the figure of Shakespeare walking in the city of London is intended to be dateable by the "algebra" method to June 16, 1604, exactly three hundred years before the date of the setting of *Ulysses*.

Stephen begins with the dramatic announcement of a specific time: "It is this hour of a day in mid June" (*U* 180). The "this" emphatically announces the particularity of the time and does so more than the earlier manuscript version "It is this hour of a June day," which Joyce revised, perhaps to emphasize the connection with the single day of mid-June on which *Ulysses* itself is set. The time of day is important since the performance in the open-air Globe took place by daylight. So, I would suggest is the date. The sentence toward which this revision seems to lead (even if it doesn't quite get there) is the wording "It is this hour of *this* June day," that is, June 16 at some time between 2:00 and 3:00 when Stephen is talking and Shakespeare, as it were, "simultaneously" walking along Fetter lane or along the bankside to the Globe.

Shakespearean tercentenary celebrations (based on the dates of his birth and death) took place in 1864 and 1916, and Joyce knew about this since he had put on Shaw's "Dark Lady of the Sonnets" (which had formed part of an appeal for it) with the English Players in Zürich in 1918 (Habicht 2001, 441–55). "It is three hundred years since [his] genius attained its full development," Brandes had written in his introduction (Brandes 1911, 1) further inviting Joyce to tie up the year as well as the date and the time of his novel with the life of Shakespeare in this way.

Joyce liked anniversaries, having *Ulysses* specially printed for his fortieth birthday. The incident of the occupation of Gibraltar that took place precisely two hundred years before 1904 is recalled in "Penelope" (*U* 710). So it is natural to expect that Joyce at least entertained the idea of dating Shakespeare's walk as the pretercentenary date of *Ulysses* itself. Diurnality materializes modernity in *Ulysses* as it does in Woolf's *Mrs Dalloway*, which closely followed it, or in more recent examples such as Don de Lillo's *Cosmopolis* or Ian McEwan's day novel *Saturday*, or indeed in the ubiquitous historical monumentality of the named day 9/11 to which these recent novels partly respond.

In the London scene-setting Stephen owes something to Brandes and to the range of familiar primary sources behind Brandes (reproduced in Dover Wilson and elsewhere) such as Hollar's *View of London*, with its two bankside theaters, and Paul Hentzer and Donald Lupton's accounts of the theaters and bear-baiting: "The flag is up on the playhouse by the bankside. The bear Sackerson growls in the pit near it" (*U* 180). To this scene he introduces a Shakespeare whose precise location in time and space can be further connected to 1604 by another historicizing detail: "—Shakespeare has left the huguenot's house in Silver street and walks by the swan mews along the riverbank. But he does not stay to feed the pen chivying her game of cygnets towards the rushes. The swan of Avon has other thoughts" (*U* 180).

For this passage, as Richard Ellmann points out (1977, 52–55, 105), Joyce borrowed specific elements from the populist biographical book *A Day with William Shakespeare* by May Byron (1913), who wrote several such books under the pseudonym "Maurice Clare." In one way this was slightly anachronistic, since that book (and Stephen's reference to the "huguenot" and "Silver street") drew on a discovery of legal documents by Charles Wallace published in 1910 and was therefore not strictly knowable to the fictional Stephen. However, both May Byron and the Wallace discovery were arguably indispensable to Joyce and his sense of modernity, since the one gave him the idea of locating Shakespeare on a single day in history (May Byron's actual date had been 1599) and the other gave him both a real itinerary for Shakespeare to walk beside the Thames on his way to the Globe and a specific location in time of 1604.

Shakespeare thus boiled down into the "single act" of walking in the city becomes not just a figure of Futurist theater but also one related to the emblematic figures of modernity in Foucault and Benjamin's readings of Baudelaire, walking in the city and, more profoundly, "recapturing something eternal that is not beyond the present instant . . . but within it," experiencing in the sense of Benjamin's *Erlebnis* "a certain hour in one's life" (Benjamin 1973, 165). Stephen's Shakespeare experiences and helps to define modernity, combining a sense of "sceptical determinism" with the hilarious atmosphere of comic condensation so present in the episode as a whole.

The approach significantly historicizes and demystifies the figure of the author by embodying him in time and space. Though couched in terms of Stephen's Aristotelianism (to which George Russell, who represents the opposite pole of idealism in the episode, promptly objects), and an appeal to Ignatius Loyola, there are just as strong gestures within it toward the modernity of the disruptions to tradition found in Futurism and the ideas of the everyday in urban cultural theory.

Stephen's vision of Shakespeare is re-enforced with a sense of the carnival chaos of the occasionally glimpsed moments in Shakespeare's sex life and that of his contemporaries and also with the phenomenological limitations of the human body.

Many early twentieth-century modernities play into the cultural construction of modernity in *Ulysses*. But the anarchic comedy of reducing "all of Shakespeare" to a "single act" in these various senses and the consequent materializing of the ghostly body of Shakespeare according to the precise time-spatial coordinates of June 16, 1604 has the effects for both Stephen and Joyce of demystifying the bardolatrous in favor of a sense of the materiality of the everyday life. Conversely, an immersion in Shakespeare and the contextual methodologies of Shakespearean biography that sit behind the composition of the chapter seems to have provided Joyce with a Ulyssean route to steer between the contrasting modernities of a Marinetti and a Benjamin and with one of the strongest means by which *Ulysses* asserts its cultural modernity through an immersion in everyday life.

8

Loving the Alien

Egoism, Empathy, Alterity, and
Shakespeare Bloom in Stephen's Aesthetics

SAM SLOTE

Frank Budgen recounts that shortly after "Lestrygonians" had been published in *The Little Review*, Joyce received a letter from a reader who was tiring of Bloom. "The writer of [the letter] wants more Stephen. But Stephen no longer interests me to the same extent" (Budgen 1972, 105). Budgen uses this exchange as a pretext to elaborate the salient features of Bloom and, coming after an account of five Bloom-centric episodes, his encomium is certainly not surprising.[1] However, it also directly precedes Budgen's summary of "Scylla and Charybdis," the last Stephen-centric episode and an episode in which Bloom barely appears, and only at the very end.[2] I, for my part, find this placement of Joyce's curt dismissal of Stephen in favor of Bloom in Budgen's book to be telling, since I would argue that Bloom is indeed a central character in "Scylla," and that this episode offers, at least in part, a theory of Bloom couched within Stephen's theory of Shakespeare.

---

1. "Bloom should grow upon the reader throughout the day. His reactions to things displayed in his unspoken thoughts should not be brilliant, but singular, organic, Bloomesque" (Budgen 1972, 105).

2. Budgen notes that he asked Joyce about Bloom's virtual absence in this episode; Joyce replied: "Bloom is like a battery that is being recharged. . . . He will act with all the more vigor when he does reappear" (Budgen 1972, 118).

Stephen begins his theory with the assertion that Shakespeare, whose son Hamnet died in childhood, was cuckolded by his wife. So, right off there is a correlation between Stephen's Shakespeare and Bloom. This particular conjunction intersects with a variety of correspondences throughout the book in a complex fashion as I have argued elsewhere.[3] Now, according to Stephen, Shakespeare modelled the character of King Hamlet after himself so that he might play that rôle on stage in order to enact a symbolic revenge against his unfaithful wife. By addressing Hamlet through the proxy of the dead king's ghost, Shakespeare addresses his dead son Hamnet: "you are the dispossessed son: I am the murdered father: your mother is the guilty queen, Ann Shakespeare, born Hathaway" (U 181).

There are several dissents to Stephen's theory. Initially, Eglinton protests at the biographical reading Stephen proposes: "She died, for literature at least, before she was born" (U 182). Eglinton thus subscribes to an aesthetic idealism where art is divorced from the material circumstances of its creation. Stephen retorts that "She died . . . sixtyseven years after she was born. She saw him into and out of the world. She took his first embraces. She bore his children and she laid pennies on his eyes to keep his eyelids closed when he lay on his deathbed" (U 182). Stephen thus counters Eglinton by apparently reinserting Hathaway back into the dialogue. For Stephen, art is not an abstracted idealism, but rather is inseparable from its material circumstances. Indeed, his refutation is not merely a simple, thetic counterstatement, but rather proceeds through concrete and specific details, such as the pennies placed on Shakespeare's eyelids on his deathbed. Stephen's retort is thus conveyed through the style of his formulation as much as through its substance. As with the elaboration of his Shakespeare theory, where he depicts the specific scene of Shakespeare onstage playing King Hamlet opposite Burbage's prince, the accumulation of "Local colour" (U 180) is fundamental to Stephen's (and Joyce's) style.

Furthermore, by invoking the material circumstances of Anne Hathaway's life and death, Stephen reminds himself of the scene of his own

3. See Slote 2008.

"Mother's deathbed" (*U* 182). Indeed, the image of Anne Hathaway placing pennies on her husband's corpse derives from Stephen's mother's funeral, as he recalls that her corpse was "bronzelidded" (*U* 182). The specific material circumstances of Stephen's life, his agenbite of inwit, thus inform his theory of Shakespeare as is presented in the library.

Eglinton, in any case, tries to refute the import of Anne Hathaway by claiming that Shakespeare's marriage was a mistake (*U* 182), an accident of life that has no bearing on art. This leads Stephen to make his famous claim that for a man of genius "errors are volitional and are the portals of discovery" (*U* 182). There are a number of resonances of this line, but for the moment suffice it to say that Anne Hathaway is important to Stephen's theory primarily insofar as he can claim her as an adulteress. In effect, she is little more than the punchline to Stephen's unoriginal joke "If others have their will Ann hath a way" (*U* 183).[4] As Mr Best says of this exchange between Stephen and Eglinton, "Yes, we seem to be forgetting her as Shakespeare himself forgot her" (*U* 183). Anne Hathaway seems to betoken a bit of a blind spot in Stephen's theory; something I'll get back to later.

The next dissent that Stephen faces in articulating his theory is the widely held view that Shakespeare modelled Prince Hamlet after himself and thus the king would be a figuration of his own father, John Shakespeare.[5] So, in identifying the ghost as Shakespeare, Stephen is blithely flying past the net of most Shakespearean scholarship:

> The corpse of John Shakespeare does not walk the night. From hour to
> hour it rots and rots. He rests, disarmed of fatherhood, having devised

---

4. Shakespeare puns on the varying resonances to his name "Will" in Sonnets 135 and 143. The pun on the name Anne Hathaway goes back at least to 1792 and Charles Dibdin's "A Love Dittie" in his novel *Hannah Hewit; or, the Female Crusoe*: "Angels must love Ann Hathaway; / She hath a way so to control, / To rapture the unprisoned soul, / And sweetest heaven on earth display, / That to be heaven Ann hath a way; / She hath a way, / Ann Hathaway—To be heaven's self Ann hath a way" (quoted in Schutte 1957, 62n5).

5. *Hamlet* was officially registered on July 26, 1602, one year after Shakespeare's father's death (Brandes 1911, 341; cf. Schutte 1957, 161–62).

that mystical estate upon his son. . . . Fatherhood, in the sense of conscious begetting, is unknown to man. It is a mystical estate, an apostolic succession, from only begetter to only begotten. On that mystery and not on the madonna which the cunning Italian intellect flung to the mob of Europe the church is founded and founded irremovably because founded, like the world, macro and microcosm, upon the void. Upon incertitude, upon unlikelihood. *Amor matris*, subjective and objective genitive, may be the only true thing in life. Paternity may be a legal fiction. Who is the father of any son that any son should love him or he any son? (*U* 198–99)

Stephen has veered away quite a bit from Shakespeare in this privileging of paternity over maternity. While motherhood may be certain, just as motherly love is, as Cranly had told Stephen in A *Portrait* (*P* 241–42), the provenance of fatherhood is uncertain. However, it is precisely because of this uncertainty that fatherhood is important for Stephen. The paternal bond is metaphysical, not physical or biological. Stephen clarifies what he means by this mystical estate: "When Rutland bacons out Hampton shakespeare or another poet of the same name in the comedy of errors wrote *Hamlet* he was not the father of his own son merely but, being no more a son, he was and felt himself the father of all his race, the father of his own grandfather, the father of his unborn grandson who, by the same token, never was born, for nature, as Mr Magee understands her, abhors perfection" (*U* 199).

Stephen defines patrimony as the essential condition for the artist and in so doing has introduced a significant modification to his biographical reading of *Hamlet*: Shakespeare is not just Hamlet's father, he is the father of all; he is even more pan-paternal than Theodore Purefoy, that most "remarkablest progenitor" (*U* 402). In a sense, it doesn't matter *who* exactly wrote Shakespeare's plays, merely that they were written by some prolific individual. Indeed, on the one hand Eglinton remarks that "of all great men, [Shakespeare] is the most engigmatic" (*U* 186), while, on the other, Best replies that "*Hamlet* is so personal" (*U* 186). As William Schutte points out, both comments are valid: the plays are personal without divulging the character of their creator (Schutte 1957, 88).

This patrilineal mode of artistic creation follows from Stephen's aesthetic theory in A *Portrait*, where he defined the artist as being independently self-creating. Of course, in A *Portrait* Stephen chose his namesake Daedalus, the "Old father, old artificer" (*P* 253), as his artistic exemplar. In chapter 5, he explicitly defines a work of art as one that is mystically infused with the personality of is creator:

> The personality of the artist passes into the narration itself, flowing round and round the persons and the action like a vital sea. . . . The personality of the artist, at first a cry or a cadence or a mood and then a fluid and lambent narrative finally refines itself out of existence, impersonalises itself, so to speak. The aesthetic image in the dramatic form is life purified in and reprojected from the human imagination. The mystery of the aesthetic like that of material creation is accomplished. The artist, like the God of the creation, remains within or behind or beyond or above his handiwork, invisible, refined out of existence, indifferent, paring his fingernails. (*P* 215)

As with the enigmatic Shakespeare, the artwork is intimately personal even as the artist remains mysterious. The other key component to Stephen's aesthetic is the realization of *claritas* in the artist's work. Stephen describes this as the "*whatness*," or *quidditas*, of the thing being represented in the only possible synthesis occasioned by the realization of its *integritas* and *consonantia*: "This supreme quality is felt by the artist when the esthetic image is first conceived in his imagination. The mind in that mysterious instant Shelley likened beautifully to a fading coal" (*P* 213).[6] According to Stephen's theory, the moment of aesthesis, *claritas*, is accomplished only through the initiative of the artist's personality, which

---

6. Stephen echoes Shelley's line again in "Scylla" as the "intense instant of imagination" (*U* 186). In "A Defence of Poetry" Shelley writes: "[T]he mind in creation is a fading coal, which some invisible influence, like an inconstant wind, awakens to transitory brightness; this power arises from within, like the colour of a flower which fades and changes as it is developed, and the conscious portions of our natures are unprophetic either of its approach or its departure" (Shelley 1977, 503–4). Joyce also cited this image in his essay on Mangan (*Joyce 2000*, 133).

withdraws from the artwork and, in so doing, permeates it entirely. The artist's imagination is thus fulfilled in the act of representing the world in full phenomenological precision. Mimetic fidelity *is* artistic fulfilment both in the sense of the fulfilment of the artwork and the fulfilment of the artist.

This theory is perfectly commensurable with Joyce's use of free indirect discourse in *A Portrait*, which is not to say that Stephen could necessarily write that novel; he is, after all, still a young man and not yet the artist. But his aesthetic theory anticipates the style of the narrative in which he is presented as a character, a style inflected by his character. So, in a sense, Stephen's aesthetic theory in *A Portrait* is a theory of the style of that novel. And, this theory is highly egocentric: the artist is the essential and focal prism between life and art. And, in being as such, he creates not just the work of art but also creates himself as an independent, self-standing, self-sufficient artist. The consequence for this is that all art is necessarily autobiographical in a rather tautological manner: the artist creates the artwork that is infused with him, and this in turn is what creates the artist as artist. The artist is father to both the work of art and to himself, or, as Mulligan mockingly puts it in "Scylla": "Himself his own father" (*U* 200).

This theory clearly follows from Joyce's 1904 essay "A Portrait of the Artist": "Our world, again, recognizes its acquaintance chiefly by the characters of beard and inches and is, for the most part, estranged from those of its members who seek through some art, by some process of the mind as yet untabulated, to liberate from the personalized lumps of matter that which is the individuating rhythm, the first or formal relation of their parts. But for such as these a portrait is not an identificative paper but rather the curve of an emotion" (*P* 258). And, in *Finnegans Wake*, Joyce satirizes this notion of the self-involved and self-creating artist with the image of Shem writing about himself on his body with an ink made from his excrement (*FW* 185.14–26).

In his important essay "Against *Ulysses*," Leo Bersani precisely identifies this comportment of the Joycean aesthetic: "Joyce miraculously reconciles uncompromising mimesis with a solipsistic structure" (Bersani 2004, 219). This perhaps aptly describes what we find in *A Portrait*, but while it may well be apposite to *Ulysses*, it misses some nuance, as I will argue shortly. And while Bersani's critique of *Ulysses* is quite negative, it is actually quite consonant with Hélène Cixous's more positive reading in *The Exile of James Joyce*, where she posits Joyce as a self-creating artist who substitutes himself for God, the ultimate father, as the creative agency.[7] The artist is thus an artist by being an egoist. Jean-Michel Rabaté expands upon this point in his book *James Joyce and the Politics of Egoism*, where he argues that Joycean egoism does not retreat into solipsism because it blends with language, in such a way as to make Joyce "the Lacanian symptom of literature" (Rabaté 2001, 23; cf. 67–69).

Returning to "Scylla," Stephen's argument, which started by positing Shakespeare as playing the rôle of King Hamlet, has now morphed into a theory of Shakespeare as the preeminent figure of a godlike artist, Coleridge's polytropic "myriadminded man" (*U* 197)[8] who encompasses all creation and, in so doing, creates himself. This would mean that Stephen's initial premise is faulty since Shakespeare, in his divine plenitude, could not be reduced to any one of his characters. As Eglinton observes: "The truth is midway. . . . He is the ghost and the prince. He is all in all" (*U* 204). Stephen relents at this and agrees: "He is. . . . The boy of act one is the mature man of act five" (*U* 204).

Shakespeare reflects and is inflected by everybody, everybody seeing their reflection in Shakespeare.[9] This pan-dimensionality of Shakespeare is hardly a point original to Joyce. As Borges has it in a footnote

---

7. "Joyce is attempting to set up a vision of his own, ex-centric as far as the Creation is concerned, a world which can escape from the Absolute which rules the world God has created. Everything which usually constitutes or contributes to the traps and net in which God holds the world and the mind captive, subjected to his Presence and Omnipotence, is endangered by Joyce's art" (Cixous 1972, 701).

8. In the *Biographia Literaria*, Coleridge writes that his own work could not surpass "the greatest genius, that perhaps human nature has yet produced, our myriad-minded Shakespeare" (Coleridge 1985, 320).

9. This happens to both Stephen and Bloom in "Circe," when they each see themselves in the face of a "beardless" Shakespeare in the mirror (*U* 528), the image of the face crowned by the antlers of a cuckold.

in his story "Tlön, Uqbar, Orbis Tertius," "All men who speak a line of Shakespeare *are* William Shakespeare" (Borges 1998, 76n4). Coleridge's myriadminded man infects the minds of myriad men.[10] Shakespeare is analogous to (the Christian) God not simply because of the sheer range of his creative output, but rather because he infuses himself throughout his creations. Shakespeare, like God, in-gathers and subsumes multiplicities, *his* multiplicities. As Eglinton observes, "When all is said Dumas *fils* (or is it Dumas *père*) is right. After God Shakespeare has created most" (*U* 204). The comment was properly made by Dumas *père*, Alexandre (Schutte 1957, 150n9). And the irony of Eglinton's confusion is that, in a sense, it confirms Stephen's construction of artistic patrimony in that father and son become indistinct (or, at the very least, their witty *aperçus* become indistinct and unattributable) in the "apostolic succession, from only begetter to only begotten" (*U* 199).[11]

After Eglinton's comment that Shakespeare is "all in all," Stephen proposes a new scene for *Hamlet* in which Shakespeare again plays, but unlike the earlier scene where Stephen cast Shakespeare as King Hamlet, here Shakespeare plays all characters. This new scene works as the revision to Stephen's Shakespeare theory as well as to his aesthetic theory from *A Portrait*. Furthermore, the scene is painted through a variety of lines and images concatenated from Shakespeare's works and days:

> Maeterlinck says: If Socrates leaves his house today he will find the sage seated on his doorstep. If Judas goes forth tonight it is to Judas his steps will tend. Every life is many days, day after day. We walk through ourselves, meeting robbers, ghosts, giants, old men, young men, wives,

---

10. Nietzsche suggests this paradox in *The Will to Power*: "The highest man would have the greatest multiplicity of drives, in the relatively greatest strength that can be endured. Indeed, where the plant 'man' shows himself strongest one finds instincts that conflict powerfully (e.g., in Shakespeare), but are controlled" (Nietzsche 1968, §966).

11. Stuart Gilbert takes a different route in explicating Eglinton's confusion by saying it "is a recall of Stephen and Sabellius' hypothesis" (Gilbert 1955, 220n). In "Telemachus," Stephen had thought about, among other heresiarchs of divine patrimony, "Sabellius who held that the Father was Himself His own Son" (*U* 21).

widows, brothers-in-love, but always meeting ourselves. The playwright who wrote the folio of this world and wrote it badly (He gave us light first and the sun two days later), the lord of things as they are whom the most Roman of catholics calls dio boia, hangman god, is doubtless all in all in all of us, ostler and butcher, and would be bawd and cuckold too but that in the economy of heaven, foretold by Hamlet, there are no more marriages, glorified man, an androgynous angel, being a wife unto himself. (*U* 204–5)

The paraphrase from Maurice Maeterlinck's *La Sagesse et la desti-née*[12] is apt because, in a review of his first play, Octave Mirabeau called him, "le Shakespeare belge," a line that Joyce alluded to in a 1907 letter to Stanislaus (*LII*, 212). Shakespeare's progeny are legion. Indeed, this passage concerns the multiplicities engendered in and by Shakespeare. If Shakespeare is all his characters, "all in all" as Eglinton said, then this omnipresence is itself present in everyone, "all in all in all of us," as Stephen says. This marks the important modification Stephen makes to his aesthetics of egoism. The artist, whether Shakespeare or Maeterlinck or Stephen or Joyce or God, is not the only focal point; egoism is multipolar. Any man can be an everyman, just as any day can be a Bloomsday, or as Stephen puts it, "Every life is many days, day after day" (*U* 204). And, as Molly explains why she chose Bloom, "as well him as another" (*U* 732). The artist is important precisely in that he is multiple, and this multiplicity is reciprocal and communal: "We walk through ourselves, meeting robbers, ghosts, giants, old men, young men, wives, widows, brothers-in-love, but always meeting ourselves" (*U* 204). In effect, Stephen here proposes an egotistical empathy, the artist-as-everyman, and, conversely, everyman-an-artist, or, at least, a potential artist.

Indeed, this sense of possibility actualized is what makes the artist an artist: "He found in the world without as actual what was in his world within as possible" (*U* 204). The artist sees his imagination (his world

---

12. "If Judas go forth to-night, it is towards Judas his steps will tend, nor will chance for betrayal be lacking; but let Socrates open his door, he shall find Socrates asleep on the threshold before him, and there will be occasion for wisdom" (Maeterlinck 1912, 31).

within) confirmed in the world outside. Stephen's formulation here is, in effect, an Aristotelian rendition of Mallarmé's line about Hamlet: "il se promène . . . , lisant au livre de lui-même" (Mallarmé 2003, 275).[13] The artist sees himself confirmed by seeing the world, but conversely, this confirmation can only occur by the artist's ability to be receptive to that world. In other words, the artist who is confirmed as an artist is an artist with an ability to empathize with that world. The artist that Stephen proposes here is the egoist open to alterity, which is thus unlike the more closed-off and withdrawn artist proposed in A *Portrait*.[14] In this way, Stephen's Shakespeare theory represents a further step in his maturation as an artist.

In this way, Stephen here proposes a theory of Bloom as well as a theory of Shakespeare. After all, as we learn in "Ithaca," one of Bloom's many possible careers is an "exponent of Shakespeare" (U 642). While Bloom may not have actualized this particular Shakespearean possibility, it is actualized in the text. As Stephen says in "Circe": "What went forth to the ends of the world to traverse not itself, God, the sun, Shakespeare, a commercial traveller, having itself traversed in reality itself becomes that self" (U 475). Just as Joyce and Budgen had extolled Bloom's Bloomish virtues, so too does Stephen in "Scylla," even though he barely knows Bloom at this point.

The possibility of empathy as indicated in Stephen's comment also impacts how Joyce reworks free indirect discourse in *Ulysses*. If in A

---

13. Best cites this at U 9. The citation is from Mallarmé's letter-essay "Hamlet et Fortinbras," which is not, as Best characterizes it, a prose poem (U 179).

14. The crossover that Stephen posits between the actual and the possible derives from Aristotle's *Poetics*, where that "Bald . . . millionaire" (U 37) writes: "the historian narrates events that have actually happened whereas the poet writes about things that might possibly occur. Poetry, therefore, is more philosophical and more significant than history, for poetry is more concerned with the universal, and history more with the individual" (Aristotle 1981, 1451b1 9–14). Stephen, on the other hand, posits an equivalence between the actual and the possible through the medium of the artist reading the book of himself in his environs. An implication of this formulation, which would be a hallmark of Joycean aesthetics, is that a precisely defined individual becomes universal. Bloom is an everyman not because he is perfectly, or even adequately, representative of all mankind, but because his specific quirks are precisely enumerated.

Portrait Stephen's theory of aesthetics reflects Joyce's use of free indirect discourse in that novel, then an analogous thing happens in "Scylla." Simply put, Joyce's use of free indirect discourse in *Ulysses* is multipolar, which is to say that it is not strictly delimited by the consciousness of any one individual. To take "Scylla" as an example, both Stephen's various discourses as well as the narrative style of the episode-as-a-whole take on a Shakespearean cant and hue (just as the style of "Lestrygonians" is literally peppered with culinary and gastronomic terms and allusions). In *A Portrait* the narrative style betrayed a tendency to the centripetal, whereas in *Ulysses* the style is both centripetal and centrifugal.

After Stephen has finished his peroration, he admits that he does not believe in his own theory (*U* 205). At this, Eglinton cannot resist interjecting a variety of other *au currant* theories about Shakespeare and *Hamlet* and sarcastically notes that, at the very least, the proponents of these theories did believe in them (*U* 205). Stephen then thinks: "I believe, O Lord, help my unbelief. That is, help me to believe or help me to unbelieve? Who helps to believe? *Egomen*. Who to unbelieve? Other chap" (*U* 205).

Stephen does not necessarily not believe in his proposed theory, and there's the rub. On the side of belief lie the egomen, or rather, the Greek word *"egomen,"* "I, for my part" or "I myself" (which is roughly equivalent to *mé fhéin*, the singular of *Sinn Féin*). And, on the side of unbelief there's everybody else, the "other chap" of alterity. Not believing thus marks the retreat of the ego and the approach of alterity, and Stephen does not know yet where to go.

This shows the flaw in Stephen's theory, which is why it would be more of a prolegomenon to Bloom than a theory of Bloom as such. Stephen concludes the proposition that the artist is "all in all in all of us" with the postulation that he would be "an androgynous alien, being a wife unto himself" (*U* 205). To this, Mulligan sarcastically cries *"Eureka!"* (*U* 205). This then leads him to his crude satire of Stephen's proposition *"Everyman His Own Wife / or / A Honeymoon in the Hand"* (*U* 208). The crass, masturbatory joke is actually quite apposite to Stephen's logic. Since his formulation of egotistical empathy is still somewhat solipsistic in that it omits the care, that is to say, the love of alterity. Stephen's theory of egotistical empathy omits love. Concomitant with the omission of love is the omission of the maternal from this theory of artistic patrimony.

As with the earlier discussion of Anne Hathaway, the omission of the maternal is a blind spot or error, which is to say that it might also be some kind of potential portal of discovery. Obviously, Stephen's omission of maternity from his theory would be informed by his agenbite of inwit over not having prayed at his mother's deathbed. Now, his agenbite of inwit can be characterized as a result of the conflict between aesthetic self-determination and independence on the one hand and filial duty to the surety of maternal love on the other.[15] In this way, Stephen's agenbite could be characterized as a symptom of the impossibility of absolute self-determination, which is to say a symptom of the impossibility of a pure, self-sufficient egoism. Stephen thus has one more net to fly by, the net of his own egoistic artistic self-determination.

Even if Stephen has not yet escaped this net, by admitting empathy into the artist's egoism, with the "all in all in all of us," he does point toward a way out. By omitting love as the condition of empathy, he does not get there yet, and this inability highlights the centrality of Bloom, the "Everyman or Noman" (U 679) in all of us.

15. See P 241–42 and U 28.

9

History and Possibility

Shakespeare and the Stage in Finnegans Wake

VINCENT CHENG

In *Ulysses*, John Eglinton (quoting Alexandre Dumas senior) asserts that "After God, Shakespeare has created most"—while Stephen Dedalus makes an equation between Shakespeare and the Creator, "the playwright who wrote the folio of this world" ("and wrote it badly," Stephen adds [*U* 204]). In *Finnegans Wake*, James Joyce confirms this notion, referring to Shakespeare as "Great Shapesphere" (295.04). To Joyce, artist and god were equivalent; the quintessential artist was the greatest bard of all, the lord of language at the Globe.

Joyce was also in the habit of equating himself—and comparing himself—with Shakespeare as fellow artist-creators and playwrights who write the folios of their worlds.[1] Furthermore, Joyce conceived of the world of *Finnegans Wake* as drama, as a Shakespearean play. Like Shakespeare, Joyce viewed the world as a stage, "the worldstage" (33.03) of the *Wake*. There are hundreds of allusions to Shakespeare and to his plays in the *Wake*; I have discussed and catalogued many of these in *Shakespeare and Joyce: A Study of "Finnegans Wake"* (Cheng 1984). Adaline Glasheen has gone so far as to assert that "Shakespeare (man, works) is the matrix of

---

This essay is extracted and adapted from several sections of the author's earlier book, *Shakespeare and Joyce: A Study of Finnegans Wake*, cited as Cheng 1984.

1. See Cheng 1984, 1.

Finnegans Wake" and that *"Finnegans Wake* is about Shakespeare" (Glasheen 1977, xxii, 260).

Foremost among the Shakespearean matrixes in the *Wake* is that of *Hamlet*, undoubtedly one of the "books at the *Wake*." There are by far more allusions to *Hamlet* than to any other play (Shakespearean or otherwise); and the parallels are more frequent, precise, and insistent: HCE as King Hamlet, Shem as the prince, Issy as Ophelia, Shaun as Laertes/Polonius. References to Hamlet are ubiquitous; and, as in the case of *Ulysses*, the themes and motifs in *Hamlet* are structural counterparts to those in *Finnegans Wake*. The other Shakespearean plays most alluded to are *Macbeth* and *Julius Caesar*, both for similar reasons: as parallels to the filial (Cad, Hosty, Shem-Shaun, Buckley, and so forth) overthrow and replacement of the father figure (HCE, Russian General, and so on). A *Midsummer Night's Dream* is important to the *Wake* largely because of the notions of the drama as a dream, the play as Bottom's dream, and the *Wake* as both the drama and the dream of all mankind. Finally, perhaps Shakespeare's own life as a man and an artist offers the most important matrix of all, for the pattern and model that Shakespeare provides becomes that which Shem-Joyce must emulate and reproduce (similarly enduring the charges of plagiarism, forgery, and madness), as well as ultimately overthrow and supplant, a filial rival replacing the patriarch at the start of a new Viconian cycle.

But why did Joyce make Shakespeare—the man and his works—so central to his dreambook of universal history? In order to apprehend his reasons more fully, we first need to understand Joyce's ideas about the contestation between history and imaginative possibility.

James Joyce's mind is that of the essential poet: it works by analogy. A defecator, a lover, a father, a poet, and God are all, by analogy, equivalent—because they each create, or produce, something. Therefore, those somethings are also, by analogy, equivalent; *Finnegans Wake*, like the letter unearthed by Biddy the hen, is a *creatio ex* shitpile, a "letter from litter" (FW 615.01). Joyce—who unlike his predecessor and fellow creator-defecator-poet Shakespeare, knew much Latin and some Greek—was aware that the Latin word for, at once, letters of the alphabet, epistolary letters, and belles lettres, was *litterae*, a felicitous correspondence to the English word "litter" and its connotations of shit and birth. Thus, to the Joycean mind, poetic creations in English "litterature" are at once bilabial speech, biological offspring, and biodegradable waste. Each implies the others; the part reflects the whole. A poet is the god and creator of his own worlds—"After God, Shakespeare has created most"—while God is but a very major poet, "the playwright who wrote the folio of this world." HCE, the archetypal father who "Haveth Childers Everywhere" (*FW* 535.34–35) and who thus also creates and populates a world, is but another version of both poet and god—of "Great Shapesphere." Joyce himself, of course, is all of these things: like Stephen Dedalus's Shakespeare, he is "all in all" (*U* 204). As a god and an artist, a poet triumphs over confining reality by creating worlds through the imagination—and each of his works is an exploration into the possible "history" of such worlds. As a god and an artist, Joyce carried the exploration of this general notion of "history" furthest in *Finnegans Wake*—with the construct of a dream, the perfect vehicle for repeated motifs and variations, for all possibilities and all history in the course of a night's dream.

The Nightmare of History

"History, Stephen said, is a nightmare from which I am trying to awake" (*U* 34). To the aspiring artist, history is a nightmare because of its destructive qualities: "Had Pyrrhus not fallen by a beldam's hand in Argos or Julius Caesar not been knifed to death. They are not to be thought away. Time has branded them and fettered they are lodged in the room of the infinite possibilities they have ousted. But can those have been possible seeing that they never were? Or was that only possible which came to pass?" (*U* 25).

In these crucial lines in the "Nestor" episode of *Ulysses*, Stephen is referring to Aristotle's theory that there is a room of infinite possibilities— if Caesar had not been knifed to death, he might have lived to a ripe old age, might have developed cancer, might even have come to America— but history limits, and chooses from that room one possibility (which is that Caesar gets knifed to death), thus destroying all others. History, then, is seen by Stephen as a usurper and a destroyer of creative potential, a restrictive force that limits other, perhaps more interesting, possibilities.

For young Stephen, those imaginative possibilities are a liberating force. The question is one of control: who is in the driver's seat, history or man? Does history control us by limiting our possibilities; or do we control history by creating new and different ones, by interpreting history in light of our own creative viewpoints? Does the father create the son; or the son, the father? Without the son, there would be no father; in the *Metamorphoses*, when Icarus dies, Daedalus (Ovid tells us) is *nec iam pater*, a "father no more." Thus, if Stephen Dedalus can just as easily create Simon Dedalus, then, as he observes later in the library, "Paternity may be a legal fiction" (*U* 199). He is free to explore Aristotle's room; and, once history is banished in favor of imagination, Leopold Bloom may as easily be Stephen's father as Simon Dedalus. Imagination neutralizes history.

Stephen now goes on, in the "Proteus" episode, to give us an example of this alternative to factual history, creating a mental voyage to his Aunt Sara's house and then for two pages having an imaginary conversation with his Uncle Richie—all of which we as readers at first assume is actually taking place. A little later, and a lot drunker, Stephen tries to pull off a trick of a greater order: in the library scene ("Scylla and Charybdis"), he once more unsheathes his Thomistic Aristotle: "Horseness is the whatness of allhorse. . . . Space, what you damn well have to see. . . . Hold to the now, the here, through which all future plunges to the past" (*U* 178). He urges himself to keep to "the now, the here," to stick to the Scylla of "hard facts" and not be swept away by the Charybdic "speculation of schoolboys" (*U* 176, 177). Still, despite A.E.'s warning that "all these questions are purely academic" (*U* 177), Stephen cannot avoid letting go of known history and speculating about Shakespeare. He devises a thorough and elaborate theory of Shakespeare's life and works—again, exploring Aristotle's room of infinite possibilities.

The fact that Stephen chooses Shakespeare as the subject of his speculative theories is significant. In *Ulysses*, history is composed of the hard facts of the external, material world—Bloom's world. In "Scylla and Charybdis," Stephen tries to break away from the nightmare of history; in *Finnegans Wake*, Joyce does so—and the nightmare becomes the dream of history, in which all possibilities, including actual reality, can be realized and explored—for history is ultimately uncertain and indeterminate, the subject of much gossip and varying interpretation. That is why Shakespeare is chosen: our knowledge of the Bard's personal life and history is so scant and meager—based on a few Stratford documents and a host of unverifiable legends—that it invites interpretation, fabrication, and the speculation of schoolboys (as well as scholars). It is ripe ground for Stephen's exercises in the artistic imagination and the exploration of possibilities. Significantly, this paucity of fact and specific detail may be precisely why Joyce finds it so easy, in the *Wake* as well, to use Shakespeare as a universal analogy, as man-father-creator-artist-god; for our knowledge of the Bard is apocryphal and neomythical, not actual nor linearly determinate: Shakespeare's little-known life, with its still possible possibilities, allows for the universalization and fecundity of Viconian history. As Samuel Goldberg writes, his is the "Myth of Shakespeare, the particular hero in whose story may be found the universal laws that hold for all his type, in whose deeds may be found a universal wisdom" (Goldberg 1961, 67). Shakespeare is as myriad-minded and faceted as HCE.

Imaginative Possibilities: *Finnegans Wake*

And so Joyce's notions in *Ulysses* about the "room of infinite possibilities" are carried out in the *Wake*, in which all history and literature are seen as uncertainty and gossip, the exploration of practically every possibility, and in which the study of the past is as uncertain as our knowledge of Shakespeare—his life, loves, plays (and their authorship), manuscripts, and so forth.

All of *Finnegans Wake* could be considered an attempt to answer the question, "What happened to HCE?" Like Hamlet, we want to know the truth; Willard Farnham has suggested that "the Hamlet problem of Hamlet problems" is "the theme of unsimple truth": "It may be said that *Hamlet* is indeed about the pursuit of revenge but most deeply about the pursuit of truth" (Farnham 1969, 931–32). Finding the "truth" (if there is one) about HCE is a matter of digging through the countless possibilities, variations, and interpretations accumulated by the middenpile of time.

Art and creation (and thus also shitpile and letter) are, for the Joyce of the *Wake* as well as for Stephen Dedalus and Aristotle, a "movement then, an actuality of the possible as possible" (*U* 25), an exploration of potential actualities from the room of infinite possibilities. The problem is the same with the story of HCE: we try to choose one version. But which one? Unfortunately, "Zot is the Quiztune" (*FW* 110.14), and Joyce, like Hamlet and Aristotle before him, knew it.

In describing the *Wake*'s explorations as "a sequentiality of improbable possibles" (*FW* 110), Joyce appeals to the dean of the Department of Possibilities and Probabilities, Aristotle ("Harrystotalies"). Joyce explains in this passage that the book explores a history of resonant uncertainty and indeterminate sequentiality, a sequentiality of improbable possibles that are as possible as anything, or as much so as the sequentiality put out by linear "history": "for utterly impossible as are all these events they are probably as like those which may have taken place as any others which never took person at all are ever likely to be" (110.14–15). Nor, as we well know, is fact or history ever certain. The twentieth century gave us relativity and quantum mechanics; but historians and novelists have known for centuries that no event ever happens in a known or exclusively certain way, for what "happens" is ultimately determined by the beholder (in the forms of gossip, criticism, history books, and so on), and nothing is ever conclusive: every generation reinterprets history, just as each generation of critics reinterprets Shakespeare. Modern physics has given us a new terminology for this literary and historical resonance, explored by such novels as *Tristram Shandy, Clarissa, The Good Soldier,* and *Absalom, Absalom!*: we are dealing with the Uncertainty Principle in literature—or what I like to call the Rashomon effect.[2] *Finnegans Wake* studies this effect by exploring

---

2. In the classic Japanese film (and novel) *Rashomon*, a sequence of events centered around a rape is reenacted four different times in four significantly different versions—as recollected by the raped woman, then by the rapist, by the woman's husband (tied to a tree and forced to witness the rape), and, finally, by an unsuspected fourth witness to the crime. Such literary relativity in shifting points of view is masterfully explored by modern writers such as Ford, Faulkner, and Durrell. Joyce would have been familiar with similar effects in Browning's *The Ring and the Book*.

all possibilities and all viewpoints which "are probably as like those which may have taken place."[3] In a sense, all of *Finnegans Wake* deals with the basic question, "What *did* happen to HCE?" What happened in the Park by the Magazine Wall? What was the crime? *Was* there a crime? What took place in the encounter with the Cad? Nothing is certain, though there are many versions of stories being bantered about. Like the question that worries Hamlet, the question of *Finnegans Wake* centers around the fact that we are dealing with unsimple truth, that we are in the dark ("as any camelot prince of dinmurk" [143.07]) and do not quite know what happened. As with some of Shakespeare's plays, this "drauma" (115.32), the gossip about HCE, is a tale of dubious accuracy and questionable authorship that has a great need for scholarship and critical interpretation; one way of looking at the *Wake* is to see it as a scholarly casebook on the HCE tale, including all the variant versions and interpretations thereof.

What *did* happen to HCE? The research done on the original manuscripts and early folios on HCE's small folly is inconclusive; all we know is that "the great fact emerges that after that historic date all holographs so far exhumed initialled by Haromphrey bear the sigla H. C. E." (*FW* 32.12–14). As with the few documents we have about Shakespeare, little else is known for certain about HCE aside from his signature. Presumably, on the "historic date," he went out and committed a crime for which he probably suffered a fall of some sort; and subsequently, he had an encounter with a younger man. Little else is known for certain, including the "historic date" itself. Much of the book explores possible variations of those events from the room of infinite possibilities.

---

3. Similarly, Clive Hart notes in *Structure and Motif* (1962) that "[i]n *Finnegans Wake* [Joyce] was particularly concerned to reproduce relativity and the uncertainty principle. The latter functions in the book exactly as it does in the physical world. The large cyclic books of the constituent material are both clearly defined and predictable, but the smaller the structural units we consider, the more difficult it is to know how they will function.... There is in fact no absolute position whatever in *Finnegans Wake*.... From whichever standpoint we may examine the Joycean phenomena, all other possible frames of reference, no matter how irreconcilable or unpalatable, must be taken into account as valid alternatives" (65–66).

Whatever it is that actually happens on that historic date, news of HCE's crime immediately spreads around town, "bruited" (*FW* 33.16) about and noised from ear to ear, until the poet Hosty collects the rumors and composes "The Ballad of Persse O'Reilly"; this signals the downfall of Earwicker. The Cad's wife whispers poisonous gossip about this profane story into the ear of her confessor: "the gossiple delivered in his epistolear" (38.23); so also the news "hushly pierce[s] the rubiend aurellum of one Philly Thurnston" (38.34–35), and goes on and on. Pouring poison into one's ear was an image that fascinated Joyce. *Earwig*, namesake of H. C. Earwicker, is, according to the *OED*, a verb meaning to whisper or to insinuate: it is also "an insect . . . that poisons the brain by penetrating the head through the ear"; an ear-whisperer, gossiper, or parasite; and a madman who has a maggot or a craze in the brain.

Joyce associated the motif of the spread of gossip by pouring slanderous poison in one's ear with *Hamlet*—for the ghost recounts that he (King Hamlet) had been killed in this manner while he slept: "And in the porches of my ears [Claudius] did pour / The leperous distilment" (I, v, 63–64). This drama, reenacted and recoursed in Hamlet's staged dumb show, obsessed Joyce. In *Ulysses*, Stephen Dedalus recalls the words of King Hamlet's ghost to the prince:

> *List! List! O List!*
> My flesh hears him; creeping, hears.
> *If thou didst ever . . .*
>   —What is a ghost? Stephen said with tingling energy . . .
> *Hamlet, I am thy father's spirit*
>
> (*U* 180)

Stephen has King Hamlet's death by poisoning on his mind all day, but especially while he is in the library, where he pours the poison of his own Shakespearean speculations (from the room of infinite possibilities) into the ears of his listeners: "They list. And in the porches of their ears I pour" (*U* 188). As with Hamlet *père*, HCE's demise as the father figure is caused by the poison poured into people's ears. That ear-piercing gossip is aptly titled "The Ballad of Persse O'Reilly," the ear-piercing (*perce-oreille*, or earwig) ballad of H. C. Earwicker; thus it is appropriate that HCE is repeatedly associated with King Hamlet. Like Hosty and like the Cad, Stephen Dedalus, a poet and a son, spreads rumors about Shakespeare, one of his own acknowledged father figures. Joyce also does this: in *Finnegans Wake* he anthologizes all sad stories and variations of the death of kings and fathers. "List! List!" becomes a call to listen to such poison, a call repeated throughout the *Wake* ad nauseam in every conceivable variation.[4] The *Wake* is a collection of all the poisonous and "gossipaceous" (195.04) variations of the HCE tale. King Hamlet's death by poison poured in his ear; the tales told about Hamlet and Shakespeare by Stephen Dedalus; every scholar's reading or retelling of *Hamlet*; H. C. Earwicker and earwigs; the rumors and gossip that bring about HCE's downfall, the various and variant versions and interpretations of HCE's tale; the stories at the *Wake* to which we, as guests and auditors, are called to list; the *Wake* itself; and, finally, every past, present, and future reading or interpretation of *Finnegans Wake*—all are related by analogy, by equating poison in the ear with gossip or speculation.

Chapter 3 of book 1, a second retelling of the "humphriad of that fall and rise" (*FW* 53.03; involving Humphrey Chimpden and the Cad), contains various versions of the story of HCE's fall and his subsequent encounter with the Cad, including several which involve a drunken Cad and a porter, like that in *Macbeth*, at a gate. This "play" is constantly subject to new interpretations. All is slander and gossip, poison poured in the porches of one's ears. Thus, this chapter is about gossip and uncertainty, about incommunicability and the impossibility of learning the truth, about the attempts of literature, scholarship, and history to state truth by fabricating varying accounts or interpretations of every incident.

---

4. In *Shakespeare and Joyce* (Cheng 1984), I have listed fifty or so variants. Here are a few examples: "Heed! Heed!" (*FW* 5.26), "List!" (13.16), "Year! Year!" (15.08–09), "Lissom! Lissom!" (21.02), "lust!" (51.09), "Lou! Lou!" (58.06), "lo! lo!" (58.18), "Hear, O hear" (68.25), "Oyeh! Oyeh!" (85.31; Oyez, oyez!), "Liss, liss!" (148.26), "List!" (238.23), "land me arrears" (278.L3, or Mark Antony's famous line in *Julius Caesar*), "Ear! Ear! . . . Eye! Eye! (409.03), and "Oyes! Oyeses! Oyesesyeses!" (604.22).

The chapter pursues the Rashomon effect, interviewing men and women on the street—including three soldiers, an English actress, an "entychologist," Shaun-Kevin, a jaunting car driver, the great cook Escoffier, a tennis player, a barmaid, a Board of Trade official, a girl detective, and so forth (FW 58–61)—and each one espouses his or her own view of the HCE tale. Though each evidence-giver has his or her own interpretation, nothing can be proved; and they are all probably "meer marchant taylor's fablings" (61.28)—mere lies and fables about a sailor and a tailor. All this Irish gossip is erroneous misunderstanding, and Joyce tells us that HCE, "the Man . . . [was] subjected to the horrors of the premier terror of Errorland (perorhaps!)"—*perhaps*, for even that is uncertain (62.23–25).

Similarly, Joyce begins chapter 8 of book 1 by trying to investigate HCE's crime: whatever it was the three soldiers tried to make out that he tried to do to the two girls in Phoenix Park (FW 196.09–11). Once again, we attempt "to make his private linen public" (196.16). Still, what *was* the crime? As always, all is uncertainty and misunderstanding, as is often pointed out in the *Wake*: "No, no, the dear heaven knows, and the farther the from it, if the whole stole stale mis betold, whoever the gulpable, and whatever the pulpous was" (396.21–24). We can only listen to (or read) the *Wake*'s compilation of all the gossipy possibilities and speculative misunderstandings of history and the Ballad of Persse O'Reilly. Thus, we are called to "List, list!" to a review of human history: "*Hirp! Hirp! For their Missed Understandings! chirps the Ballat of Perce-Oreille*" (175.27–28). As such a compilation, the *Wake* is thus an exploration of the "Notpossible!" (175.05).

The Letter From Litter

"Learned scholarch[s]" also engage in such explorations. Scholarship and artistic creation, connected by the role of language (*litterae* as "litterature" and letters), are both concerned with finding, if possible, the right interpretation from the dungheap of infinite possibilities. Joyce was clearly aware of the similarity between reading the *Wake* and researching purple passages of literature; a twentieth-century foliowright, he describes his own "problem passion play" (FW 32.32) as "the purchypatch of hamlock"

(31.23–24),[5] "the patchpurple of the massacre" (111.02), "theirs porpor patches!" (200.04), "paupers patch" (316.23), and a "puling sample jungle of woods" (112.04)—a pure and simple jumble of words. Joyce further emphasizes this similarity by his repeated references to holographs, folios, librettos, original manuscripts, and Shakespearean scholars and ghosters.

Finnegans Wake is Joyce's attempt to compile these error-possibilities of HCE's comedy of errors—in other words, all history. A problem play has purple patches that engender much critical speculation and scholarly research; in this sense, *Finnegans Wake* is, like the letter unearthed by Biddy the hen, an attempt to dig into the middenheap and find the "gossiple" truth. Throughout the *Wake*, Biddy the hen scrabbles for evidence in the littermound, keeping her "kiribis pouch filled with litterish fragments" (*FW* 66.25–26). As chapter 8 of book 1 ("Anna Livia Plurabelle") opens, Biddy sifts through all the possibilities of HCE's crime, the tale of "Don Dom Dombdomb and his wee follyo" (197.18): HCE's folly in the park is made equivalent (history=literature) to Shakespearean folios. Joyce's works are like Shakespeare's; and HCE himself is like Shakespeare the man, for little is known for certain about the lives and histories of either.

The problem play of *Finnegans Wake* is, like the letter unearthed by Biddy the hen, an attempt to dig the truth out of the middenheap of possibilities. Like the hen, Joyce faces in chapter 4 of book 1 the question of whether or not to attempt wading through all the muddy misinterpretations, like some Shakespearean scholar, to find the original manuscript and learn the truth. The issue is, Hamlet-like, to dig or not to dig, like the gravedigger in *Hamlet*, into the graveyard of past literature and history for his style and his subject matter; Joyce describes his technique as the "mating of a grand stylish gravedigging with secondbest buns" (*FW* 121.32). Digging for old skulls, like that of Yorick, is like the scholarly digging that unearthed Shakespeare's will, which left Anne Hathaway his "secondbest bed." Similarly, Biddy the hen digs out of the graveyard of "litterature"

---

5. The "problem plays" is a term first used by F. S. Boas (1896) to describe four Shakespearean plays containing great problems of interpretation; these include *Hamlet* ("the purchypatch of hamlock"), a play full of purple passages (also commonly known as purple patches).

alphabetical letters, belles lettres, and postal letters; thus, it is only appropriate that Biddy's discovery from the litter pile is a letter, literally a "letter from litter" (615.01).

Chapter 5 of book 1 concerns the letter, scholarship, and textual studies. Here again, Joyce tries to equate his works (the letter as the *Wake* and as all of literature) with those of Shakespeare—especially *Hamlet*—including "disjointed times" (*FW* 104.05), "Ophelia's Culpreints" (105.18), "the drame of Drainophilias" (110.11), "me ken or no me ken Zot is the Quiztune" (110.14), "from tham Let Rise till Hum Lit" (114.19), "dummpshow" (120.07–08), "very like a whale's egg" (120.11), "his Claudian brother" (121.01), and "a grand stylish gravedigging" (121.32).

The chapter begins with a catalogue of possible names for the letter (*FW* 104–7), an exploration into the many possibilities for titling the "untitled mamafesta" (104.04). The speaker then begins a lecture on the letter and on scholarship about the letter. He raises the question of textual scholarship. As with Shakespeare, some plays may have been written by forgers, "claimants," or collaborators. The chapter pursues several of the many possibilities.

On page 110 the speaker launches into a sort of "Proteus" episode (from *Ulysses*), quoting Hamlet's famed soliloquy, referring to Aristotle's room of infinite possibilities, and wondering whether the possibilities explored in the letter were likely ones. The speaker begins to talk about the "original hen" (*FW* 110.22) and the object at which she is scratching, "a goodish-sized sheet of letter-paper originating by tranship from Boston (Mass.)" (118.08–10). The hen has uncovered the celebrated letter, and the rest of the paragraph records its contents: a talky letter, its contents are commonplace and it sports a large teastain. The speaker now discusses the condition of the manuscript, flavoring his words with Stephen's Aristotelian-Thomistic aesthetics ("Horseness is the whatness of allhorse" [*U* 178], and so on). He admits that the letter is a jumble of words, that he hasn't "the poultriest notions" (112.05) of what it is about; and that, actually, it is fair game for Gypsy scholars ("Zingari schoolerm" [112.07]).

He therefore calls for us, as literary scholars, to make inspection of the letter and to study the hearsay of literature (*FW* 112.29). The speaker launches into a textual study of the missive, noting that the characters slide up and down on the page in a pattern of fall and *ricorso*, and that the letter resembles the problem play of *Hamlet* ("tham Let" and "Hum Lit"): "But by writing thithaways end to end and turning, turning and end to end hithaways writing and with lines of litters slittering up and louds of latters slettering down, the old semetomyplace and jupetbackagain from tham Let Rise till Hum Lit" (114.16–19; "thithaways" and "hithaways" may refer to Anne Hathaway). In these lines, Joyce predicts that the *Wake* will eventually attain a literary prominence like that of *Hamlet* (see also Cheng 1984, 108–9).

Because there are an infinite number of possible meanings for the letter's sequentiality of improbables, scholarly study of this work arrives at different interpretations in differing schools of criticism. The speaker follows with an imitation of psychoanalytic criticism (*FW* 115), like that of Freud or Shakespearean critic Ernest Jones, and then one of Marxist criticism (116). The message (and language) of this Viconian letter (the *Wake*) could be "anythongue athall" (117.15–16); yet, while we may have doubts about its sense, "we must vaunt no idle dubiosity as to its genuine authorship and holusbolus authoritativeness" (118.04). The speaker then argues—as some Shakespearean scholars have done on the issue of authorship—that the fact is that the affair was done once and for all, and someone wrote it down, regardless of subjective phenomenology; he goes on to compare the letter with the Bible and the Book of Kells, admitting that it looks pretty blurred and stained. Equated with Joyce's works, the letter is similar to great literature, and specifically to Shakespeare's *Hamlet*. The professor, in his textual study of the Wakean letter, concludes about this "dummpshow" (120.07—the dumb show on the middendump): it is a "prepronominal *funferal* [the *Wake* as a funeral and fun-for-all], engraved and retouched and edgewiped and pudden-padded, very like a whale's egg farced with pemmican as were it sentenced to be nuzzled over a full trillion times for ever and a night till his noddle sink or swim by that ideal reader suffering from an ideal insomnia" (120.09–14). This work, like Shakespeare's, has been retouched and worked over; and, like the plays or the *Wake*, it is meant to be puzzled over for a trillion nights by that ideal dreambook and insomniac reader. Finally, the passage describes the *Wake*'s Protean qualities as an exploration of infinite possibilities, which, like the cloud observed by

Hamlet and Polonius, takes on many shapes, "Very like a whale" (III, ii, 367)—this line has been quoted before, by Stephen, in, appropriately, the "Proteus" episode (U 41), *Ulysses's* exploration of infinite possibilities.

Like Shakespearean folios, then, or like littermounds, works of literature are comedies of errors, compilations of misunderstandings. In *Finnegans Wake*, Joyce's "lifewand" makes "the dumb speak" (195.05), exploring the infinite possibilities neglected by history and time, those imaginative alternatives that allow a cloud to become a whale.

All the World's a Stage

Joyce conceived of *Finnegans Wake* as essentially dramatic, a Shakespearean play acted out on the "worldstage" (FW 33.03) by the archetypal family members of a dramatic company. What I call the "dramatic metaphor"—that is, that all the world is a stage and all the figures of history merely players—underlies all the "action" in *Finnegans Wake*, Joyce's chronicle of history. Joycean history, as we have seen, is an exploration into many possibilities; in the *Wake* these possibilities take on the forms of various plays, particularly Shakespearean plays, each recreating a different view of the possibilities of history. Joyce sets his dream of all-history in the context of the dramatic milieu: the dream as drama.

Like Shakespeare before him, Joyce had increasingly come to think of an artist as a playwright and a creator-god, and of the artist's works as a stage peopled by his creations, "all the charictures in the drame" (FW 302.21–32). In *A Portrait of the Artist as a Young Man* Stephen Dedalus had proclaimed that, in the dramatic form, "the artist, like the God of the creation, remains within or behind or beyond or above his handiwork, invisible, refined out of existence, indifferent, paring his fingernails" (P 215). Joyce was fond of the metaphor of the artist as both playwright and god. Creating his own worlds, a poet is a god and a father; God is the playwright who penned "the folio of this world"; Shakespeare, God, HCE, and Joyce, are all, like Hamlet's father (with whom, according to Stephen, Shakespeare identifies), "all in all" (U 204).

The metaphor of playwright as god becomes even more recurrent and insistent in the *Wake*, Joyce's chronicle of the world and world history. The

prime mover behind the force of destiny is a playwright, "the composi-
tor of the farce of dustiny" (*FW* 162.02–03); this production of the play
about Viconian history is presented by "the producer (Mr John Baptister
Vickar)"—Joyce as the author of the *Wake* and God as the author of history, alias Giambattista Vico and John the Baptist (255.27). God-Shake-
speare-Joyce-HCE is a "worldwright" (14.19) and a "puppetry producer"
(219.07–08); like Prospero, he is a "pageantmaster" (237.13) and the "god
of all machineries" (253.33). In the *Wake*, the most recurrent symbol for
the creator-father-god figure is, however, Michael Gunn, manager of Dublin's Gaiety Theatre, and father of Joyce's friend Selskar Gunn; repeatedly
HCE is referred to as, or compared with, Michael Gunn, in the role of
manager of his worldstage. In chapter 1 of book 2, that most "dramatic"
of *Wake* chapters, HCE is introduced as "HUMP (Mr Makeall Gone)"; as
stage managers, Michael Gunn and God can both make all things come
or go. At the end of the same chapter, after loud applause, the exiting HCE
is described as "Gonn the gawds, Gunnar's gustspells" (257.34); Gunn as
god is gone; the play, Gunn's and God's gospels, is over. In 481.19 Joyce
describes HCE as a builder of cities, a populator and a patriarch: "We
speak of Gun, the farther"—HCE as Gunn and God the Father. So also
he is described in 434.08–10 as "the big gun," waiting "for Bessy Sudlow"
(Michael Gunn's real wife, and an actress in his troupe at the Gaiety)
to serve him his dinner. In keeping with the theme of Viconian *ricorso*,
HCE will also become, in a felicitous coinage, the "cropse of our seedfa-
ther" (55.08)—the corpse will become the earth-laden seed and father of
future crops and generations. Thus, finally, in this "worldwright" metaphor, HCE is a "gunnfodder" (242.10): at once Brecht's cannonfodder; a
phallic gun; Michael Gunn, a father and a creator, a grandfather, and the
fodder for future Gunns, guns, and generations. Even after death, after
Makeall Gone has made all gone (himself being but cannonfodder), even
then will there be the "Hereweareagain Gaieties of the Afterpiece"—a
joyous play (*pièce*) at the Gaiety in our afterlife. This will be supervised
by this new Gaiety's manager, Michael Gunn, "the Royal Revolver of
these real globoes" (455.25–26), the god and gun who makes this world
revolve, the stage manager of the Globe Theatre and the global world.
As "Makeall Gone," "Gun, the farther," "gunnfodder," and "the big gun,"

Joyce is a playwright-god whose phallic gun is the creative pen of Shem the Penman.

The Dramatic Metaphor

In *Finnegans Wake*, Joyce repeatedly makes the punning equation between "dream" and "drama" (see Cheng 1984, 35–38). The *Wake's* "prepossessing drauma" (*FW* 115.32) is both a traumatic dream sequence, the nightmare of history, and the archetypal family drama, *The Mime of Mick, Nick and the Maggies* (see Cheng 1984, 49–53). A poet-playwright—by analogy, HCE and all men—dreams the nightmare of all time, the "drema" (*FW* 69.14) of the world. The metaphor of the world as stage, the dramatic metaphor, is suggested recurrently in *Finnegans Wake*, and most insistently in the two passages (30–33 and 219–21) in which Dublin's Gaiety Theatre is aptly transformed into the Globe.

James Atherton has observed that "one of Joyce's favourite images for the world, or the *Wake*, is the stage—although the famous quotation is never made" (Atherton [1959] 2009, 149). Of course, few direct quotations are made in *Finnegans Wake* without being refracted through puns and double meanings. Pages 30 to 33, however, contain a cluster of allusions to Shakespeare and to the stage, most conspicuous of which is the description of HCE as "our worldstage's practical jokepiece" (33.02–03). Clearly, this is a direct reference to *As You Like It's* Jaques (the "jokepiece"?), who said, "All the world's a stage, / And all the men and women merely players" (II, vii, 139–40). As a drama on the worldstage, HCE's story is a nightly reenactment, to which the public is invited, of an archetypal story, a "druriodrama" (50.06) in this Drury Lane world of ours.

The reader first sees HCE, like the "old gardener" Adam in his "prefall paradise," sitting about in his garden "under his redwood tree" (*FW* 30.13–15), as the king approaches. These lines again echo *As You Like It* and "Under the greenwood tree" (II, v, 1), in a context which informs that the world has been a stage from the beginning of time, and that the Green World of the Forest of Arden (in which Jaques makes his "worldstage" metaphor), Shakespeare's correlative for the world of dramatic romance, is none other than Eden and all gardens. "Under the greenwood tree," a song sung by Jaques and Amiens (549.31— "amiens"), is Shakespeare's invitation to this Green World: "Under the greenwood tree, / Who loves to lie with me. . . . / Come hither, come hither, come hither" (II, v, 1–5).

So here also, at the beginning of chapter 2 in book 1, is Joyce's own "come hither," his invitation to attend the play about HCE, a production to be "staged by Madame Sudlow" (*FW* 32.10) at the King Street Theatre ("king's treat house" in 32.26). Bessy Sudlow (so named in 434.08) and Michael Gunn managed the Gaiety Theatre—on King Street in Dublin—where Christmas pantomimes were annually produced. This particular "pantalime" (32.11), to be staged by the proprietress, bears certain resemblances to Shakespearean plays performed at the Globe, particularly *Hamlet*. Admission to sit in the "pit stalls and early amphitheatre" (33.10) is two bits ("two pitts" in 32.11). The seating choices are "Pit, prommer and parterre, standing room only" (33.12). The habitual theatregoers are all out tonight to see our "worldstage's practical jokepiece," HCE: "Habituels conspicuously emergent" (33.13; emphasis added). Like *Hamlet*, this piece is a "problem passion play" (32.32): *Hamlet* is one of the "problem plays"—and the *Wake* is a "passion play" (since, as Joyce said, book 3 was written in the form of the fourteen stations of the Cross). *Hamlet*'s presence is strong in these pages, with references to "Offaly" (31.18), "hamlock" (31.24), and "metheg in your midness" (32.05). This problem play at the Gaiety/Globe may well be "the purchypatch of hamlock" (31.23–24), the purple patch of *Hamlet*. In any event, history is seen as a play or pantomime presented on a worldstage.

This pantomime of the *Wake* is the drama of history, in its "homedromed and enliventh performance . . . of the millentury, running strong since creation" (*FW* 32.31–33). It is an archetypal family drama: it is the tragedy of HCE's fall and his falling-out with his wife ("*A Royal Divorce*" [a play about Napoleon and Josephine] and "Napoleon the Nth" in 32.33 and 33.02) and his daughters ("*The Bo Girl*" [Michael Balfe's *The Bohemian Girl*] and "*The Lily*" in 32.35). Brothers ("our red brother" in 31.25) and sisters ("his inseparable sisters, uncontrollable nighttalkers, Skertsiraizde with Donyahzade" in 32.07–09—Scheherazade and Dunyazade, skirt-raised sisters from the *Arabian Nights*) are also here, as is the Holy Trinity, "the triptychal religious family symbolizing puritas of doctrina, business per usuals, and the purchypatch of hamlock" (31.22–23).

The World as Family Drama and Stage Company

This drama is a family affair. Joyce pursues this analogy in the *Wake* by frequently referring to the characters in the drama of the *Wake* as both family members and actors in a stage company. The drama on this world-stage is "real life"—or history—and the roles are played by a theater company (whether the Gunns, Porters, Bonapartes, Hamlets, or Holy Trinity) whose cast members are the archetypal family itself: "Real life behind the floodlights as shown by the best exponents of a royal divorce" (FW 260n3). The cast members are, as we know, the members of HCE-Porter-Gunn's household, and their Gaiety Theatre globe-stage is none other than the publican's inn and residence in Chapelizod; thus, the word "house" is used throughout the *Wake* in three senses: domestic, tavernal, and theatrical. The cast is first introduced on page 13 of the *Wake*: the family members are an "alderman" (older man) with a hump ("bulbenboss") and a stutter, or Humphrey-HCE; his wife, ALP, a poor old woman; his daughter Issy, an "auburn mayde"; and his twin sons, the Pen and the Post, Shem and Shaun. There are five so far in the cast, and yet that is not all. This household troupe is actually a "howthold of nummer seven" (242.05), having two additional, non–family members in the household: a male servant (Sickerson, Sanderson, etc.) and a female servant (Kate). At the start of chapter 1 of book 2, the performance of *The Mime of Mick, Nick and the Maggies* is prefaced by the proper theatrical introductions of the cast: "featuring: GLUGG (Mr Seumas McQuillad). . . . IZOD (Miss Butys Pott). . . . CHUFF (Mr Sean O'Mailey). . . . ANN (Miss Corrie Corriendo). . . . HUMP (Mr Makeall Gone). . . . SAUNDERSON. . . . KATE" (219.21–221.12)—that is, Shem the Penquill, Issy the Beauty Spot, Shaun the Post, Anna Livia (the running—*corriendo*—waters of the Liffey), HCE–Michael Gunn, Saunderson, and Kate. These are the elements of our domestic drama, "the family umbroglia" (284.04).

In an acting troupe of only seven members, each actor or actress must be able to assume a number of roles on call, depending on the particular family imbroglio being performed that evening; thus, each member is symbolic of a family "type," able to be recast into almost any old play or version of a royal divorce. "Like the newcasters in their old plyable of *A Royenne Devours*" (FW 388.07), they must be ready to take over history's old plays, each actor performing the role assigned to him by the "worldwright" and puppetry producer. This concept is important and fundamental. The notion of an archetypal cast performing different plays, or different interpretations of an archetypal play, corresponds marvelously with Joyce's concept of history as a resonant exploration of different possibilities. As the *Wake* is about history, the different variations (and possibilities) of reality and history become the different plays in the repertoire performed by the acting troupe and family, "the whole stock company of the old house" (510.17), where each member is able to act the part for his "type" in each new play. The *Wake* is thus full of references to stock companies and acting troupes, with the same basic "types" playing different roles under each character "type." There could be no better model for Wakean history and Viconian *ricorso*. HCE can be the same basic actor under the various historical guises of Adam, Tim Finnegan, Finn MacCool, Shakespeare, and so forth; the filial usurper (Cad, Hosty, Paul Horan, etc.), "Under the name of Orani . . . may have been the utility man of the troupe capable of sustaining long parts at short notice" (9.19–21). The family is a house troupe, which performs "with nightly redistribution of parts and players by the puppetry producer and daily dubbing of ghosters" (219.06–08).

Pages 323 and 324 provide an excellent illustration of how *Finnegans Wake* is presented as a stage drama played by "the whole stock company of the old house": "tummelumpsk . . . that bunch of palers. . . . Toni Lampi. . . . ghustorily spoeking, gen and gang, dane and dare, like the dud spuk of his first foetotype. . . . And ere he could catch or hook or line to suit their saussyskins, the lumpenpack. . . . Sot! . . . change all that whole set. Shut down and shet up. Our set, our set's allohn" (323.28–324.16).

Fritz Senn has pointed out that this passage (quoted in part) refers to a particular stage performance of *Hamlet* in Dublin at the Crow Street Theatre. Referring to "the versatility of the Dublin stock companies" (and quoting from Samuel Fitzpatrick's *Dublin: A Historical and*

Topographical Account of the City [1907], one of Joyce's source books for
the *Wake*), Senn writes:

> "At Crow Street Digges ['Digges' in 313.26] was playing 'Hamlet' and
> ruptured a blood vessel. The play was immediately stopped and *She
> Stoops to Conquer* substituted for it. The manager's apologies hav-
> ing been accepted, the performers, who were all in the house, hast-
> ily dressed and went on. A gentleman in the pit had left the building
> immediately before the accident to Digges, for the purposes of buying
> oranges. He was delayed for some little time, and having left 'Hamlet'
> in conversation with the 'Ghost,' found on his return the stage occupied
> by 'Tony Lumpkin' and his companions at the Three Jolly Pigeons. He
> at first thought he had mistaken the theatre, but an explanation showed
> him the real state of affairs" (Fitzpatrick, 256–57). In *FW*, all actors play
> multiple parts, often simultaneously, and we [readers] all think, again
> and again, that we have mistaken the theatre. In particular, Joyce used
> the incident in the paragraph beginning 323.25, where *She Stoops* and
> *Hamlet* are among the things that go on at the same time. (1962, 6)

With much going on at once, the passage on pages 323 and 324 is
a murky one at best; in context, it seems that HCE, in the role of the
Norwegian Captain, has momentarily left the tavern for the outhouse
(much as the spectator at Crow Street goes out to buy oranges), and
returns to find the set (tavern=theater=house, of course) completely
changed, as happened with *She Stoops to Conquer* and *Hamlet*. This
historic worldstage seems to be constantly changing sets, exploring new
and different variations and possibilities. The drinkers at the tavern have
suddenly become "that bunch of palers" (a bunch of players); Sheridan's
Tony Lumpkin appears as "tummelumpsk" and "Toni Lampi." The first
play concerned Danish ghosts: both the ghost of King Hamlet, King of
Denmark ("ghustorily spooking . . . dane and dare") daring his son on (a
father spooking and speaking, "like the dud spuk," to his firstborn, "his
first foetotype"); and Ibsen's *Ghosts* (*Gengangere* in Dano-Norwegian;
here, "gen and gang"). However, suddenly the set has changed back to
Tony Lumpkin and the Three Jolly Pigeons—back to the "lumpenpack"
accompanied by the shout: "Sot! . . . change all that whole set. Shut

down and shet up. Our set, our set's allohn"—our set's all one in the versatile drama of all-history. (The prop men, crying to shut down and set up, seem to be Sinn Feiners: ourselves, ourselves alone.) Change the set, but the show (and history) must go on, "like the newcasters in the old plyable" (388.07). For the nightly shows put on by this stock company and family troupe consist of the infinite possibilities of all history, new castings of a pliable old play. The archetypal family drama is a tale renewed and reenacted nightly on the worldstage, a daily dubbing of *Hamlet* (and all family dramas) at the Globe.

10

"An Upstart Crow, Beautified with Our Feathers"

Finnegans Wake, Hamlet, *and the Problem of Context*

PAUL FAGAN

Throughout book 3, chapter 3 of *Finnegans Wake*, the Four Masters cross-examine a somnolent Yawn on the text's most problematic details, namely, its characters, its themes, and its content. To the extent that this strange ad hoc analysis (part psychoanalysis, part séance) stands as a double for the unusual encounter between the *Wake* and its readers, it is appropriate that the Masters are less than successful in their critical endeavors: their inquiry does not clarify the terms by which we might distinguish reading the *Wake* from *mis*reading the *Wake*, but rather yields results that are "baffling," "complex," even "outright demented" (Rabaté 2007, 385). As text, Yawn responds to this treatment at his readers' hands with a mixture of defensive pugnacity and mocking irony: "I can psoakoonaloose myself any time I want . . . without your interferences" (FW 522.34–35).[1] And yet, given the scene's strangely narcissistic function, the self-description that Yawn offers under this coercion is revealing. Inquiring about "crazyheaded Jorn," the four receive the cryptic advice *"ex ugola lenonem"* (513.07–08), a Wakean reworking of the Latin *tanquam ex ungue leonem*

---

1. As my analysis is limited exclusively to *Finnegans Wake*, I will hereafter dispense with the convention of including the abbreviation FW before page and line numbers—all such in-text citations are to be understood as referring to the *Wake*.

("we know the lion by his claw"), a maxim that is echoed throughout the text.[2] If Yawn's advice to his inquisitors doubles as guidance for the *Wake's* readers, then it suggests that even the *Wake's* most obscure details can lead us to "the right context" in which its seemingly kaleidoscopic forms can cohere in a recognizable whole.

However, this idea of "the right context" has been one of the most contested issues in *Wake* studies. As Fritz Senn underlines, when reading any particular passage "we often suffer from context amnesia, not for lack of attention, but because of bewilderment" (1990, 69). The impression of the *Wake* as "a middenhide hoard of objects" (19.08) is further compounded in the text's many lists,[3] wherein "the *Wake* itself appears to offer almost nothing but trash and refuse, rubbish, odds and ends, middenheaps" (Senn 1990, 62). For Ruben Borg, this recurring self-reflexive motif of the *Wake* as a loose collection of (potentially infinite) random details reveals the text's most central tensions: "One expects a catalogue to be able to perform a synthesis of all items included within it . . . But what the unity of this unit depends on is precisely what the *Wake* will refuse to

2. Most notoriously, this was Johann Bernoulli's pronouncement upon inspecting Isaac Newton's anonymously submitted solution to a challenge Bernoulli had posed to the readers of *Acta Eruditorum* in June 1696 (Brewster 1832, 179). We find this sentiment echoed in the analysis of "The Reverend Letter" in book 1, chapter 5 of the *Wake*, when the exegete speculates "why, pray, sign anything as long as every word, letter, penstroke, paperspace is a perfect signature of its own?" (115.06–08). Elsewhere, during the relation of the Burrus and Caseous episode in book 1, chapter 6, we are informed that "It was aptly and corrigidly stated (and it is royally needless for one ex ungue Leonem to say by whom)" (162.28–29).

3. For example, book 1, chapter 7 presents a page-and-a-half list of items littered on the floor, walls, and doorways of Shem's house, from "burst loveletters, telltale stories, stickyback snaps [and] doubtful eggshells" to "worms of snot, toothsome pickings, cans of Swiss condensed bilk [and] highbrow lotions" (183.11–184.02). See also the two pages of "abusive names" hurled at HCE (71.10–72.16), the three-page list of presents delivered by ALP to her children (210.6–212.19), the four pages of potential titles for ALP's Letter (103.5–107.7), and the mammoth fourteen-page list supposedly of the attributes of "Finn Mc Cool" (125.10–139.14).

provide: some evidence of the pertinence of all accumulated objects to the whole, and the sense that the collection of epithets, nouns, clichéd expressions is not utterly random and unmotivated" (2007, 80).

Critics who contest this conceptualization of the *Wake* as an unsynthesized (and ultimately unsynthesizeable) accumulation of objects generally assert that its allusive and highly suggestive language provides just enough anchorage by which to fix the floating chain of signifieds and guide the reader toward the "correct" meaning or myth. In line with this assumption, such critics have developed an ad hoc hermeneutic for reading this peculiar text. This matrix text model, as I shall refer to it, attempts to overcome the fundamental problem of relating text to context when reading the *Wake* by conceptualizing the work's perceived intertextual echoes and resonances as imbedded clues that reveal a cunningly concealed matrix. Once uncovered, this matrix functions as a fixed and recoverable metacontext, the correct identification of which will unlock the work's manifold mysteries, reveal its overall structuring principle, and invest its neologisms with meaning. By shifting focus from the work's indeterminable linguistic blends to its determinable allusive targets, any unit of Wakean text might be afforded meaning by the manner in which it yields to the concerns, themes, and structure of the proposed matrix. This is a way of looking at any detail of the *Wake* and proclaiming, "we know the lion by his claw."

I propose to re-engage this debate by testing the matrix text hermeneutic model through an extended reflection on the specific, and prominent, contention that Shakespeare's *Hamlet* enjoys the status of structuring matrix text in the *Wake*'s allusive complex. My interest in returning to this particular way of reading the *Wake*, even as it has undergone a steady line of critique by more recent critical engagements,[4] lies not in advocating its

---

4. Borg is representative of this line of critique: "there is . . . no interpretive key, no preconceived plan by which to redeem the excesses of *Finnegans Wake*. The work realizes its own organizing principles as a structure in constant progress . . . As a perpetual work in progress the *Wake* has no origin; rather, it invents its own origin as it unfolds" (2007, 83).

validity or exposing its shortcomings *per se*. Rather, I wish to advance the case that the model is worth attending to exactly because an "elucidation of the relationship of [its] methodology to its own necessity" (De Man 1983, xix) reveals what is at stake in the rhetoric of validity and authenticity that continues to inform the critical discourse surrounding the *Wake*.

Shakespeare's specter at the *Wake* is a particularly auspicious image for this inquiry: as Helen Sword notes, "Shakespeare raises the dual hermeneutic specters of overdetermination and indeterminacy" insofar as "his murky features mirror the interpretive paradoxes of every age or culture that has tried to lay claim to his image" (2002, 50).[5] As I interrogate the claim that *Hamlet* is the *Wake's* structuring matrix text par excellence, Sword's thesis offers the guiding coordinates for my considerations of how the *Wake's* own "murky features" disclose the variously anchored yet radically contingent mechanisms of context, and thus "mirror the interpretive paradoxes" of diverse critical attempts to lay claim to its image. I ultimately propose that Shakespeare's presence at the *Wake* offers less a structuring principle than a paradigmatic site for reflecting upon the ways in which acts of reading, when faced with the *Wake's* radical contextual potentiality, attempt to position conceived contexts as essential (substantial, objective, deterministic) rather than contingent (conceptual, subjective, unnecessary). And by revealing the stakes of such claims to insight, the *Wake* challenges us to acknowledge the contingency of our readings in order to disavow their authority.

---

5. Sword traces the claims and counterclaims of this historical hermeneutic battle over the right to speak the "truth" about Shakespeare with authority in the following illuminating terms: "Throughout much of the eighteenth century . . . England's struggle to establish a coherent national identity found simultaneous expression in the canonization and bowdlerization of Shakespeare's plays, seemingly contradictory symptoms . . . of a single appropriative impulse. Victorian England's troubled obsession with erosions of religious and patriarchal authority led, similarly, both to the rise of empiricist biography and to a compensatory proliferation of alternate authorship theories. Most recently, postmodern America's tendency to counter deconstructive impulses with commodity fetishization has resulted in a radical disjunction between scholarly and popular representations of the Bard" (2002, 50).

Entering the Matrix

That the critical canon of *Finnegans Wake* is heavy on blindness and too light on insight, Clive Hart claims, is demonstrated by careful attention to its similarities to, and divergences from, Shakespeare's treatment at the hands of his scholars: "Critics of *Finnegans Wake* have too often used the book to pursue their own obsessions. That is not, of course, a phenomenon peculiar to Joyce studies. Critics of Shakespeare . . . have been quite as aberrant in their pronouncements. The difference, in the case of Shakespeare studies, is that there the plain sense of the text keeps pulling the reader back to the common center, whereas we have no common center to which to relate ideas generated by *Finnegans Wake*" (1992, 15).

Hart is here echoing a central principle of discourse analysis: that "there must be an appeal to a common context of shared knowledge or otherwise no communication can take place at all" (Widdowson 2007, 21). The matrix text model for reading *Finnegans Wake* is the most prominent attempt to claim not only the hypothetical value but also the existence of such a "common center to which to relate ideas generated by *Finnegans Wake*" (Hart 1992, 15). The development of the model dates back to James Atherton's seminal 1959 study of Wakean allusions *The Books at the Wake*, which marries the *Wake*'s highly allusive tendencies to the explicative structural promise of Joseph Campbell and Henry Morton Robinson's *A Skeleton Key to Finnegans Wake* (1944). Atherton proposes that the sources for *Finnegans Wake* can be divided into those from which Joyce lifted a handful of words and phrases "chosen not for what they said but for the way in which they said them," and those from which "Joyce took not only words but ideas . . . which could provide him with the theoretical structure he required" (2009, 27).[6] This promise of "theoretical structure" has

---

6. The model's champions are also emboldened by the perceived successes of the Homeric matrix for reading *Ulysses* (1922)—as first made public in Stuart Gilbert's *James Joyce's Ulysses*—by which, ostensibly, "the wealth of information assembled by Joyce is saved from meaninglessness by direct association with the universal structures of myth, so that, for all the stylistic virtuosity, and the coincidences which permeate the narrative, nothing in this monumental novel appears to have been left to chance" (Borg 2007, 82).

become so central to *Wake* studies that there are few analyses of the text that do not explicitly or implicitly incorporate its basic premises.

From the outset, Shakespeare and his works have held a privileged position in this tradition. Building on pioneering articles on the *Wake*'s Shakespearean allusions by William Peery (1951) and M. J. C. Hodgart (1953), Atherton contends that the work contains "at least one quotation from every single play by Shakespeare" (2009, 45). The argument that the volume and consistency of Shakespearean allusions reveal their thematic, structural, and contextualizing influence over the *Wake* was first proposed by Adaline Glasheen, in her oft-cited assertions that "Shakespeare (man, works) is the matrix of FW" and that "*Finnegans Wake* is about Shakespeare" (1977, 260, xxi). For François Laroque, the belief "that Shakespeare and his oeuvre lie at the core of the proliferating text of [*Finnegans Wake*] has now become established fact" (2013, 57).

In his exceptionally researched 1984 monograph *Shakespeare and Joyce*, Vincent Cheng takes up and refines Glasheen's Shakespearean matrix model with the contention that "Shakespeare provides some of the . . . most central . . . matrixes in the *Wake*, and certainly the most important one in terms of Shem-Joyce's vision of himself as an artist" (1984, 6). While he investigates the *Wake*'s engagements with plays and poems across the Shakespeare canon, as well as with the Bard's contested biography and reception, ultimately Cheng insists that "foremost among these Shakespearean matrixes is that of *Hamlet*" (1984, 6). With the conviction that "Joyce found in *Hamlet* an all-encompassing matrix for his purposes," *Shakespeare and Joyce* builds the case that "*Hamlet* is a structural matrix in *Finnegans Wake*, a central and symbolic framework for the action" that is constructed with the "scaffoldings of allusion" (1984, 72, 54, 11).[7]

---

7. While I propose to submit this claim for the matrical status of *Hamlet* in the *Wake* to a rigorous test, it must be underlined that without Cheng's thoroughly researched study any work on Shakespearean allusions in the *Wake* would be a very poor thing indeed, and his book remains the authoritative study and work of reference in the field. Cheng's broader analysis touches on many points of encounter between Shakespeare and the *Wake*, such as the functions of the dramatic metaphor, filial rivalry, plagiarism, and cyclical history. Given the focus of this essay, however, only those elements of Cheng's

Cheng clearly lays out the foundation and rationale for the claim that *Hamlet* allusions in the *Wake* constitute a structuring and contextualizing matrix: "There are by far more allusions to *Hamlet* than to any other play (Shakespearean or otherwise); and the parallels are more frequent, precise, and insistent: HCE as King Hamlet, Shem as the Prince, Shaun as Laertes-Polonius. References to *Hamlet* are ubiquitous; and . . . the themes and motifs in *Hamlet* are structural counterparts to those in *Finnegans Wake*" (1984, 6–7). Three principles of legitimatization can be observed here: (1) frequency of allusion; (2) fidelity of character correspondence; and (3) the structuring potential of the thematic resonances.

According to the first principle, the volume and consistency of *Hamlet* allusions constitute the proof of, and key to, its status as a matrix that synthesizes the *Wake*'s heterogeneous allusive complex under one all-encompassing metacontext. Signaling the correct "common context of shared knowledge" (Widdowson 2007, 21), these recurring echoes enable communication by anchoring the *Wake*'s polysemes and structuring its content into a system of (relatively) stable characters, relationships, and themes.[8] Considering these criteria alongside the Wakean critical canon, however, we find that the sheer volume and frequency of diverse echoes and resonances throughout the *Wake* lead to any number of potentially equally valid claims for the matrical authority of any particular constella-

---

argument that are paradigmatic of the matrix text approach have been highlighted for analysis. My primary purpose is not to critique the individual instance of Cheng's analysis per se, but rather to reflect on the consequences of running his impressively researched and compiled index of Shakespeare allusions in the *Wake* through the software of the matrix text hermeneutic model.

8. The model is evocative of Michael Riffaterre's theory that the poetic text is structured around an absent "matrix" that underlies and structures the text but does not appear explicitly therein, with the poem itself constituting a "greater or lesser expansion of the matrix's components" (Riffaterre 1978, 12). In Riffaterrean terms, then, the contention that *Hamlet* provides a structuring matrix for the *Wake* rests upon the presupposition that the repetition of echoes and correspondences with *Hamlet* pushes the reader toward the "text not present in the linearity" (Riffaterre 1978, 12) of the *Wake*, pointing toward the absent matrix that determines the text's structure and thus its full significance.

tion of allusions. Cheng's principles of legitimatization also support Frances Motz Boldereff's claim that "in *Finnegans Wake* [Joyce] has given us an accurate account of Ireland from her beginning," as "there is not a single page of *Finnegans Wake* which does not contain a direct reference to Ireland" (1959, iii, xi); Harry Burrell's insistence that "the third chapter of Genesis . . . is the narrative base of *Finnegans Wake*" because "virtually every page has the Bible story as its basic level of communication" (1996, 7); Donald Phillip Verene's articulation of the widely held assertion that as "Joyce alludes to Vico throughout" the *Wake*, the *Scienza nuova* is "fundamental . . . in the thematic and structural sense" (1987, 85); and John Bishop's declaration that it seems "impossible for any reader seriously interested in coming to terms with *Finnegans Wake* to ignore *The Interpretation of Dreams*," as Freud's text "is everywhere implicit" (1986, 16).

Such contextual potentiality and plurality open up the *Wake* once again to decentered undecidability, necessitating the introduction of a distinguishing "hierarchy of allusion." Organizing his revelations of Shakespearean correspondences in the *Wake* along the lines of Atherton's assertion that Wakean allusions can be categorized into the lexical and the structural, Cheng asserts that "the scaffolding in *Finnegans Wake* is in fact multiplex" (1984, 6), being composed of three major Shakespearean matrixes: *Hamlet*, *Macbeth/Julius Caesar*, and *A Midsummer Night's Dream*. However, *Hamlet* is "foremost" among these matrixes in so far as "its thematic relevance to the book is comprehensive and manifold; thus *Hamlet* allusions are discovered throughout the *Wake*, not merely in occasional 'clusters' built around single themes (as with allusions to *Macbeth*, *Julius Caesar*, and *A Midsummer Night's Dream*)" (Cheng 1984, 54). By virtue of its sheer allusive frequency, *Hamlet* is approached as a metacontext that synthesizes *Finnegans Wake* as a whole, while allusions to *Macbeth/Julius Caesar* or *A Midsummer Night's Dream* are allowed only limited and localized signifying possibility owing to their confinement to a "single theme" (respectively, familial power struggles and the thematics of dreaming). However, as Cheng acknowledges, this hierarchical structure is troubled by "shared" or "multiplex" allusions which present a "coupling of two verbal echoes" (Cheng 1984, 10). How, by these criteria, shall we approach strings of Wakean text such as "frai is frau" (94.15), in which a reader may detect traces of both Hamlet's "frailty thy name is woman" (I, ii, 146; German *Frau*) and *Macbeth's* "fair is foul and foul is fair" (I, i, 10). Or the *Wake's* final paragraph, in which the lines "Take. Bussoftlhee, mememormee! Till thousendsthee. Lps. The keys to. Given! A way" (628.14–15) appear to weave together echoes of *Hamlet* ("But soft! methinks I scent the morning air" [I, v, 58]) and *Measure for Measure* ("O, take those lips away"; "Little have you to say / When you depart from him, but, soft and low, 'Remember now my brother'" [VI, I, 6, 67–69])? Are we to infer that the *Hamlet* allusions operate in a thematically and structurally significant way in which the simultaneous Shakespeare allusions may not? As I will presently argue, Cheng's suggestion that "context provides the best clue" (1984, 10) for resolving such instances fails to rigorously confront the methodological complications that arise here. However, for now it is worth highlighting that it appears that if the matrix text model's "frequency criterion" hinges upon a selective elision of the multiplicity and heterogeneity of the Wakean allusive complex, then its concomitant "hierarchization criterion" passes over the text's allusive simultaneity.

Given these complications for the case that allusive frequency substantiates the exclusive claim of any one hierarchically privileged text to contextualize and synthesize the *Wake's* whole, most proponents of the model further support their proposed matrix by highlighting significant character correspondences between the *Wake* and the structuring text. For Cheng, "Shakespearean allusion becomes a leitmotif by which the reader can identify the presence of a character" (1984, 9). Once again, Glasheen's model offers the prototype in the form of thirteen pages of schematized character correspondences (1977, lxxii–lxxxiv). The argument for the supreme importance of *Hamlet* for the *Wake* is thus pinned on the "frequency, precision and insistence" of the character correspondences, which cast HCE as King Hamlet, ALP as Gertrude, Shem as Prince Hamlet, Shaun as Laertes (and/or Polonius), and Issy as Ophelia (Cheng 1984, 6–7). Even if *Hamlet* and *Macbeth* possess similarly Wakean themes of the overthrow of a father figure "which results in a power struggle between two filial figures" (Cheng 1984, 7), only *Hamlet* possesses a constellation of characters that can be made to correspond directly to the *Wake's* five notoriously protean central characters; *Macbeth,* for example, has no obvious Issy correspondent. Thus parallels with *Hamlet* shape and define the *Wake*'s *dramatis personae* and their relations in ways that other allusive targets do not.

However, a closer look at the makeup of allusions throughout the *Wake* reveals a high degree of noncorrespondence throughout Glasheen's index of suggested character counterparts. With regard to the *Wake*'s *Hamlet* constellation, we find that it is Shaun, and not Shem, who regards "home" as a place "where it is nobler in the main to supper than the boys and errors of outrager's fortune" (434.04–05).[9] Cheng accommodates such instances of noncorrespondence for Shem and Shaun by evoking the concept of "Shakespearean reversals" that solicit "a tension between form and function," thereby "housing a meaning that defies the ostensibly familiar" (1985, 60–61).

While Cheng's analysis of such Shakespearean role reversals between the notoriously interchangeable twins is germane and rigorously supported by appropriate examples, by casting a wider net we find that its logic does not account for the great deal of less tidy noncorrespondences. For instance, ALP's closing monologue in book 4 echoes the Ghost's parting words to his son in *Hamlet* act 1, scene 5, throughout. These resonances take a number of forms, as in ALP's repeated motif "soft morning,"[10] her persistent urges to "list,"[11] and her final plea to "mememormee" (628.14).[12] As ALP's words echo King Hamlet's and not Gertrude's, the anticipated

---

9. Echoing Hamlet's contemplation of "whether 'tis nobler in the mind to suffer / The slings and arrows of outrageous fortune" (III, i, 57–58).

10. Suggesting the ghost's "But soft, methinks I scent the morning air" (I, v, 58); as in ALP's "Soft morning" (619.20), "the softest morning" (621.08), "So soft this morning, ours" (628.08), and "Bussoftlhee" (628.14).

11. Evoking the ghost's "List, list, O, list!" (I, v, 22); collocated with the "soft morning" echo in "Soft morning, city! Lsp! . . . Lpf! . . . Lispn!" (619.20–22), and resonating in approximations such as "Lst!" (621.17), "Lss" (624.06), and, perhaps, "Lps" (628.15).

12. Echoing the ghost's parting plea to Hamlet to "Remember me!" (I, v, 91). Note how this allusion is collocated with the King Hamlet "soft morning" allusions in "it is the softest morning that ever I can ever remember me" (621.08) and "Bussoftlhee, mememormee!" (628.14).

character identifications, as outlined by the rules of allusive correspondence, are disappointed.

If we posit that, in line with Cheng's theory of Shakespearean reversals, it is appropriate that ALP should swap roles with her husband's *Hamlet* counterpart, we still need to account for the fact that it is ALP, advising
Issy on affairs of the heart in her role as "gramma" (268.24) in book 2,
chapter 2, who poses the prince's question "to me or not to me. Satis thy
quest on" (269.19–20).[13] If we want to look for evidence of localized reversals between mother and daughter, we must ultimately admit that even this
character correspondence between ALP and Hamlet is not locally stable
in the text, as Issy herself, in the same "Nightlessons" chapter, echoes the
prince's assertion that "there's a divinity that shapes our ends" (V, ii, 10)
when she speaks of a "diminitive that chafes our ends" (278.F2). How well,
then, can the proposed structural *Hamlet* model hold up if the purported
character correspondences are not universal, "frequent, precise, and insistent" (Cheng 1984, 6), but rather local, sporadic, transient, and fluid?

In order to accommodate such moments of noncorrespondence to
the proposed matrix text, Cheng offers an alternative reading of the function of some *Hamlet* echoes in the *Wake* by turning to the potential contexts provided by the allusion's immediate co-text. Cheng examines the
Wakean clause "to begin properly SPQueaRking" (455.28) in this manner. He asserts that the simultaneous echoes of Horatio's "the graves stood
tenantless and the sheeted dead / Did squeak and gibber in the Roman
streets" (I, i, 115–16) and of SPQR (the historical abbreviation signifying
the Senate and People of Rome) are best understood as amplifications
of the themes of Apocalypse and the Last Day with which the relevant
Wakean passage is concerned (1984, 11). Regarding the allusion to Hamlet's assertion that "though I am native here / And to the manner born,
it is a custom / More honored in the breach than the observance" (I, iv,
14–16) in "manorwombanborn" (55.10), Cheng insists that "we need not
worry . . . about all the meanings and implications of the Shakespearean
lines themselves, nor about how Joyce might be reflecting or commenting

---

13. Echoing Hamlet's "To be or not to be—that is the question" (III, i, 56).

upon them—for he is not. He is merely picking up the verbal echo of 'to the manhor bourne' to fashion a pun which suits his own context: in this passage the taverner HCE, defending himself against accusations leveled at him, is claiming to be a gentleman and a nobleman, one not only born to the manner and customs of the nobility, but, literally, born in a baronial manor" (Cheng 1984, 12).

A number of previously cited concerns present themselves. For instance, if the portmanteau "manorwombanborn" may also evoke a schematic image of *Macbeth*'s "none of woman born / Shall harm Macbeth" (IV, i, 86–87), then yet again the text's simultaneous allusion to *Hamlet* and *Macbeth* seems to trouble any clear differentiation between global and local allusive functions. Yet, I want to argue that it is in this particular move of his argument that we find in Cheng's reading what Paul De Man characterizes as the "constitutive discrepancy, in critical discourse, between the blindness of the statement and the insight of the meaning" (De Man 1983, 110).

Faced with the challenge of such global noncorrespondence, or reversals, Cheng here makes a significant turn to the potential contexts provided by the allusion's immediate co-text, even as this move seems to undermine directly the matrix model's more structuralist and universalist metacontextual claims. Significantly, the contradiction between a localized contextual approach to this *Hamlet* allusion as it is anchored by its co-text and the assertion of the metacontextual force of others is not reconciled in Cheng's analysis, even as it exposes the possibility that in each case of an inferred *Hamlet* echo, co-textual justifications present themselves that do not require or support such overarching schematic patterns. For instance, if ALP's "Soft morning, city!" (619.20) monologue in the *Wake*'s *ricorso* suggests a potentially immediate co-textual narrative force insofar as it depicts the speaker "passing out" (627.34) as the *Wake*'s night is coming to an end, then the Ghost's words—a parting farewell on his return to purgatory, brought on by the cock's crow that signals the night's end—could be inferred as providing a congenial local context, without the need to justify breaking from a series of externally imposed rules of character correspondence between ALP and Gertrude.

The issue of co-text raises the crucial problem of the *Wake's* grammar as it relates to context. Recent work on the *Wake's* approach to sentence structure has shown that if we "make a distinction between techniques that strain the order for which [the equation between meaningful thought and logical proposition] stands . . . and techniques that dispense with it altogether" we find that the *Wake's* language tends not toward radical ungrammaticality but rather "syntactic impracticality" (Borg 2007, 79–80).[14] As Cheng's insight of the contextualizing potential of co-text reveals, some semblance of semantic information can be discerned from treating the Wakean text as syntactically and semantically predictable, while acknowledging its "deliberate rejection of any principle of good measure" (Borg 2007, 80). Thus, pragmatic interpretations of Wakean passages can be attempted by utilizing conceived allusions (to *Hamlet,* etc.) to anchor and contextualize the local information provided by the passage's exploitations of the English linguistic code. In this approach— which is perhaps somewhat closer to what we more conventionally term "reading"—focus is shifted from a discussion of what an allusion to *Hamlet* means for the structural principles of *Finnegans Wake* globally to a consideration of how such resonances might be influenced by, and in turn influence, their immediate co-text.

A case in point: at the outset of his lustful and reproachful sermon to Issy in book 3, chapter 2, Jaun recounts an anecdote from "Father Mike, P.P." concerning "how he [Father Mike] had been confarreating teat-a-teat with two viragos intactas about . . . what a lawful day it was, there and then, for a consommation with an effusion" (432.10–14), expanding, a few lines down, that this "consommation" is a "fate's to be wished for" (432.33; cf.

14. Margot Norris has likewise noted "we can . . . concede that, in spite of its many portmanteaus and neologisms, the *Wake* exhibits general linguistic compatibility with English" (2009, 225) insofar as a significant number of its sentences exhibit a tendency toward analytic language syntax: SVO word order, prenoun adjectives, a preference for grammatical relationships over inflectional morphemes, etc. Thus, to the extent that any line of the *Wake* can be shown to exploit such analytic grammar, it becomes syntactically predictable, if not necessarily deterministic. See also Thwaites (2001, 168).

Cheng 1984, 170). Tracing the digressive grammar of the Wakean passage, an immediate narrative context can be conceived. Father Mike's anecdote concerns his marrying (confarreation as a ceremony of ancient Roman patrician marriage) a couple (*virgo intacta*, of course) and informing them what a "lawful day" their wedding day is for consummating their love with an emission (and an effusive one at that). As his words do not echo Laertes or Polonius, but rather Hamlet's characterization of death as "a consummation / Devoutly to be wished" (III, i, 63–64),[15] Jaun's allusion does not adhere to the model of intertextual character correspondence, nor does it seem to offer a fixed evocation of the Wakean night or *Hamlet*'s thematic elements. The echo does, however, provide a potential contextual space in which to infer Jaun's deeper purpose for relating the story. While dutifully passing on the good Father's advocacy of pre-marital abstinence to Issy, encouraging her to wait for that "lawful day" to consummate, Jaun's *Hamlet* allusion implies that such a sexual union with his sister is exactly the "consummation" for which he himself is devoutly wishing—an implication supported by a number of coinciding double entendres, such as rendering *tête-à-tête* as "teat-a-teat." Significantly, here, elision may be just as revealing as allusive fidelity, and it is telling that the "devoutly" of the *Hamlet* quote is entirely absent from Jaun's less than pious sermon.

An alternative hermeneutic possibility, implied but unstated in the unfolding of the matrix text model, thus presents itself—one that constitutes an understanding of such echoes as potentially locally contextual, rather than deterministically matrical. For instance, the *Wake*'s first major *Hamlet* allusion occurs with the declaration that Finnegan was "of the first . . . to bare arms and a name" (5.05; cf. Cheng 1984, 113). In a reading that conceives either a localized or global presence of Shakespeare's play, it can be persuasively inferred that the line alludes to the scene in which the two clowns, digging Ophelia's grave, punningly infer that Adam was the first to bear arms, as "scripture says Adam digged. Could he dig without arms?"

15. See Cheng 1984, 170. Expanding on a suggestion first made by Hodgart (1953, 741), Cheng further proposes that Jaun's entire sermon to Issy parallels Laertes' address to Ophelia in *Hamlet* act 1, scene 3 (Cheng 1984, 69–72).

(V, i, 28–36). If the function of the allusion is to evoke an absent matrix as metacontext in order to guide the reader toward the structure and themes of *Finnegans Wake*, or to schematize its characters and their relationships, the text could just as easily allude to *any* quote from *Hamlet* with the same result—the allusions would be interchangeable, and their positions in the text purely arbitrary (which, of course, they might be). Finnegan is, however, the first Man in the *Wake's* universe, as Adam, and is about to be waked and buried. *Hamlet*, it would seem, has been bypassed as a thematic signifier or structural matrix in order to facilitate the conditions for a potential contextual space within which Adam may be collocated with grave digging, concerns relevant to the local Wakean narrative context if not globally to the Shakespearean play.

And yet, while considering the "arms and a name" clause within a Hamletian context places Shakespeare's play in a privileged position for anchoring and shaping the passage's meaning, is it not equally persuasive to posit an alternative conceptual context? Within a different cognitive environment of schematic knowledges and biases, might not the line evoke a schematic image of the opening line of Virgil's *Aenid* ("I sing of arms and the man")? Or, perhaps, an image of Vico's *giganti*, who engaged in primal acts of arming and naming, which could be activated just as legitimately if the reader's contextual frame has been influenced by the many Vichian elements of the immediate co-text.[16] Correspondingly, the details of Yawn's "Father Mike" anecdote do not lead inevitably to a Hamletian context and pragmatic inference of a desired sexual consummation. For example, if the co-occurring phrase "larries ate pignatties" (432.15) evokes the image of *Lares et Penates*, the Roman gods of hearth and home related to the domestication of the religious ritual of libation (the act of pouring the first few drops of wine onto the household altar in religious offering) then the "consommation with an effusion" (432.10–14) that Mike and Jaun desire may just as easily be a drink (French, *consommation*). Thus, it

16. For example, the density of heraldic terms in the paragraph ("His crest of huroldry," 5.06, etc.) might evoke Vico's assignation of heraldry as the language of the "heroic age."

appears that the insight of a localized rather than structural context suffers from its own blindness to the radically subjective and contingent nature of context itself: these anchored contextual spaces are not only local and nondeterministic, but are also, it seems, strictly unnecessary.

A common understanding of the function of context might consider the notion that "we know the lion by his claw" to be intuitive and unproblematic. However, this model for the relation of text to context in the process of creating pragmatic inferences is complicated by the radical inaccessibility and contingency of the unique contexts that individual readers bring to bear upon any text. In Ludwig Wittgenstein's oft-referenced aphorism that "if a lion could talk, we wouldn't be able to understand it" (2009, 235[e]), he highlights that while the relationship between the signifier and signified (between the claw and the lion, as it were) is impossible without relation to context, this context is not referential or substantial—not a mapping of shared, recoverable, and duplicable conditions "on the ground"—but rather a conceptual and subjective aspect of an individual cognitive environment shaped by its schematic biases, knowledges, and experiences.[17] As H. G. Widdowson insists, the context within which one infers the pragmatic significance of textually encoded semantic details (even those which are as impractical as the *Wake*'s) "cannot simply be the situation in which it occurs but the features of the situation that are taken as relevant." Context is "not what is *perceived* in a particular situation, but what is *conceived* as relevant." In other words, "context is not an external set of circumstances but a selection of them internally represented in the mind" (Widdowson 2007, 20–22).[18] Or, as the *Wake* advises its readers: "wipe your glosses with what you know" (304n3).

---

17. A schema, in this context, refers to a mental structure of preconceived ideas (comprising worldviews, archetypes, stereotypes, social roles, scripts) used to organize current knowledge and provide a framework for future understanding. Widdowson characterizes such schemata as the conceptual systems which constitute "the customary and conventional ways in which [a person's] socio-cultural reality is structured" into a "set of default assumptions" concerning how the world is perceived to work (2007, 53).

18. Even as the contingency of readers' positions in the literary event has become a critical commonplace, the purely conceptual nature of context is concealed from many

To the extent that *Finnegans Wake* solicits readings that bring their own conceptual contexts to bear upon the text, what it offers is not a total rupture of the operations of discourse, whereby coded meaning is related to conceived contexts in order to allow or hinder interlocutors to infer and share pragmatic meaning. Instead, by revealing context as a conceptual rather than a substantial force, the *Wake* exposes the radical contingency, and thus the problem, of context in all discourse. If the *Wake* is a space of extreme polysemantic simultaneity, this is because it is a space of radical contextual potentiality. And in the process of forging the conditions of such potentiality, the text demonstrates both the absence of the necessity of any given context and the fact that any particular context exists without having to do so in order for the text to engender meaning. As Derek Attridge suggests: "*Finnegans Wake* may not be an aberration of the literary but an unusually thoroughgoing exemplification of the literary, of the very conditions of existence of *Middlemarch* or *Sons and Lovers* as literary texts—namely the impossibility of ever being limited by originating intention, or external reference, or constraining context" (2004, 232).

How, then, shall we reappraise the matrix text model in light of its conflict with this problem of the contingency of context? Let us reconsider another representative example. In her study *The Steadfast "Finnegans Wake": A Textbook* (1994), Grace Eckley proffers W. T. Stead's mediumistic discourse as the *Wake's* structuring matrix. Eckley's line of argument, as summarized by Helen Sword, is a familiar one: "Earwicker's concealed identity as Stead . . . is Joyce's much-vaunted 'weapon of silence,' the key that neatly unlocks all the secrets of an otherwise enigmatic novel" (Sword 2002, 71). In her *Ghostwriting Modernism* (2002), Sword compares the

---

in their procedural readings to the extent that discourse communities tend to share broad, but by no means immutable, normative, or deterministic, points of reference. To tweak Wittgenstein's analogy, if a lion with a perfectly functioning knowledge of the grammar, lexicon, and morphology of the English language were to read *Hamlet*, there is no guarantee, given his schematic biases, knowledges, and experiences, that he would read it as a tragic tale of mourning and revenge in the Kingdom of Denmark, and not, for example, as a manual for hunting wildebeest. (Often, it seems, the hapless reader of *Finnegans Wake* feels that she finds herself in the position of just such a lion reading *Hamlet*.)

hermeneutic model through which Eckley arrives at her thesis to that of suspicious critical responses to Shakespeare's authorship of the works attributed to him:

> Eckley's critical methodology—she reads even the most trivial details as evidence of encoded textual secrets . . . —bears an all-too-uncanny resemblance to that of the numerous anti-Stratfordians who have deployed anagrams, cryptograms, rearrangements of key passages, and even communications from the dead to "prove" that the true author of Shakespeare's plays was someone other than Shakespeare. Indeed, almost as if to anticipate approaches and claims such as Eckley's, *Finnegans Wake* contains numerous references to Shakespearean cryptograms, forgers, claimants, imitators, and alternate authorship theories . . . Where Eckley tries to decode *Finnegans Wake* by means of a single skeleton key, Joyce himself invokes cryptic specters and closeted skeletons that are clearly meant to raise multiple interpretations rather than lay them comfortably to rest. (2002, 71)[19]

Close attention to the logic of the matrix text model, its blindness and its insight, bears out Sword's stance that the *Wake* is more invested in creating the conditions for, and testing the operations of, a kind of radical contextual potentiality than coaxing the reader toward an enlightening absent matrix. My claim is that through its constant return to the motif of *tanquam ex ungue leonem*, the *Wake* willfully solicits and stages these

---

19. In a less generous mood, Martha Fodaski Black opens her review of Eckley's study with the charge that rather than successfully identifying the lion by his claw, "Eckley is like the blind man who felt the elephant's tail and concluded that the earth's largest mammal was a reptile" (1995, 441). Beyond the fact that its tone reveals that something more fundamental than analytical rigor is at stake in how it perceives Eckley's proposed model for reading the *Wake*, Black's review is informative to my argument at two other junctures: first when it critiques Eckley's monograph as "an overdetermined reading of Joyce's quintessentially indeterminate text," and second, and even more tellingly, when it comments that Eckley's reading "is more bemusing than amusing" as "Joyceans who accept the idea that *Finnegans Wake* concerns real people know that more important characters—like the *Hamlet* cast—will upstage Eckley's double man" (1995, 443/441).

critical conflicts, thereby exposing the means by which readings present a given context as natural and necessary, rather than contingent, in order to claim the authority to speak the "truth" about the text with a force that commands credulity. Given the plurality of potential pragmatic readings to which the Wakean critical canon attests, the question becomes not which reading offers the true or justified explication, or by what criteria we might distinguish reading the *Wake* from *mis*reading the *Wake*, but rather what is at stake when we make claims to authentic readings by presenting our conceived contexts as substantial? And what types of contexts and insights are these claims attempting to disqualify?

In part, the critical record suggests that this conflict between overdetermination and indeterminacy is staged between readers who hold stakes in more fundamental disagreements about structure and play, analogy and alterity, which relate to aesthetic, ethical, and ideological concerns that arise, in many ways, prior to the text. However, the *Wake* is not merely a kind of Rorschach test. Rather, following Sword's point that its "cryptic specters and closeted skeletons . . . are clearly meant to raise multiple interpretations rather than lay them comfortably to rest" (2002, 71), I would argue that the *Wake* is more a kind of textual machine for generating *mis*readings.

In revealing the dual operation of context as both contingent and inevitable—given both the general impossibility of sidestepping context in expressing a stance on the text and the *Wake*'s superabundance, rather than poverty, of potential contextual anchors—the *Wake* challenges us to encounter fully this problem of context, rather than to decide the dispute in favor of one side or the other by sanctioning certain kinds of reading. And toward fully staging this undecidability, matrix text readings are not superfluous to conversations on the *Wake*—mere misreadings to be consigned to the dustbin of history—but rather integral. The most attentive response to the *Wake*'s unusual forms might be neither to insist upon the necessity of a particular pragmatic reading nor to assert the possibility of foregoing contextualized reading altogether, but rather to formulate and present such readings while simultaneously disavowing their authority.

Returning to Hart's characterization of the problem of context as it relates to *Finnegans Wake* from this vantage point, we find that his argument is, in fact, paradigmatic of the solicited conflict between overde-termination and indeterminacy.[20] Even as he calls for a critically rigorous contemplation of the text's meaning through "hypotheses about its nature and purpose," Hart admits that there is no "common center" to the *Wake* (Hart 1992, 15). And in the light of the more radical problem of context staged in and by the *Wake*, Hart's call for a critical response to the text that uncovers a "common center" that he simultaneously concedes does not exist takes on added significance. It suggests that the *Wake*'s reader is "to double business bound" (*Hamlet* III, iii, 41).

Exiting the Matrix

In deference to this double business, I will conclude by performing my own matrix text reading in which I want to attend more closely to how such an act might illuminate the problem of context that I am suggest-ing *Finnegans Wake* forces us to confront. To that end, I will explore the possibilities provided by a single allusive unit, the relatively transparent "any camelot prince of dinmurk" (143.07), as a motivated manipulation of the reader's schematic knowledge in order to activate a potential, but by no means determined, Hamletian conceptual context that might shape pragmatic interpretation.[21]

Despite the initial impression that the rather long and involved ninth question of the Quiz chapter (143.03–28)—in which we find the "any camelot prince of dinmurk" (143.07) *Hamlet* echo—constitutes a series of unrelated and ungrammatical clauses, a consideration of its potential exploitations of the English linguistic code suggests that the sentence is

20. Indeed, as Hart notes, Joyce himself was the *Wake*'s first reader to apply this dual hermeneutic to the text, through his "frequent vacillations between the total com-mitment to the unconscious response and the rational semirepudiations of that commit-ment—the claim that explication and hard work are necessary" (1992, 17).

21. As such close analysis necessitates constant reference to the allusion's co-text and peculiar grammar, it is recommended that the interested reader keep the passage (143.03–28) close at hand as a reference. For a complementary, and much more detailed, close reading of the passage's syntactic and Shakespearean elements, see Slote 1994.

indeed syntactically predictable, despite the extremely hypotactic nature of its grammar. Investigating its simultaneous syntactic conformity and impracticality, Sam Slote characterizes the long sentence as paradigmatic of the *Wake's* tension between overdetermination and indeterminacy. Singling out the passage "for its especially convoluted syntax," Slote parses the "six syntactic parts or main syntagms" of its "twisted syntax" in pursuit of "a more substantial and precise reading." Such close attention to detail, however, ultimately reveals that the sentence's many digressions "away from the subject—the ostensive syntactic concern" offer a "breakdown in syntactic structure" that "destabilizes the status of the question" (Slote 1994, 69–70). And yet, by observing Tony Thwaites's advice that "sometimes the only way to follow the structure of a *Wake* sentence is to keep one's finger firmly on the grammatical subject until the verb arrives" (2001, 168), we find that, among a number of slightly divergent possibilities, the line can be parsed as "if a human being . . . were . . . accorded . . . with an earsighted view of old hopeinhaven . . . then what would that fargazer seem to seemself to seem seeming of . . . ?" (143.03–27).

By considering the *Hamlet* allusion "any camelot prince of dinmurk" in isolation from this potential main clause, the echo loses the force of its possible syntagmatic relations, and critics, by necessity, utilize the allusion to reflect on the source material. Thus, working outside the frame of the immediate Wakean co-text, Cheng offers a pragmatic interpretation of "any camelot prince of dinmurk" with the observation that "what worries Hamlet and makes him hesitate is that he is in the dark (a prince of dinmurk)" (1984, 57). The alluded-to text, rather than the alluding, provides the sole context in which interpretation is attempted, despite Cheng's assertion that "rarely does an allusion to another work involve interpreting the material alluded to" (1984, 11). The upshot is that what the allusion suggests about the "human being" at the Wakean sentence's core, who is "as hapless behind the dreams of accuracy as any camelot prince of dinmurk" (143.06–07), remains unexplored.

Placing the allusion back into its co-text, we read: "Now, *to be* on anew and *basking* again in the panaroma of all flores of speech, if a human being duly fatigued by his dayety in the sooty, having plenxty off time on his gouty hands and vacants of space at his sleepish feet and as hapless behind the dreams of accuracy as *any camelot prince of dinmurk*" (143.03–07; emphasis added). If a Hamletian conceptual context has been activated in a particular reader's cognitive environment by the impending "prince of dinmurk" allusion, then the opening "to be" might be anagnostically invested with added allusive potential, thus evoking a schematic image of Hamlet's fourth soliloquy and its famous consideration of whether it is better "to be or not to be" (III, i, 57; cf. Cheng 1984, 65–66).

This inference is not only suggested by the evocative lexical element of "any camelot prince of dinmurk," but appears to be encoded in the very grammar of the passage. As Slote highlights, the lexical unit "being" in "human being" is "yoked as both a qualification of the ostensive subject (the human) and as an indefinite present participle" (1994, 72). If we privilege this latter grammatical function in our reading, then, following on from the gerund forms "being" and "having," for the line to make syntactic sense it should read: "if a human[,] *being* duly fatigued by his dayety in the sooty, *having* plenxty off time on his gouty hands . . . and [*being*] as hapless behind the dreams of accuracy as any camelot prince of dinmurk" (143.04–07; emphasis added).

The gerund "being" is grammatically necessary in the final clause, yet, as in the case of Jaun's "devoutly," conspicuous by its absence. If the conceived *Hamlet* allusion opens up a contextual space within which this absent "being" might contribute to an understanding of the line as treating a dichotomy of states of being and not being ("to be or not to be"), it assumes added relevance if one notices that the clause in which the "human" is "being" deals with waking hours during his day in the city ("his dayety in the sooty"), and that in the clause in which it is *not* being, the "human" is "hapless behind the dreams of accuracy" (143.04–07). As Hamlet compares the loss of being through death to sleep, so, it seems, the Wakean passage concerns the human being's "ingredient and egregiunt whights and ways" (143.10–11)[22] in a construction that moves from

---

22. That is to say, its entering ("ingredient" from Latin *in-gradia*, "to walk in") and exiting (Latin *egredi*, "to step out") of nights and days ("whights and ways").

the active voice to the passive—from a human who is "being" during his "dayety in the sooty," to one who, in sleep, might be "accorded . . . with an ear-sighted view of old hopeinhaven" (143.09–10).

If this schematic image of a sleeper's journey from dusk till dawn has been activated by keying the line's lexical and grammatical features into a contextual space opened up by the *Hamlet* allusion, then any number of the passage's diverse details can begin to appear pertinent to this interpretation. As Horatio has heard how "the cock, that is the trumpet to the morn, doth . . . awake the god of day" and force King Hamlet's ghost to "[fade] on the crowing of the cock" (I, i, 132–39), so the human being's night lasts "till intempestuous Nox should catch the gallicry and spot lucan's dawn" (143.16–17),[23] when the "gallicry" (cockcrow) reawakens the Wakean passage's "dayety" (a deity of the day).

Once this schematic image has been activated, we find we are no longer bound to our original parsing of the line's grammar in order to argue for the validity of this reading, as this signification of *not* being in sleep might be inscribed into other potential parsings such as: "if a human being . . . were at this auctual futule preteriting *unstant*" (143.03/07–08; emphasis added; cf. Slote 1994, 74). As a negation of the Latin *instant*, the present participle of *instare* ("to be present"), "unstant" presents us with a "human being" who is not present at a non-instant. Thus, as it ceases "to be," the "human being" enters "the states of suspensive exanimation" (143.08–09; Latin *exanimatus*, "to deprive of life") to become "a none" (143.15) and a "nihilant" (143.20; Latin *nihil*, "nothing"). In this context, Cheng intriguingly suggests that as the question centers on what this human (not) being would "seem to seemself to seem seeming of" (143.26–27), the line finally evokes Hamlet's rebuke to Gertrude: "Seems, madam? Nay, it is, I know not 'seems'" (I, ii, 76; Cheng 1984, 129). This inference provides the ground for a satisfying reversal of the dichotomy of

23. In other words, the sleeper's "Nox" (Latin, "night") lasts until the "gallicry" (the cry of the Latin *gallus*, "cock") signals dawn's shining ("lucan's," from the Latin *lucens*, "shining").

being and seeming set up in the *Hamlet* quote, suggesting that the sleeping "human being," lying still as a corpse, possesses all of the uncanny qualities of "seeming" and none of "being" (cf. McCarthy 1980, 76).

Thus, we find that the development of the question's subject from a "human being" to a "fargazer" hinges upon this central comparative image of "any camelot prince of dinmurk": any one of a series of passive, disindividualized sleepers or corpses who have made the transition from being to not being. Presented as a performance in which the "principal" character ("prince") is absent ("unstant," a "none") and in a state of "seeming," sleep or death becomes a case of "Hamlet without the Prince."

As the conceived context allows us to invest these details with successful pragmatic inferences, increasingly we feel that really we do "know the lion by his claw." However, lest we consider all instances of lexical units such as "to be" or "seems" to allude to *Hamlet*, we must admit that this context is in no way deterministically encoded in the text itself. Furthermore, given that most readers possess routine knowledge that cocks crow at dawn, the "gallicry" that brings "lucan's dawn" may constitute an allusion to *Hamlet* only within a particular conceptualization, which is by no means inevitable, absolute, or even necessary for arriving at the pragmatic inference that these crowing cocks signify the end of night. Indeed, these schematic images might not be activated at all if the text's lexical and grammatical encodings are interpreted within the potential contextual spaces opened up by any of its other echoes. If allusions to the Vichian cycle ("the course of his tory will had been having recourses" [143.12]) anchor the text to a context of ricorso and rebirth, then these lexically and grammatically encoded juxtapositions of "being" and "not being" might be interpreted as signifying a cyclical pattern of death and resurrection. Had the allusions to other Shakespearean plays ("hereby hang of the Hoel of it" [143.15], for example, echoing *As You Like It*'s "thereby hangs a tale" [II, ii, 26–28]) or biblical tales (Jacob and Esau; Shem, Ham, and Japhet) shaped the contextual space through their conceived relevance, the inferred pragmatic significance of these lexical and grammatical elements would have been different again. In a passage that boasts such a plenitude of literary allusion, the *Hamlet* echo offers merely one potential, but ultimately unnecessary, contextual anchor. It bears the capacity to influence what information is and is not conceived as relevant, without presiding exclusively over the passage. Perhaps this is why the *Wake*'s response to the question of what the "human being" would "seem to seemself to seem seeming of" is "Answer: A collideorscape!" or kaleidoscope (143.28). In the end, it transpires that the camel in "any camelot prince of dinmurk" is much like Hamlet's amorphous cloud, which may seem "in shape of a camel," "like a weasel," or "very like a whale" (III, ii, 361–67), depending on the vantage point of the reader.

The case that I am making is that Joyce's text highlights the impossibility of fixing meaning due to the plurality of potential conceptual contexts in any given instance of discourse, and thus exposes the struggle for authority at stake in competing attempts to fix a particular context as natural and determined. And yet, it also acknowledges the necessity of formulating such readings, while impressing the imperative that we admit the contingency of our own readings in order to disavow their authority. Jean-Michel Rabaté highlights the centrality of this stance to Joyce's aesthetic and politico-ethical project:

> Stephen is eager to avoid any subjective reduction of his theory to its position of enunciation . . . This is . . . the attitude one sees him taking at the end of his Shakespeare discussion in "Scylla and Charybdis" in *Ulysses* when he confesses that he does not believe in his own theory. The really "sublime" moment occurs when the author of the theory can renounce the paternity of the discourse, cutting as it were the umbilical cord linking the words to their enunciator, thus letting the theory follow its own course. (Rabaté 2001, 78)

For many readers, this creation of a space of radical self-reflexive, and antiauthoritarian, potentiality and undecidability is not enough. Hart characterizes not only the desirability but also the necessity of some form of matrix text or center in the following terms:

> The exploration of rich implications in *Hamlet* is unproblematical because there is little doubt about the underlying thrust of the text. The first scene is about people waiting for a ghost, not about baking a cake. But in large parts of *Finnegans Wake* such simple certainties are, even

now, wholly lacking. Some passages may well be about ghosts and cakes and many other things simultaneously, but they are not about anything and everything we may care to name—or, if they are, there is almost literally no book to read and nothing of interest to take us out of our own minds. (1992, 30)

Against Hart's pessimistic view I offer the idea that the *Wake*'s significance lies, in part, in exactly this program of dismantling the rhetorical strategies of authority by laying bear the problem of context and exposing the degree to which all reading occurs in "our own minds." If "Shakespeare and his oeuvre lie at the core of the proliferating text" of *Finnegans Wake* (Laroque 2013, 57), it might be because Joyce's text, too, is an upstart crow beautified with our feathers.

Works Cited

Contributors

Index

Works Cited

Akrigg, G. P. V. 1968. *Shakespeare and the Earl of Southampton*. London: Hamish Hamilton.

Aristotle. 1981. *Poetics*. Translated by Leon Golden. Tallahassee: Florida State Univ. Press.

Atherton, James S. (1959) 2009. *The Books at the Wake: A Study of Literary Allusions in James Joyce's Finnegans Wake*. Reprint, Carbondale, IL: Southern Illinois Univ. Press.

Attridge, Derek. 2004. *Peculiar Language: Literature as Difference from the Renaissance to James Joyce*. London: Routledge.

Attridge, Derek, and Marjorie Howes, eds. 2000. *Semicolonial Joyce*. Cambridge: Cambridge Univ. Press.

Bacon, Francis. 2002. *Francis Bacon: The Major Works*. Edited by Brian Vickers. Oxford: Oxford Univ. Press.

Ball, Robert Hamilton. 1968. *Shakespeare on Silent Film: A Strange Eventful History*. London: George Allen and Unwin.

Bamber, Linda. 1982. *Comic Women, Tragic Men. A Study of Gender and Genre in Shakespeare*. Stanford: Stanford Univ. Press.

Bénéjam, Valérie. 2008. "Charades and Gossip: The Minimalist Theatre of Joyce's *Dubliners*." *Journal of the Short Story in English* 51: 51–66.

Benjamin, Walter. 1973. *Illuminations*. London: Fontana.

Bersani, Leo. 2004. "Against *Ulysses*." In *James Joyce's Ulysses: A Casebook*, edited by Derek Attridge, 201–29. Oxford: Oxford Univ. Press.

Bevington, David, ed. 1998. *Troilus and Cressida*, by William Shakespeare. The Arden Shakespeare, 3d series. London: Bloomsbury Academic.

Bishop, John. 1986. *Joyce's Book of the Dark: Finnegans Wake*. Madison, WI: Univ. of Wisconsin Press.

Black, Martha Fodaski. 1995. Review of *The Steadfast "Finnegans Wake": A Textbook*, by Grace Eckley. *James Joyce Quarterly* 32, no. 2 (winter): 441–46.

Bloom, Harold. 1994. *The Western Canon*. London: Papermac.

Boas, Frederick S. 1896. *Shakespeare and His Predecessors*. 3d impr. London: John Murray.

Boldereff, Frances Motz. 1959. *Reading Finnegans Wake*. Woodward, PA: Classic Nonfiction Library.

Borges, Jorge Luis. 1998. "Tlön, Uqbar, Orbis Tertius." In *Collected Fictions*, translated by Andrew Hurley, 68–81. New York: Viking.

Booker, Keith. 1995. *Joyce, Bakhtin, and the Literary Imagination*. Ann Arbor: Michigan Univ. Press.

Borg, Ruben. 2007. *The Measureless Time of Joyce, Deleuze and Derrida*. London: Continuum.

Brandes, Georg. (1898) 1911. *William Shakespeare: A Critical Study*. Reprint, London: Heinemann.

Brewster, David. 1832. *The Life of Sir Isaac Newton*. New York: J. & J. Harper.

Brown, Richard. 1985. *James Joyce and Sexuality*. Cambridge: Cambridge Univ. Press.

———. 1997. "'Shakespeare Explained': James Joyce's Shakespeare from Victorian Burlesque to Postmodern Bard." In *Shakespeare and Ireland*, edited by Mark Thornton Burnett and Ramona Wray, 91–114. London: Palgrave Macmillan.

———. 1999. "Translation and Self-Translation through the Shakespearean Looking-Glasses in Joyce's *Ulysses*." In *Translating Life: Studies in Transpositional Æesthetics*, edited by Shirley Chew and Alistair Stead, 339–59. Liverpool: Liverpool Univ. Press.

Budgen, Frank. 1972. *James Joyce and the Making of Ulysses*. Oxford: Oxford Univ. Press.

Burkdall, Thomas. 2001. *Joycean Frames: Film and the Fiction of James Joyce*. London: Routledge.

Burnham, Michelle. 1990. "'Dark Lady and Fair Man': The Love Triangle in Shakespeare's Sonnets and Ulysses." *Studies in the Novel* 22, no. 1: 43–56.

Burrell, Harry. 1996. *Narrative Design in Finnegans Wake: The Wake Lock Picked*. Miami: Univ. Press of Florida.

Byron, May ("Maurice Clare"). 1913. *A Day With William Shakespeare*. London: Hodder and Stoughton.

Campbell, Joseph, and Henry Morton Robinson. 1944. *A Skeleton Key to Finnegans Wake*. New York: Harcourt, Brace.

Canning, A. S. 2004. *Shakespeare Studied in Eight Plays*. 1903. Reprint, London: Kessinger.

Cheng, Vincent J. 1984. *Shakespeare and Joyce: A Study of Finnegans Wake*. University Park and London: Penn State Univ. Press; and Gerrards Cross: Colin Smythe.

———. 1985. "Shakespearean Reversals in *Finnegans Wake*." *English Language Notes* 22, no. 3: 58–61.

———. 1995. *Joyce, Race, and Empire*. New York: Cambridge Univ. Press.

Cixous, Hélène. 1972. *The Exile of James Joyce*. Translated by Sally A. J. Purcell. New York: David Lewis.

Cole, Douglas. 1980. "Myth and Anti-Myth: The Case of *Troilus and Cressida*." *Shakespeare Quarterly* 31, no. 1: 76–84.

Coleridge, Samuel Taylor. 1985. *Samuel Taylor Coleridge*. Edited by H. J. Jackson. Oxford: Oxford Univ. Press.

Costello, Peter. 1992. *James Joyce, The Years of Growth: 1882–1915*. New York: Pantheon Books.

Crispi, Luca. 2004. "Manuscript Timeline 1905–1922." *Genetic Joyce Studies*, issue 4 (spring). http://www.antwerpjamesjoycecenter.com/GJS4/GJS4%20Crispi.htm.

Dante Alighieri. 1952. *The Divine Comedy of Dante Alighieri*. Translated by Charles Eliot Norton. Chicago: William Benton.

De Man, Paul. 1983. *Blindness and Insight: Essays in the Rhetoric of Contemporary Criticism*. 2d edition, rev. Introduction by Wlad Godzich. Minneapolis: Univ. of Minnesota Press.

Diamond, William. 1925. "Wilhelm Meister's Interpretation of Hamlet." *Modern Philology* 23, no. 1: 89–101.

Dodds, E. R. (1951) 2004. *The Greeks and the Irrational*. Reprint, Berkley: Univ. of California Press.

Dollimore, Jonathan, and Alan Sinfield, eds. 1985. *Political Shakespeare: New Essays in Cultural Materialism*. Manchester: Manchester Univ. Press.

Dowden, Edward. (1875) 1880. *Shakespere: A Critical Study of His Mind and His Art*. Reprint, New York: Harper and Brothers.

———. 1877. *Shakespeare Primer*. London: Macmillan.

———. (1893) 1906. *Introduction to Shakespeare*. Reprint, New York: Charles Scribner and Sons.

Eckley, Grace. 1994. *The Steadfast "Finnegans Wake": A Textbook*. Lanham: Univ. Press of America.

Eco, Umberto. 1989. *The Aesthetics of Chaosmos. The Middle Ages of James Joyce*. Translated by Ellen Esrock. Cambridge: Harvard Univ. Press.

Einboden, Jeffrey. 2005. "The Genesis of Weltliteratur: Goethe's *West-Östlicher Divan* and Kerygmatic Pluralism." *Literature and Theology* 19, no. 3: 238–50.

Eliot, T. S. (1919) 1975. "Hamlet." In *Selected Prose of T. S. Eliot*, edited by Frank Kermode, 45–49. Reprint, London: Faber and Faber.

———. 1923. "Ulysses, Order, and Myth." *The Dial* 75 (Nov.): 480–83.

Ellmann, Maud. 2003. "The Sixth Act: Shakespeare after Joyce." In *Shakespeare and Comedy*, edited by Peter Holland, 137–45. Vol. 56 of *Shakespeare Survey*. Cambridge: Cambridge Univ. Press.

Ellmann, Richard. 1972. *Ulysses on the Liffey*. London: Faber and Faber.

———. 1977. *The Consciousness of Joyce*. London: Faber and Faber.

———. 1982. *James Joyce*, new and rev. ed. New York: Oxford Univ. Press.

Farnham, Willard. 1969. "Introduction" to *Hamlet*. In *William Shakespeare: The Complete Works*, edited by Harbage et al., 931–32. Baltimore: Penguin Books.

Felperin, Howard. 1990. *The Uses of the Canon: Elizabethan Literature and Contemporary Theory*. Oxford: Clarendon.

Forker, Charles R., ed. 2002. *Richard II*, by William Shakespeare. The Arden Shakespeare. London: Thomson Learning.

Forkner, Ben. 2000. "Joycean Drama and the Remaking of Yeats's Irish Theatre in 'Ivy Day in the Committee Room.'" *Journal of the Short Story in English* 34: 89–108.

Foucault, Michel. 1984. "What is Enlightenment?" In *The Foucault Reader*, edited by Paul Rabinow, 39–42. London: Penguin.

French, Marilyn. 1981. *Shakespeare's Division of Experience*. New York: Summit.

Freud, Sigmund. (1909 [1908]) 1977. "Family Romances." In *On Sexuality*, edited by Angela Richards, 219–25. Vol. 7 of *The Pelican Freud Library*. Reprint, Harmondsworth: Penguin.

Fuchs, Dieter. 2011. "'Poor Penelope. Penelope Rich': Sir Philip Sidney's *Astrophil and Stella* as a Source for the Rewriting of the Odysseus-Archetype in James Joyce's *Ulysses*." *James Joyce Quarterly* 48, no. 2: 350–56.

Furbank, P. N. 1966. *Italo Svevo, the Man and the Writer*. London: Secker and Warburg.

Garber, Marjorie. 2005. *Shakespeare After All*. New York: Anchor/Random House.

Gay, Penny. 2002. "Women and Shakespearean Performance." In *The Cambridge Companion to Shakespeare on Stage*, edited by Stanley Wells and Sarah Stanton, 155–73. Cambridge: Cambridge Univ. Press.

Genette, Gérard. 1972. *Figures III*. Paris: Seuil.

Gibson, Andrew. 2002. *Joyce's Revenge: History, Politics, and Aesthetics in Ulysses*. Oxford: Oxford Univ. Press.

Gifford, Don, with Robert J. Seidman. 1988. *Ulysses Annotated: Notes for James Joyce's Ulysses*. Berkeley: Univ. of California Press.

Gilbert, Stuart. 1955. *James Joyce's "Ulysses."* New York: Vintage.

Gillespie, Gerald. 1992. "Afterthoughts of Hamlet: Goethe's Wilhelm, Joyce's Stephen." In *Comparative Literary History as Discourse*, edited by Mario J. Valdés, Daniel Javitch, and A. Owen Aldridge, 287–304. Bern: Peter Lang.

Gillespie, Michael Patrick. 1983. *Inverted Volumes Improperly Arranged: James Joyce and his Trieste Library*. Ann Arbor, Michigan: UMI Research Press.

Gillespie, Michael Patrick, and Erik Bradford Stocker, eds. 1986. *James Joyce's Trieste Library: A Catalogue of Materials at the Harry Ransom Humanities Research Center The Univ. of Texas at Austin*. Austin: Harry Ransom Humanities Research Center.

Girard, René. 2000. *A Theatre of Envy: William Shakespeare*. Exeter: Short Run.

Glasheen, Adaline. 1977. *Third Census of "Finnegans Wake."* Berkeley: Univ. of California Press.

Goethe, Johann Wolfgang von. 1995. *Wilhelm Meister's Apprenticeship*. Edited by Eric A. Blackall in cooperation with Victor Lange. Vol. 9 of *Goethe: The Collected Works*. Princeton: Princeton Univ. Press.

———. 1998. *Werke*. Edited by Erich Trunz. Band 7: *Wilhelm Meisters Lehrjahre*. München: Deutscher Taschenbuch Verlag.

Goldberg, S. L. 1961. *The Classical Temper: A Study of James Joyce's "Ulysses."* New York: Barnes and Noble.

Greenblatt, Stephen. 1980. *Renaissance Self-Fashioning: From More to Shakespeare*. Chicago: Univ. of Chicago Press.

———, ed. 1982a. *Genre* 15, no. 1–2.

———, ed. 1982b. *The Power of Forms in the English Renaissance*. Norman: Pilgrim Books.

Greenfield, Matthew A. 2000. "Fragments of Nationalism in *Troilus and Cressida*." *Shakespeare Quarterly* 51, no. 2: 181–200.

Groden, Michael. 1977. *Ulysses in Progress*. Princeton: Princeton Univ. Press.

———. 2007. "Joyce at Work on 'Cyclops': Toward a Biography of *Ulysses*." *James Joyce Quarterly* 44, no. 2: 217–45.

Groden, Michael, Hans Walter Gabler, A. Walton Litz, and Danis Rose, eds. 1978. *The James Joyce Archive*, Vol. 3. New York: Garland.

Gruber Benco, Aurelia. 1972. "Between Joyce and Benco." *James Joyce Quarterly* 9, no. 3 (Joyce & Trieste issue): 328–33.

Habicht, Werner. 2001. "Shakespeare Celebrations in Times of War." *Shakespeare Quarterly* 52, no. 4: 441–55.

Harris, Frank. 1909. *The Man Shakespeare and His Tragic Life-Story.* London: Frank Palmer.

Hart, Clive. 1962. *Structure and Motif in "Finnegans Wake."* Evanston: Northwestern Univ. Press.

———. 1992. *"Finnegans Wake* in Adjusted Perspective." In *Critical Essays on James Joyce's Finnegans Wake,* edited by Patrick A. McCarthy, 15–33. New York: G.K. Hall.

Haverkamp, Anselm. 2006. "The Ghost of History: Hamlet and the Politics of Paternity." *Law and Literature* 18, no. 2: 171–97.

Hayman, David. 1974. "Cyclops." In *James Joyce's Ulysses: Critical Essays,* edited by Clive Hart and David Hayman, 243–76. Berkeley: Univ. of California Press.

Henke, Suzette. 1990. *James Joyce and the Politics of Desire.* New York: Routledge.

Hodgart, Matthew J. C. 1953. "Shakespeare and Finnegans Wake." *The Cambridge Journal* 6, no. 12: 735–52.

Holderness, Graham, ed. 1992. *Shakespeare's History Plays: Richard II to Henry V.* New Casebook Series. London: Macmillan.

———. 2000. *Shakespeare: The Histories.* London: Macmillan.

Homer. 1982. *The Odyssey.* Translated by Robert Fitzgerald. New York: Knopf.

Howard, Tony. 2007. *Women as Hamlet: Performance and Interpretation in Theatre, Film and Fiction.* Cambridge: Cambridge Univ. Press.

Howe, Susanne. 1930. *Wilhelm Meister and his English Kinsmen: Apprentices to Life.* New York: Columbia Univ. Press.

Jenkins, Harold, ed. 1982. *Hamlet,* by William Shakespeare. The Arden Shakespeare. London: Thomson Learning.

Jones, Ernest. 1911. *Das Problem des Hamlet und der Ödipus-Komplex.* Übersetzt von Paul Tausig. Schriften zur angewandten Seelenkunde, 10. Leipzig: Franz Deuticke. (This is the title taken from Gillespie, 132; the title reprinted in Ellmann [1977, 114] reads: *Das Problema des Hamlet und des Ödipus-Komplex*).

Joyce, James. (1914) 1996. *Dubliners.* Edited by Robert Scholes and A. Walton Litz. Reprint, London: Penguin.

———. (1916) 1964. *A Portrait of the Artist as a Young Man.* Reprint, New York: Viking.

———. (1922) 1993. *Ulysses.* Edited by Jeri Johnson. Reprint, Oxford: Oxford Univ. Press.

———. (1939) 1959. *Finnegans Wake.* Reprint, New York: Viking.

———. (1944) 1963. *Stephen Hero.* Reprint, New York: New Directions.

———. 1966. *Letters of James Joyce.* Vol. 1, edited by Stuart Gilbert. Vols. 2 and 3, edited by Richard Ellmann. New York: Viking.

———. 1968. *Giacomo Joyce.* Edited by Richard Ellmann. London: Faber & Faber.

———. 1977–79. *The James Joyce Archive,* 63 vols. Edited by Michael Groden, Hans Walter Gabler, A. Walton Litz, and Danis Rose. New York: Garland.

———. (1921) 1979. *Exiles.* London: Jonathan Cape. Reprint, London: Panther/ Granada.

———. 1992. *Poems and Exiles.* Edited by J. C. C. Mays. New York: Penguin Books.

———. 2000. *Occasional, Critical and Political Writings.* Edited by Kevin Barry. Oxford: Oxford Univ. Press.

Joyce, Stanislaus. 1908 (Feb. 10). Triestine Book of Days. Unpublished manuscript held at the McFarlin Library, Univ. of Tulsa.

Kimball, Jean. 1988. "'Lui, C'Est Moi': The Brother Relationship in 'Ulysses.'" *James Joyce Quarterly* 25, no. 2 (winter): 227–35.

Kirby, Michael. 1971. *Futurist Performance.* New York: E. P. Dutton.

Kosters, Onno. 2010. "Review of Brown, Richard, *A Companion to James Joyce.*" *European English Messenger* 19, i (spring): 65–69.

Laman, Barbara. 2004. *James Joyce and German Theory: "The Romantic School and All That."* Madison, NJ: Fairleigh Dickinson Univ. Press.

Laroque, François. 2013. "'As Great Shapesphere puns it': The Name Game in Shakespeare and Joyce." In *Renascent Joyce,* edited by Daniel Ferrer, Sam Slote, and André Topia, 57–68. Gainesville: Univ. Press of Florida.

Lawrence, Karen. 1981. *The Odyssey of Style in Ulysses.* Princeton: Princeton Univ. Press.

Lee, Sir Sidney. 1898. *A Life of William Shakespeare.* London: Macmillan.

Leverenz, David. 1980. "The Woman in Hamlet." In *Representing Shakespeare,* edited by Murray Schwartz and Copélia Kahn, 122–40. Baltimore: Johns Hopkins Univ. Press.

Lounsbury, Thomas R. 1902. *Shakespeare and Voltaire*. New York: Charles Scribner's Sons.

Lovejoy, Arthur O. (1936) 1948. *The Great Chain of Being: A Study of the History of an Idea*. 3d impr. Cambridge, MA: Harvard Univ. Press.

Lukács, Georg. 1968. *Goethe and His Age*. London: Merlin.

Lupton, Julia Reinhard. 1997. "Othello Circumcised: Shakespeare and the Pauline Discourse on Nations." *Representations*, no. 57 (winter): 73–89. Berkeley: Univ. of California Press.

Maeterlinck, Maurice. 1912. *Wisdom and Destiny*. Translated by Alfred Sutro. New York: Dodd, Mead.

Mallarmé, Stéphane. 2003. *Œuvres complètes*, Vol. 2. Edited by Bertrand Marchal. Paris: Gallimard.

Marinetti, Filippo Tommaso. 1909. *Enquête Internationale sur le Vers Libre et Manifeste du Futurisme*. Milan: Editions de "Poesie."

———. 1910. "Futurist Speech to the English." In *Let's Murder the Moonshine: Selected Writings*, edited by R. W. Flint, 67–73. New York: Farrar, Strauss and Giroux.

———. *The Futurist Cookbook*. Edited by Lesley Chamberlain. London: Trefoil.

Massey, Gerald. 1866. *Shakespeare's Sonnets Never Before Interpreted*. London: Longmans.

Mays, J. C. C. 1992. *James Joyce, Poems and Exiles*. New York: Penguin Books.

McCarthy, Patrick A. 1980. *The Riddles of Finnegans Wake*. Cranbury, NJ: Associated Univ. Presses.

McCourt, John. 2000. *The Years of Bloom: James Joyce in Trieste 1904–1920*. Dublin: Lilliput.

———, ed. 2010. *Roll Away the Reel World: James Joyce and Cinema*. Cork: Cork Univ. Press.

Morley, John. (1871) 1886. *Voltaire*. London: Macmillan.

Nietzsche, Friedrich. 1910. *The Joyful Wisdom*. Translated by Thomas Common. Vol. 10 of *The Complete Works of Friedrich Nietzsche*. London: T. N. Foulis.

———. 1968. *The Will to Power*. Edited by Walter Kaufmann; translated by Walter Kaufmann and R. J. Holingdale. New York: Vintage.

Nolan, Emer. 1995. *James Joyce and Nationalism*. London: Routledge.

Norris, Margot. 2009. "Possible Worlds Theory and the Fantasy Universe of *Finnegans Wake*." In *James Joyce*, edited by Harold Bloom, 221–39. Bloom's Modern Critical Views. New York: Infobase.

Orgel, Stephen, ed. 1987. The Oxford Shakespeare: The Tempest. Oxford Univ. Press.

Palmer, Kenneth, ed. 1989. *Troilus and Cressida*, by William Shakespeare. The Arden Shakespeare. London: Routledge.

Pearson, Roberta E. and Uricchio, William. 2004. "Shakespeare and the Cultural Debate." In *The Silent Film Reader*, edited by Lee Grieveson and Peter Krämer, 145–55. London: Routledge.

Peery, William. 1951. "Shakhisbeard at *Finnegans Wake*." *Univ. of Texas in English* 30: 243–57.

Plock, Vike Martina. 2010. *Joyce, Medicine, and Modernity.* Gainesville: Univ. Press of Florida.

Quillian, William H. 1975. "Shakespeare in Trieste: Joyce's 1912 *Hamlet* Lectures." *James Joyce Quarterly* 12, no. 1–2: 7–63.

Rabaté, Jean-Michel. 2001. *James Joyce and the Politics of Egoism.* Cambridge: Cambridge Univ. Press.

———. 2007. "The Fourfold Root of Yawn's Unreason: Chapter III.3." In *How Joyce Wrote Finnegans Wake: A Chapter-by-Chapter Genetic Guide*, edited by Luca Crispi and Sam Slote, 384–409. Madison, WI: Univ. of Wisconsin Press.

Restivo, Giuseppina. 2004. "Country Time As She Likes It: The Country Ideology and the New Gentry in Shakespeare's As You Like It." In *International Shakespeare: the Comedies*, edited by Patricia Kennan and Mariangela Tempera, 41–73. Bologna: Clueb.

———. 2007. "Shylock and Equity in Shakespeare's Merchant of Venice." In *The Concept of Equity, An Interdisciplinary Assessment*, edited by Daniela Carpi, 223–49. Heidelberg: Universitätsverlag.

———. 2010. "La tempesta e la storia: ipotesi pre-illuministe" ("The Tempest and History: Pre-enlightenment Outlooks"). In *Strehler e oltre, il Galileo di Brecht e La tempesta di Shakespeare*, edited by Giuseppina Restivo, Renzo Crivelli, Anna Anzi, 219–68. Bologna: Clueb.

Riffaterre, Michael. 1978. *Semiotics of Poetry.* Bloomington: Indiana Univ. Press.

Rohrbach, Carl. 1859. *Shakespeare's Hamlet erläutert.* Berlin: Schneider.

Said, Edward W. 2003. *Orientalism.* London: Penguin.

Schneider, Erik. 2004. "Towards Ulysses: Some unpublished Joyce documents from Trieste." *Journal of Modern Literature* 27, no. 4: 1–16.

Schutte, William M. 1957. *Joyce and Shakespeare. A Study in the Meaning of Ulysses.* New Haven: Yale Univ. Press.

Senn, Fritz. 1962. "'Notes' on Dublin Theatres." A *Wake Newslitter*, old series, no. 2 (April): 5–8.

———. 1990. "Vexations of Group Reading: 'Transluding from the Otherman.'" In *Finnegans Wake: Fifty Years*, edited by Geert Lernout, 61–78. Amsterdam: Rodopi.

Serpieri, Alessandro. 1978. *"Othello," l'Eros negato. Psicoanalisi di una proiezione distruttiva.* Milan: Edizioni il Formichiere.

Shakespeare, William. 1969. *The Complete Works*. Edited by Alfred Harbage. Baltimore: Penguin Books.

Shaw, George Bernard. 1914. *The Doctor's Dilemma and The Dark Lady of the Sonnets.* Leipzig: Tauchnitz.

Shelley, Percy B. 1977. *Shelley's Poetry and Prose.* Edited by. Donald H. Reiman and Sharon B. Powers. New York: Norton.

Sidney, Sir Philip. 1962. "Astrophil and Stella." In *The Poems of Sir Philip Sidney*, edited by William A. Ringler Jr. Oxford: Clarendon.

Slataper, Scipio. 1944. *Ibsen.* Florence: Sansoni.

Slote, Sam. 1994. "Needles in the Camel's Eye: Concerning a Time of the 'Collideorscape.'" In *Finnegans Wake: Teems of Times*, edited by Andrew Treip, 69–80. Amsterdam: Rodopi.

———. 2008. "1904: A Space Odyssey." *Joyce Studies Annual* (2008): 163–71.

Spoo, Robert. 1989. "Teleology, Monocausality and Marriage in *Ulysses*." *ELH* 56, no. 2 (summer): 439–62.

Stanford, William B. 1963. *The Ulysses Theme: A Study in the Adaptability of a Traditional Hero.* 2d ed. Oxford: Blackwell.

Stone, Lawrence. 1972. *The Causes of the English Revolution 1529–1642.* London: Routledge & Kegan Paul.

Svevo, Italo. (1923) 1987. *La Coscienza di Zeno.* Reprint, Pordenone: Edizioni Studio Tesi.

———. 1972. *James Joyce.* Translated by Stanislaus Joyce. New York: City Lights.

Sword, Helen. 2002. *Ghostwriting Modernism.* Ithaca, NY: Cornell Univ. Press.

Tanner, Tony. 1979. *Adultery in the Novel, Contract and Trasgression.* Baltimore: Johns Hopkins Univ. Press.

Tennyson, Alfred Lord. 1986. "Ulysses." In *The Norton Anthology of English Literature*, edited by M. H. Abrams. 5th ed. New York: Norton.

Thwaites, Tony. 2001. *Joycean Temporalities: Debts, Promises, and Countersignatures.* Gainesville: Univ. Press of Florida.

Tillyard, E. M. W. (1942) 1972. *The Elizabethan World Picture*. Reprint, Harmondsworth: Penguin.

———. (1944) 1966. *Shakespeare's History Plays*. Reprint, Harmondsworth: Penguin.

Vaglio, Carla Marengo. 2006. "Noisetuning: Joyce and Futurism." In *Joyce's Victorians*, edited by Franca Ruggieri, 331. Vol. 9 of *Joyce Studies in Italy*. Rome: Bulzoni Editore.

Verene, Donald Phillip. 1987. *Vico and Joyce*. Albany: State Univ. of New York Press.

Viktus, Daniel J. 1997. "Turning Turk in *Othello*: The Conversion and Damnation of the Moor." *Shakespeare Quarterly* 48, no. 2 (summer): 145–76.

Vining, Edward P. 1881. *The Mystery of Hamlet. An Attempt to Solve an Old Problem*. Philadelphia: J. B. Lippincott.

Voltaire, Francois-Marie Arouet. 1973. Voltaire to Bernard Joseph Saurin, Dec. 4, 1765. In *The Complete Works of Voltaire*, Vol. 113. Edited by Theodore Besterman. Letter D13025. Banbury Oxfordshire: Cheney and Sons.

Walkowitz, Rebecca. 2006. *Cosmopolitan Style: Modernism Beyond the Nation*. New York: Columbia Univ. Press.

Wallace, Nathaniel Preston. 2005. "Shakespeare Biography and the Theory of Reconciliation in Edward Dowden and James Joyce." *ELH* 72, no. 4 (winter): 799–822.

Watson, G. J. 1987. "The Politics of *Ulysses*." In *Joyce's Ulysses: The Larger Perspective*, edited by Robert D. Newman and Weldon Thornton, 39–58. Newark: Univ. of Delaware Press.

Weimann, Robert. 1978. *Shakespeare and the Popular Tradition in the Theater: Studies in the Social Dimension of Dramatic Form and Function*. Baltimore: Johns Hopkins Univ. Press.

———. 2000. *Author's Pen and Actor's Voice: Playing and Writing in Shakespeare's Theatre*. Cambridge: Cambridge Univ. Press.

Welch, Robert. 1989. "Constitution, Language and Tradition in Nineteenth-Century Irish Poetry." In *Tradition and Influence in Anglo-Irish Poetry*, edited by Terence Brown and Nicholas Greene, 6–30. Basingstoke: Palgrave Macmillan.

Widdowson, H.G. 2007. *Discourse Analysis*. Oxford Introductions to Language Study. Oxford: Oxford Univ. Press.

Wilde, Oscar. (1921) 2003. *The Portrait of Mr. W. H.* Reprint, London: Hesperus.

Wilson, John Dover. 1911. *Life in Shakespeare's England*. Cambridge: Cambridge Univ. Press.

Wilson, Richard, ed. 1992. *New Historicism and Renaissance Drama*. London: Longman.

Wittgenstein, Ludwig. 2009. *Philosophische Untersuchungen / Philosophical Investigations*. Edited by P. M. S. Hacker and Joachim Schulte, translated by G. E. M. Anscombe, P. M. S. Hacker, and Joachim Schulte. Rev. 4th ed. Oxford: Wiley-Blackwell.

Contributors

VALÉRIE BÉNÉJAM is *Maître de Conférences* in English literature at the University of Nantes. She is a regular participant at James Joyce International Symposiums and a trustee of the International James Joyce Foundation. She has written many articles about Joyce, and co-edited with John Bishop a collection of essays, *Making Space in the Works of James Joyce* (Routledge, 2011), on the issue of Joyce's representations, across his work, of spatiality and space. She is currently working on a monograph about Joyce's fiction and theatricality entitled *Joyce's Novel Theatre*.

RICHARD BROWN is a reader in modern literature at the University of Leeds. He has published several articles on Joyce and contemporary British fiction, and four books on Joyce: *James Joyce and Sexuality* (Cambridge, 1985), *James Joyce: A Postculturalist Perspective* (Macmillan, 1992), *Joyce, "Penelope" and the Body* (Rodopi, 2006) and, most recently, the 450-page *Companion To James Joyce* (Blackwell, 2008).

VINCENT CHENG is the Shirley Sutton Thomas Professor of English at the University of Utah. His scholarship addresses the intersections of twentieth-century literature, Irish studies, postcolonial studies, race studies, and contemporary culture. His books include *Inauthentic: The Anxiety Over Culture and Identity* (Rutgers Univ. Press, 2004), *Joyce, Race, and Empire* (Cambridge Univ. Press, 1995), *Shakespeare and Joyce: A Study of Finnegans Wake* (Penn State Univ. Press, 1984), *"Le Cid": A Translation in Rhymed Couplets* (Univ. of Delaware Press, 1987), and (as editor) *Joyce in Context* (Cambridge Univ. Press, 1992) and *Joycean Cultures* (Univ. of Delaware Press, 1999).

PAUL FAGAN is a lecturer at the University of Vienna. He is cofounder and president of the *International Flann O'Brien Society* and is co–general editor of the society journal *The Parish Review*. He is also co-editor of the essay collection

Flann O'Brien: Contesting Legacies (Cork Univ. Press, 2014) with Ruben Borg and Werner Huber. Fagan has published in journals such as *Joyce Studies in Italy* and *Partial Answers*, and has forthcoming book chapters in collections with Rodopi, Cork University Press, and Manchester University Press.

DIETER FUCHS is associate professor of Anglophone literatures and cultural studies at the Anglo-German Department of the Technical University of Koszalin. His main research areas include Shakespeare and early modern studies, James Joyce and Irish studies, and literary and cultural theory. He has published many articles on Joyce, Shakespeare, and Renaissance culture, and the monograph *Joyce und Menippos: A Portrait of the Artist as an Old Dog* (Koenigshausen and Neumann, 2006).

JOHN MCCOURT is associate professor of English at the Università Roma Tre. He specializes in Joyce Studies and in nineteenth- and twentieth-century Irish literature. The cofounder of the Trieste Joyce School, he is widely published and best known for *The Years of Bloom: Joyce in Trieste 1904–1920* (Univ. of Wisconsin Press/Lilliput Press, 2000). He has just completed *Writing the Frontier: Anthony Trollope between Britain and Ireland*, which will be published by Oxford University Press in 2015.

LAURA PELASCHIAR is a lecturer in English literature at the University of Trieste. She is Director of the Trieste Joyce School and has written widely on Northern Irish literature and James Joyce. In 1998 she published her monograph *Writing the North: The Contemporary Novel in Modern Ireland* (Edizioni Parnaso) and in 2009 *Ulisse Gotico* (Pacini Editore). She is currently completing *Gothic Joyce*, a monograph that studies the Gothic in all of Joyce's texts.

VIKE MARTINA PLOCK is a senior lecturer in English literature at the University of Exeter. She is the author of *Joyce, Medicine, and Modernity* (Univ. Press of Florida, 2010) and the editor of a special issue of the *James Joyce Quarterly* on the topic of Joyce and physiology (2009). Currently, she is completing a research monograph on interwar women writers and fashion provisionally entitled *En Vogue: Women Writers, Fashion, and the Fictions of Modernity*.

GIUSEPPINA RESTIVO is professor emeritus at the University of Trieste. Her main research areas are contemporary English theater, Shakespeare's theater, and Shakespeare and the law. Her publications include two volumes on Edward Bond and Samuel Beckett; essays on Beckett (the last one in H. Bloom ed., *Samuel Beckett*, Chelsea House, 2011); three edited volumes on *Hamlet, Othello* and *The Tempest*; and essays on Shakespeare and the law (in *The Merchant of Venice, As You Like It, Hamlet, King Lear* and *The Tempest*), the last contribution being the voice "The law in Shakespeare's theatre" for the *Cambridge University Guide to Shakespeare*, forthcoming in 2015.

SAM SLOTE is associate professor in the School of English at Trinity College Dublin. His most recent book is *Joyce's Nietzschean Ethics* (Palgrave, 2013). In addition to Joyce and Beckett, he has written on Virginia Woolf, Vladimir Nabokov, Raymond Queneau, Dante, Mallarmé, and Elvis.

Index